Mometrix
TEST PREPARATION

OAE

Health (023)

Secrets Study Guide

DEAR FUTURE EXAM SUCCESS STORY

First of all, **THANK YOU** for purchasing Mometrix study materials!

Second, congratulations! You are one of the few determined test-takers who are committed to doing whatever it takes to excel on your exam. **You have come to the right place.** We developed these study materials with one goal in mind: to deliver you the information you need in a format that's concise and easy to use.

In addition to optimizing your guide for the content of the test, we've outlined our recommended steps for breaking down the preparation process into small, attainable goals so you can make sure you stay on track.

We've also analyzed the entire test-taking process, identifying the most common pitfalls and showing how you can overcome them and be ready for any curveball the test throws you.

Standardized testing is one of the biggest obstacles on your road to success, which only increases the importance of doing well in the high-pressure, high-stakes environment of test day. Your results on this test could have a significant impact on your future, and this guide provides the information and practical advice to help you achieve your full potential on test day.

Your success is our success

We would love to hear from you! If you would like to share the story of your exam success or if you have any questions or comments in regard to our products, please contact us at **800-673-8175** or **support@mometrix.com**.

Thanks again for your business and we wish you continued success!

Sincerely,
The Mometrix Test Preparation Team

Need more help? Check out our flashcards at:
http://MometrixFlashcards.com/OAE

Written and edited by the Mometrix Exam Secrets Test Prep Team
Printed in the United States of America

TABLE OF CONTENTS

Introduction

Thank you for purchasing this resource! You have made the choice to prepare yourself for a test that could have a huge impact on your future, and this guide is designed to help you be fully ready for test day. Obviously, it's important to have a solid understanding of the test material, but you also need to be prepared for the unique environment and stressors of the test, so that you can perform to the best of your abilities.

For this purpose, the first section that appears in this guide is the **Secret Keys**. We've devoted countless hours to meticulously researching what works and what doesn't, and we've boiled down our findings to the five most impactful steps you can take to improve your performance on the test. We start at the beginning with study planning and move through the preparation process, all the way to the testing strategies that will help you get the most out of what you know when you're finally sitting in front of the test.

We recommend that you start preparing for your test as far in advance as possible. However, if you've bought this guide as a last-minute study resource and only have a few days before your test, we recommend that you skip over the first two Secret Keys since they address a long-term study plan.

If you struggle with **test anxiety**, we strongly encourage you to check out our recommendations for how you can overcome it. Test anxiety is a formidable foe, but it can be beaten, and we want to make sure you have the tools you need to defeat it.

Secret Key #1 – Plan Big, Study Small

There's a lot riding on your performance. If you want to ace this test, you're going to need to keep your skills sharp and the material fresh in your mind. You need a plan that lets you review everything you need to know while still fitting in your schedule. We'll break this strategy down into three categories.

Information Organization

Start with the information you already have: the official test outline. From this, you can make a complete list of all the concepts you need to cover before the test. Organize these concepts into groups that can be studied together, and create a list of any related vocabulary you need to learn so you can brush up on any difficult terms. You'll want to keep this vocabulary list handy once you actually start studying since you may need to add to it along the way.

Time Management

Once you have your set of study concepts, decide how to spread them out over the time you have left before the test. Break your study plan into small, clear goals so you have a manageable task for each day and know exactly what you're doing. Then just focus on one small step at a time. When you manage your time this way, you don't need to spend hours at a time studying. Studying a small block of content for a short period each day helps you retain information better and avoid stressing over how much you have left to do. You can relax knowing that you have a plan to cover everything in time. In order for this strategy to be effective though, you have to start studying early and stick to your schedule. Avoid the exhaustion and futility that comes from last-minute cramming!

Study Environment

The environment you study in has a big impact on your learning. Studying in a coffee shop, while probably more enjoyable, is not likely to be as fruitful as studying in a quiet room. It's important to keep distractions to a minimum. You're only planning to study for a short block of time, so make the most of it. Don't pause to check your phone or get up to find a snack. It's also important to **avoid multitasking**. Research has consistently shown that multitasking will make your studying dramatically less effective. Your study area should also be comfortable and well-lit so you don't have the distraction of straining your eyes or sitting on an uncomfortable chair.

The time of day you study is also important. You want to be rested and alert. Don't wait until just before bedtime. Study when you'll be most likely to comprehend and remember. Even better, if you know what time of day your test will be, set that time aside for study. That way your brain will be used to working on that subject at that specific time and you'll have a better chance of recalling information.

Finally, it can be helpful to team up with others who are studying for the same test. Your actual studying should be done in as isolated an environment as possible, but the work of organizing the information and setting up the study plan can be divided up. In between study sessions, you can discuss with your teammates the concepts that you're all studying and quiz each other on the details. Just be sure that your teammates are as serious about the test as you are. If you find that your study time is being replaced with social time, you might need to find a new team.

Secret Key #2 – Make Your Studying Count

You're devoting a lot of time and effort to preparing for this test, so you want to be absolutely certain it will pay off. This means doing more than just reading the content and hoping you can remember it on test day. It's important to make every minute of study count. There are two main areas you can focus on to make your studying count.

Retention

It doesn't matter how much time you study if you can't remember the material. You need to make sure you are retaining the concepts. To check your retention of the information you're learning, try recalling it at later times with minimal prompting. Try carrying around flashcards and glance at one or two from time to time or ask a friend who's also studying for the test to quiz you.

To enhance your retention, look for ways to put the information into practice so that you can apply it rather than simply recalling it. If you're using the information in practical ways, it will be much easier to remember. Similarly, it helps to solidify a concept in your mind if you're not only reading it to yourself but also explaining it to someone else. Ask a friend to let you teach them about a concept you're a little shaky on (or speak aloud to an imaginary audience if necessary). As you try to summarize, define, give examples, and answer your friend's questions, you'll understand the concepts better and they will stay with you longer. Finally, step back for a big picture view and ask yourself how each piece of information fits with the whole subject. When you link the different concepts together and see them working together as a whole, it's easier to remember the individual components.

Finally, practice showing your work on any multi-step problems, even if you're just studying. Writing out each step you take to solve a problem will help solidify the process in your mind, and you'll be more likely to remember it during the test.

Modality

Modality simply refers to the means or method by which you study. Choosing a study modality that fits your own individual learning style is crucial. No two people learn best in exactly the same way, so it's important to know your strengths and use them to your advantage.

For example, if you learn best by visualization, focus on visualizing a concept in your mind and draw an image or a diagram. Try color-coding your notes, illustrating them, or creating symbols that will trigger your mind to recall a learned concept. If you learn best by hearing or discussing information, find a study partner who learns the same way or read aloud to yourself. Think about how to put the information in your own words. Imagine that you are giving a lecture on the topic and record yourself so you can listen to it later.

For any learning style, flashcards can be helpful. Organize the information so you can take advantage of spare moments to review. Underline key words or phrases. Use different colors for different categories. Mnemonic devices (such as creating a short list in which every item starts with the same letter) can also help with retention. Find what works best for you and use it to store the information in your mind most effectively and easily.

Secret Key #3 – Practice the Right Way

Your success on test day depends not only on how many hours you put into preparing, but also on whether you prepared the right way. It's good to check along the way to see if your studying is paying off. One of the most effective ways to do this is by taking practice tests to evaluate your progress. Practice tests are useful because they show exactly where you need to improve. Every time you take a practice test, pay special attention to these three groups of questions:

- The questions you got wrong
- The questions you had to guess on, even if you guessed right
- The questions you found difficult or slow to work through

This will show you exactly what your weak areas are, and where you need to devote more study time. Ask yourself why each of these questions gave you trouble. Was it because you didn't understand the material? Was it because you didn't remember the vocabulary? Do you need more repetitions on this type of question to build speed and confidence? Dig into those questions and figure out how you can strengthen your weak areas as you go back to review the material.

Additionally, many practice tests have a section explaining the answer choices. It can be tempting to read the explanation and think that you now have a good understanding of the concept. However, an explanation likely only covers part of the question's broader context. Even if the explanation makes perfect sense, **go back and investigate** every concept related to the question until you're positive you have a thorough understanding.

As you go along, keep in mind that the practice test is just that: practice. Memorizing these questions and answers will not be very helpful on the actual test because it is unlikely to have any of the same exact questions. If you only know the right answers to the sample questions, you won't be prepared for the real thing. **Study the concepts** until you understand them fully, and then you'll be able to answer any question that shows up on the test.

It's important to wait on the practice tests until you're ready. If you take a test on your first day of study, you may be overwhelmed by the amount of material covered and how much you need to learn. Work up to it gradually.

On test day, you'll need to be prepared for answering questions, managing your time, and using the test-taking strategies you've learned. It's a lot to balance, like a mental marathon that will have a big impact on your future. Like training for a marathon, you'll need to start slowly and work your way up. When test day arrives, you'll be ready.

Start with the strategies you've read in the first two Secret Keys—plan your course and study in the way that works best for you. If you have time, consider using multiple study resources to get different approaches to the same concepts. It can be helpful to see difficult concepts from more than one angle. Then find a good source for practice tests. Many times, the test website will suggest potential study resources or provide sample tests.

Practice Test Strategy

If you're able to find at least three practice tests, we recommend this strategy:

Untimed and Open-Book Practice

Take the first test with no time constraints and with your notes and study guide handy. Take your time and focus on applying the strategies you've learned.

Timed and Open-Book Practice

Take the second practice test open-book as well, but set a timer and practice pacing yourself to finish in time.

Timed and Closed-Book Practice

Take any other practice tests as if it were test day. Set a timer and put away your study materials. Sit at a table or desk in a quiet room, imagine yourself at the testing center, and answer questions as quickly and accurately as possible.

Keep repeating timed and closed-book tests on a regular basis until you run out of practice tests or it's time for the actual test. Your mind will be ready for the schedule and stress of test day, and you'll be able to focus on recalling the material you've learned.

Secret Key #4 – Pace Yourself

Once you're fully prepared for the material on the test, your biggest challenge on test day will be managing your time. Just knowing that the clock is ticking can make you panic even if you have plenty of time left. Work on pacing yourself so you can build confidence against the time constraints of the exam. Pacing is a difficult skill to master, especially in a high-pressure environment, so **practice is vital**.

Set time expectations for your pace based on how much time is available. For example, if a section has 60 questions and the time limit is 30 minutes, you know you have to average 30 seconds or less per question in order to answer them all. Although 30 seconds is the hard limit, set 25 seconds per question as your goal, so you reserve extra time to spend on harder questions. When you budget extra time for the harder questions, you no longer have any reason to stress when those questions take longer to answer.

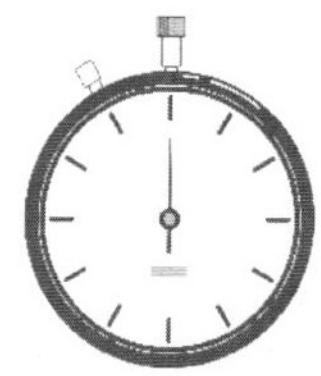

Don't let this time expectation distract you from working through the test at a calm, steady pace, but keep it in mind so you don't spend too much time on any one question. Recognize that taking extra time on one question you don't understand may keep you from answering two that you do understand later in the test. If your time limit for a question is up and you're still not sure of the answer, mark it and move on, and come back to it later if the time and the test format allow. If the testing format doesn't allow you to return to earlier questions, just make an educated guess; then put it out of your mind and move on.

On the easier questions, be careful not to rush. It may seem wise to hurry through them so you have more time for the challenging ones, but it's not worth missing one if you know the concept and just didn't take the time to read the question fully. Work efficiently but make sure you understand the question and have looked at all of the answer choices, since more than one may seem right at first.

Even if you're paying attention to the time, you may find yourself a little behind at some point. You should speed up to get back on track, but do so wisely. Don't panic; just take a few seconds less on each question until you're caught up. Don't guess without thinking, but do look through the answer choices and eliminate any you know are wrong. If you can get down to two choices, it is often worthwhile to guess from those. Once you've chosen an answer, move on and don't dwell on any that you skipped or had to hurry through. If a question was taking too long, chances are it was one of the harder ones, so you weren't as likely to get it right anyway.

On the other hand, if you find yourself getting ahead of schedule, it may be beneficial to slow down a little. The more quickly you work, the more likely you are to make a careless mistake that will affect your score. You've budgeted time for each question, so don't be afraid to spend that time. Practice an efficient but careful pace to get the most out of the time you have.

Secret Key #5 – Have a Plan for Guessing

When you're taking the test, you may find yourself stuck on a question. Some of the answer choices seem better than others, but you don't see the one answer choice that is obviously correct. What do you do?

The scenario described above is very common, yet most test takers have not effectively prepared for it. Developing and practicing a plan for guessing may be one of the single most effective uses of your time as you get ready for the exam.

In developing your plan for guessing, there are three questions to address:

- When should you start the guessing process?
- How should you narrow down the choices?
- Which answer should you choose?

When to Start the Guessing Process

Unless your plan for guessing is to select C every time (which, despite its merits, is not what we recommend), you need to leave yourself enough time to apply your answer elimination strategies. Since you have a limited amount of time for each question, that means that if you're going to give yourself the best shot at guessing correctly, you have to decide quickly whether or not you will guess.

Of course, the best-case scenario is that you don't have to guess at all, so first, see if you can answer the question based on your knowledge of the subject and basic reasoning skills. Focus on the key words in the question and try to jog your memory of related topics. Give yourself a chance to bring the knowledge to mind, but once you realize that you don't have (or you can't access) the knowledge you need to answer the question, it's time to start the guessing process.

It's almost always better to start the guessing process too early than too late. It only takes a few seconds to remember something and answer the question from knowledge. Carefully eliminating wrong answer choices takes longer. Plus, going through the process of eliminating answer choices can actually help jog your memory.

Summary: Start the guessing process as soon as you decide that you can't answer the question based on your knowledge.

How to Narrow Down the Choices

The next chapter in this book (**Test-Taking Strategies**) includes a wide range of strategies for how to approach questions and how to look for answer choices to eliminate. You will definitely want to read those carefully, practice them, and figure out which ones work best for you. Here though, we're going to address a mindset rather than a particular strategy.

Your odds of guessing an answer correctly depend on how many options you are choosing from.

Number of options left	5	4	3	2	1
Odds of guessing correctly	20%	25%	33%	50%	100%

You can see from this chart just how valuable it is to be able to eliminate incorrect answers and make an educated guess, but there are two things that many test takers do that cause them to miss out on the benefits of guessing:

- Accidentally eliminating the correct answer
- Selecting an answer based on an impression

We'll look at the first one here, and the second one in the next section.

To avoid accidentally eliminating the correct answer, we recommend a thought exercise called **the $5 challenge**. In this challenge, you only eliminate an answer choice from contention if you are willing to bet $5 on it being wrong. Why $5? Five dollars is a small but not insignificant amount of money. It's an amount you could afford to lose but wouldn't want to throw away. And while losing $5 once might not hurt too much, doing it twenty times will set you back $100. In the same way, each small decision you make—eliminating a choice here, guessing on a question there—won't by itself impact your score very much, but when you put them all together, they can make a big difference. By holding each answer choice elimination decision to a higher standard, you can reduce the risk of accidentally eliminating the correct answer.

The $5 challenge can also be applied in a positive sense: If you are willing to bet $5 that an answer choice *is* correct, go ahead and mark it as correct.

Summary: Only eliminate an answer choice if you are willing to bet $5 that it is wrong.

Which Answer to Choose

You're taking the test. You've run into a hard question and decided you'll have to guess. You've eliminated all the answer choices you're willing to bet $5 on. Now you have to pick an answer. Why do we even need to talk about this? Why can't you just pick whichever one you feel like when the time comes?

The answer to these questions is that if you don't come into the test with a plan, you'll rely on your impression to select an answer choice, and if you do that, you risk falling into a trap. The test writers know that everyone who takes their test will be guessing on some of the questions, so they intentionally write wrong answer choices to seem plausible. You still have to pick an answer though, and if the wrong answer choices are designed to look right, how can you ever be sure that you're not falling for their trap? The best solution we've found to this dilemma is to take the decision out of your hands entirely. Here is the process we recommend:

Once you've eliminated any choices that you are confident (willing to bet $5) are wrong, select the first remaining choice as your answer.

Whether you choose to select the first remaining choice, the second, or the last, the important thing is that you use some preselected standard. Using this approach guarantees that you will not be enticed into selecting an answer choice that looks right, because you are not basing your decision on how the answer choices look.

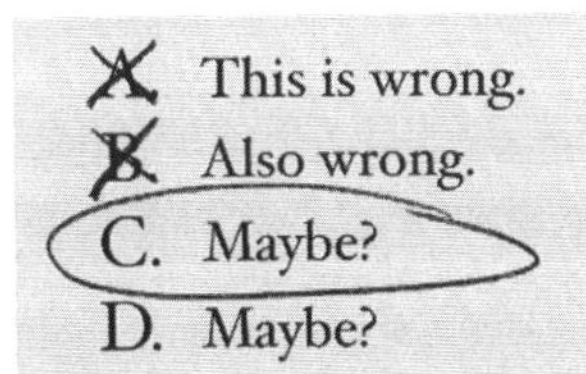

This is not meant to make you question your knowledge. Instead, it is to help you recognize the difference between your knowledge and your impressions. There's a huge difference between thinking an answer is right because of what you know, and thinking an answer is right because it looks or sounds like it should be right.

Summary: To ensure that your selection is appropriately random, make a predetermined selection from among all answer choices you have not eliminated.

Test-Taking Strategies

This section contains a list of test-taking strategies that you may find helpful as you work through the test. By taking what you know and applying logical thought, you can maximize your chances of answering any question correctly!

It is very important to realize that every question is different and every person is different: no single strategy will work on every question, and no single strategy will work for every person. That's why we've included all of them here, so you can try them out and determine which ones work best for different types of questions and which ones work best for you.

Question Strategies

✓ Read Carefully

Read the question and the answer choices carefully. Don't miss the question because you misread the terms. You have plenty of time to read each question thoroughly and make sure you understand what is being asked. Yet a happy medium must be attained, so don't waste too much time. You must read carefully and efficiently.

✓ Contextual Clues

Look for contextual clues. If the question includes a word you are not familiar with, look at the immediate context for some indication of what the word might mean. Contextual clues can often give you all the information you need to decipher the meaning of an unfamiliar word. Even if you can't determine the meaning, you may be able to narrow down the possibilities enough to make a solid guess at the answer to the question.

✓ Prefixes

If you're having trouble with a word in the question or answer choices, try dissecting it. Take advantage of every clue that the word might include. Prefixes can be a huge help. Usually, they allow you to determine a basic meaning. *Pre-* means before, *post-* means after, *pro-* is positive, *de-* is negative. From prefixes, you can get an idea of the general meaning of the word and try to put it into context.

✓ Hedge Words

Watch out for critical hedge words, such as *likely, may, can, often, almost, mostly, usually, generally, rarely*, and *sometimes*. Question writers insert these hedge phrases to cover every possibility. Often an answer choice will be wrong simply because it leaves no room for exception. Be on guard for answer choices that have definitive words such as *exactly* and *always*.

✓ Switchback Words

Stay alert for *switchbacks*. These are the words and phrases frequently used to alert you to shifts in thought. The most common switchback words are *but, although*, and *however*. Others include *nevertheless, on the other hand, even though, while, in spite of, despite*, and *regardless of*. Switchback words are important to catch because they can change the direction of the question or an answer choice.

⊘ Face Value

When in doubt, use common sense. Accept the situation in the problem at face value. Don't read too much into it. These problems will not require you to make wild assumptions. If you have to go beyond creativity and warp time or space in order to have an answer choice fit the question, then you should move on and consider the other answer choices. These are normal problems rooted in reality. The applicable relationship or explanation may not be readily apparent, but it is there for you to figure out. Use your common sense to interpret anything that isn't clear.

Answer Choice Strategies

⊘ Answer Selection

The most thorough way to pick an answer choice is to identify and eliminate wrong answers until only one is left, then confirm it is the correct answer. Sometimes an answer choice may immediately seem right, but be careful. The test writers will usually put more than one reasonable answer choice on each question, so take a second to read all of them and make sure that the other choices are not equally obvious. As long as you have time left, it is better to read every answer choice than to pick the first one that looks right without checking the others.

⊘ Answer Choice Families

An answer choice family consists of two (in rare cases, three) answer choices that are very similar in construction and cannot all be true at the same time. If you see two answer choices that are direct opposites or parallels, one of them is usually the correct answer. For instance, if one answer choice says that quantity *x* increases and another either says that quantity *x* decreases (opposite) or says that quantity *y* increases (parallel), then those answer choices would fall into the same family. An answer choice that doesn't match the construction of the answer choice family is more likely to be incorrect. Most questions will not have answer choice families, but when they do appear, you should be prepared to recognize them.

⊘ Eliminate Answers

Eliminate answer choices as soon as you realize they are wrong, but make sure you consider all possibilities. If you are eliminating answer choices and realize that the last one you are left with is also wrong, don't panic. Start over and consider each choice again. There may be something you missed the first time that you will realize on the second pass.

⊘ Avoid Fact Traps

Don't be distracted by an answer choice that is factually true but doesn't answer the question. You are looking for the choice that answers the question. Stay focused on what the question is asking for so you don't accidentally pick an answer that is true but incorrect. Always go back to the question and make sure the answer choice you've selected actually answers the question and is not merely a true statement.

⊘ Extreme Statements

In general, you should avoid answers that put forth extreme actions as standard practice or proclaim controversial ideas as established fact. An answer choice that states the "process should be used in certain situations, if..." is much more likely to be correct than one that states the "process should be discontinued completely." The first is a calm rational statement and doesn't even make a definitive, uncompromising stance, using a hedge word *if* to provide wiggle room, whereas the second choice is far more extreme.

✓ Benchmark

As you read through the answer choices and you come across one that seems to answer the question well, mentally select that answer choice. This is not your final answer, but it's the one that will help you evaluate the other answer choices. The one that you selected is your benchmark or standard for judging each of the other answer choices. Every other answer choice must be compared to your benchmark. That choice is correct until proven otherwise by another answer choice beating it. If you find a better answer, then that one becomes your new benchmark. Once you've decided that no other choice answers the question as well as your benchmark, you have your final answer.

✓ Predict the Answer

Before you even start looking at the answer choices, it is often best to try to predict the answer. When you come up with the answer on your own, it is easier to avoid distractions and traps because you will know exactly what to look for. The right answer choice is unlikely to be word-for-word what you came up with, but it should be a close match. Even if you are confident that you have the right answer, you should still take the time to read each option before moving on.

General Strategies

✓ Tough Questions

If you are stumped on a problem or it appears too hard or too difficult, don't waste time. Move on! Remember though, if you can quickly check for obviously incorrect answer choices, your chances of guessing correctly are greatly improved. Before you completely give up, at least try to knock out a couple of possible answers. Eliminate what you can and then guess at the remaining answer choices before moving on.

✓ Check Your Work

Since you will probably not know every term listed and the answer to every question, it is important that you get credit for the ones that you do know. Don't miss any questions through careless mistakes. If at all possible, try to take a second to look back over your answer selection and make sure you've selected the correct answer choice and haven't made a costly careless mistake (such as marking an answer choice that you didn't mean to mark). This quick double check should more than pay for itself in caught mistakes for the time it costs.

✓ Pace Yourself

It's easy to be overwhelmed when you're looking at a page full of questions; your mind is confused and full of random thoughts, and the clock is ticking down faster than you would like. Calm down and maintain the pace that you have set for yourself. Especially as you get down to the last few minutes of the test, don't let the small numbers on the clock make you panic. As long as you are on track by monitoring your pace, you are guaranteed to have time for each question.

✓ Don't Rush

It is very easy to make errors when you are in a hurry. Maintaining a fast pace in answering questions is pointless if it makes you miss questions that you would have gotten right otherwise. Test writers like to include distracting information and wrong answers that seem right. Taking a little extra time to avoid careless mistakes can make all the difference in your test score. Find a pace that allows you to be confident in the answers that you select.

⊘ Keep Moving

Panicking will not help you pass the test, so do your best to stay calm and keep moving. Taking deep breaths and going through the answer elimination steps you practiced can help to break through a stress barrier and keep your pace.

Final Notes

The combination of a solid foundation of content knowledge and the confidence that comes from practicing your plan for applying that knowledge is the key to maximizing your performance on test day. As your foundation of content knowledge is built up and strengthened, you'll find that the strategies included in this chapter become more and more effective in helping you quickly sift through the distractions and traps of the test to isolate the correct answer.

Now that you're preparing to move forward into the test content chapters of this book, be sure to keep your goal in mind. As you read, think about how you will be able to apply this information on the test. If you've already seen sample questions for the test and you have an idea of the question format and style, try to come up with questions of your own that you can answer based on what you're reading. This will give you valuable practice applying your knowledge in the same ways you can expect to on test day.

Good luck and good studying!

Personal Health and Wellness

Human Anatomy and Physiology

Body Systems

Functions of the human body can be divided into the following body systems.

- **Cardiovascular**: Pumps blood throughout the body via the heart and blood vessels
- **Respiratory**: Regulates gas exchange (oxygen intake and carbon dioxide expulsion)
- **Digestive**: Transforms food into energy and eliminates solid waste
- **Urinary**: Removes waste and toxins from the blood and expels them from the body through urine
- **Endocrine**: Releases hormones into the bloodstream to control metabolism, growth, and reproduction
- **Immune and Lymphatic Systems**: Defends against all foreign substances
- **Integumentary**: Skin prevents moisture loss, regulates temperature, protects from sunburn, and senses pain, pressure, touch, hot and cold
- **Musculoskeletal**: Skeletal muscles move the body, smooth muscles control the physical functioning of internal organs, and cardiac muscle pumps blood. The skeleton supports and shapes, protects internal organs, stores minerals, and produces blood cells
- **Nervous**: Controls movement, memory, and senses and communicates with the outside world
- **Reproductive**: Allows continuation of the human species through reproduction and childbearing and differentiates the sexes

Note that different models may have overlapping approaches to the body systems. For instance, the excretory system is not listed above, but the functions of the excretory systems overlap and are covered by the urinary and digestive systems.

The Three Primary Body Planes

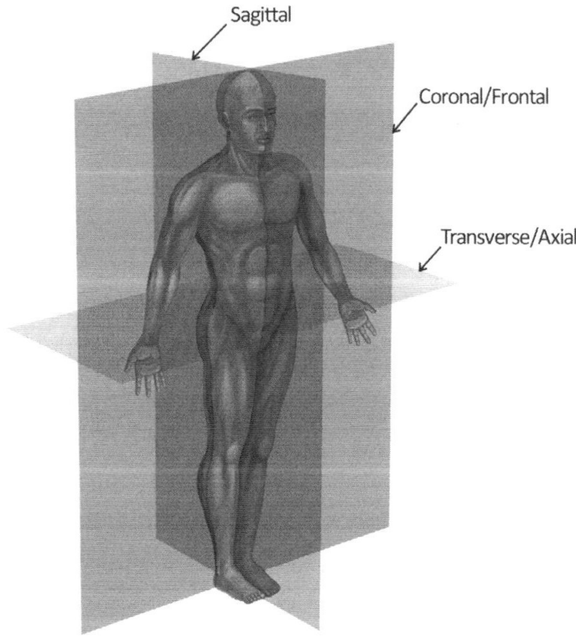

The **transverse (or horizontal) plane** divides the patient's body into imaginary upper (*superior*) and lower (*inferior or caudal*) halves.

The **sagittal plane** divides the body, or any body part, vertically into right and left sections. The sagittal plane runs parallel to the midline of the body.

The **coronal (or frontal) plane** divides the body, or any body structure, vertically into front and back (*anterior* and *posterior*) sections. The coronal plane runs vertically through the body at right angles to the midline.

Cardiovascular System

The main functions of the **cardiovascular system** are gas exchange, the delivery of nutrients and hormones, and waste removal. The cardiovascular system consists primarily of the heart, blood, and blood vessels. The **heart** is a pump that pushes blood through the arteries. **Arteries** are blood vessels that carry blood away from the heart, and **veins** are blood vessels that carry blood back to the heart. The exchange of materials between blood and cells occurs in the **capillaries**, which are the smallest of the blood vessels.

Review Video: Functions of the Circulatory System
Visit mometrix.com/academy and enter code: 376581

Review Video: Mnemonics for Heart Anatomy and Physiology
Visit mometrix.com/academy and enter code: 849489

Review Video: Electrical Conduction System of the Heart
Visit mometrix.com/academy and enter code: 624557

Review Video: How the Heart Functions
Visit mometrix.com/academy and enter code: 569724

Heart Chambers and Valves

There are four chambers of the heart that have valves separating them and regulating a one-way flow of blood between the chambers.

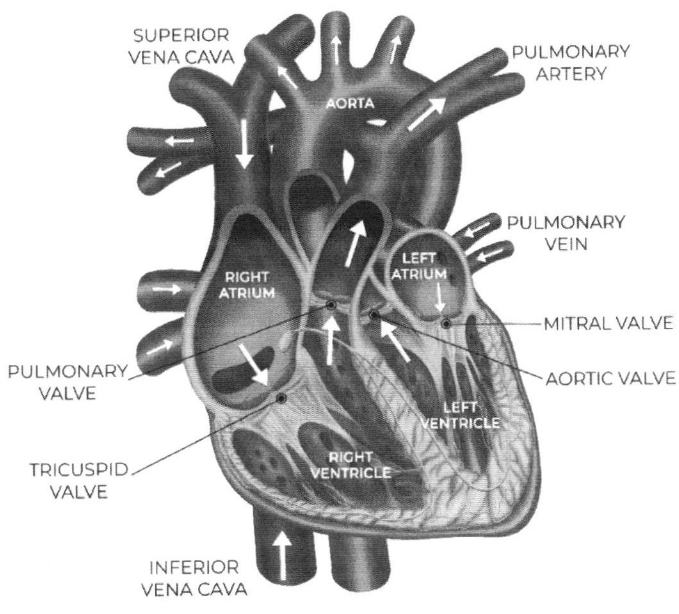

RESPIRATORY SYSTEM

The primary function of the **respiratory system** is to move air in and out of the body in order to facilitate the exchange of oxygen and carbon dioxide. The respiratory system consists of the nasal passages, pharynx, larynx, trachea, bronchial tubes, lungs, and diaphragm. **Bronchial tubes** branch into **bronchioles**, which end in clusters of alveoli. The **alveoli** are tiny sacs inside the lungs where gas exchange takes place. When the **diaphragm** contracts, the volume of the chest increases, which reduces the pressure in the **lungs**. Then, air is inhaled through the nose or mouth and passes through the pharynx, larynx, trachea, and bronchial tubes into the lungs. When the diaphragm relaxes, the volume in the chest cavity decreases, forcing the air out of the lungs. The respiratory system works jointly with the **cardiovascular system** by taking **oxygenated blood** (red blood cells) and distributing them through arteries and capillaries. **Deoxygenated blood** (carbon dioxide) is transported via the venous system back to the lungs to be exhaled. The respiratory system also functions to enhance speech and smell.

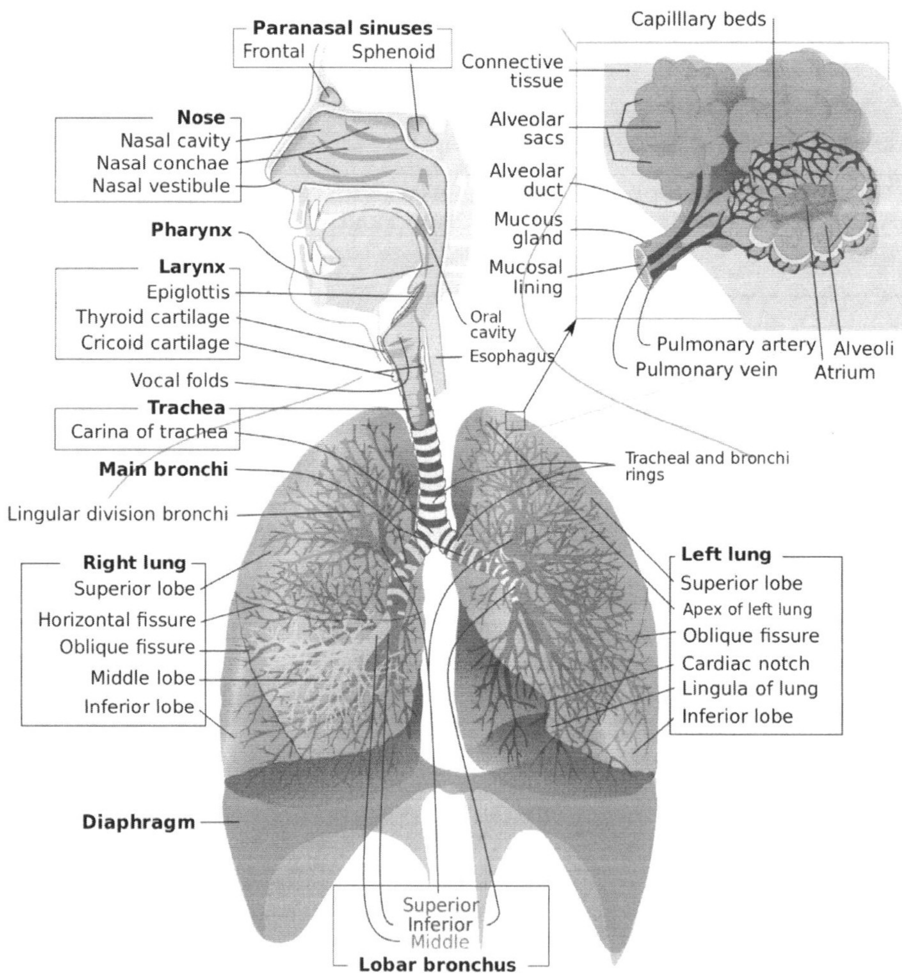

> **Review Video: Respiratory System**
> Visit mometrix.com/academy and enter code: 783075
>
> **Review Video: Pulmonary Circuit**
> Visit mometrix.com/academy and enter code: 955608

Digestive System

The main function of the **digestive system** is to process the food that is consumed by an organism. This includes mechanical and chemical processing. Depending on the organism, **mechanical processes**, the physical process of breaking food into smaller pieces, can happen in various ways. Mammals have teeth to chew their food, while many animals such as birds, earthworms, crocodilians, and crustaceans have a gizzard or gizzard-like organ that grinds their food. **Chemical digestion** includes breaking food into simpler nutrients that the body can use for specific processes. While chewing, saliva (which contains special enzymes) is secreted to begin the breakdown of starches. Many animals such as mammals, birds, reptiles, amphibians, and fish have a stomach that stores and absorbs food. Gastric juice containing enzymes and hydrochloric acid is mixed with the food. The intestine or intestines absorb nutrients and reabsorb water from the undigested material. Additionally, many animals have a liver, gallbladder, and pancreas, which aid in digestion of proteins and fats. Undigested wastes are eliminated from the body through an anus or cloaca.

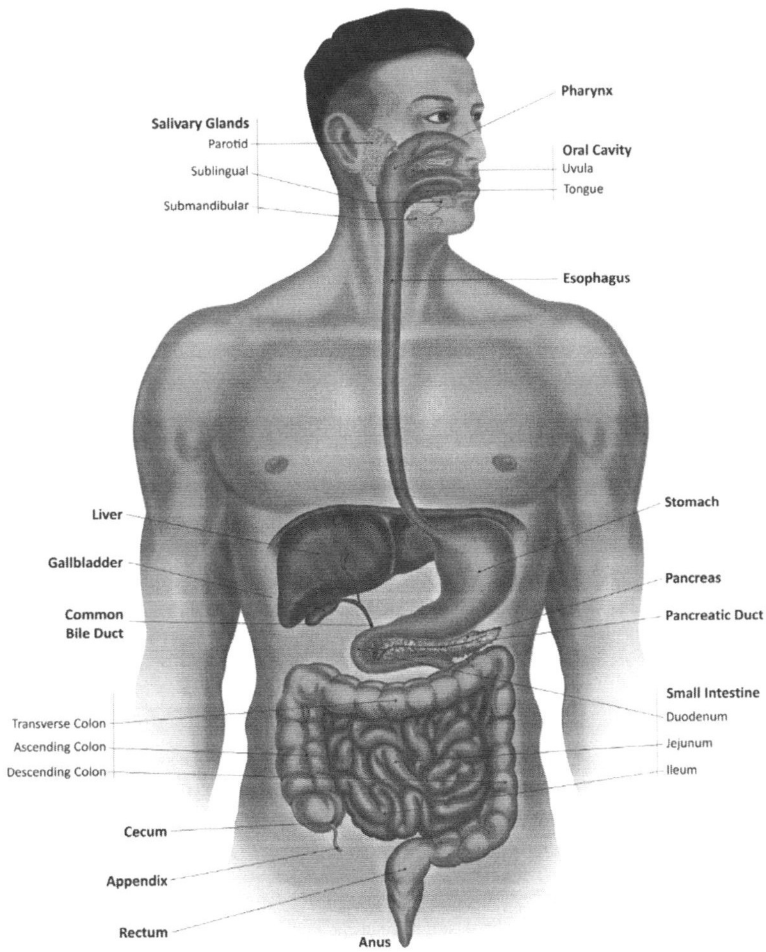

Review Video: Gastrointestinal System
Visit mometrix.com/academy and enter code: 378740

Urinary System

The **urinary system** consists of the bladder, kidneys, ureter, and urethra. Their main function is to eliminate waste products by expelling urine. This system also maintains homeostatic balance of water by excreting excess urine, maintaining electrolytes in the blood stream, and regulating blood pH levels. This balance of water is crucial to body functioning as dehydration can lead to low blood pressure, which in turn can result in metabolic shock. **Metabolic shock** is characterized by low blood pressure that affects the kidneys, liver, and brain. **Dehydration** can also affect the muscular system resulting in cramps from poor thermal regulation and altered fluid movement across tissue membranes.

Kidneys

The **kidneys** are involved in blood filtration, pH balance, and the reabsorption of nutrients to maintain proper blood volume and ion balance. The **nephron** is the working unit of the kidney. The parts of the nephron include the glomerulus, Bowman's capsule, and loop of Henle. Filtration takes place in the nephron's **glomerulus.** Water and dissolved materials such as glucose and amino acids pass on into the Bowman's capsule. Depending on concentration gradients, water and dissolved materials can pass back into the blood primarily through the proximal convoluted tubule. Reabsorption and water removal occur in the **loop of Henle** and the conducting duct. Urine and other nitrogenous wastes pass from the kidneys to the bladder and are expelled.

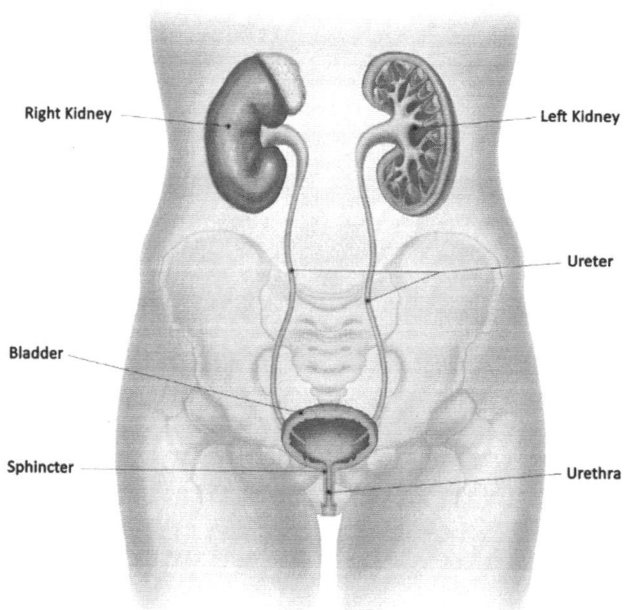

Review Video: Urinary System
Visit mometrix.com/academy and enter code: 601053

ENDOCRINE SYSTEM

The **endocrine system** consists of several ductless glands, which secrete hormones directly into the bloodstream. The **pituitary gland** controls the functions of the other glands in the system, regulates skeletal growth, and initiates the development of reproductive organs. The **pineal gland** regulates sleep cycles. The **thyroid gland** regulates metabolism and works with the **parathyroid glands** to help regulate the calcium level in the blood. The **adrenal glands** secrete the emergency hormone epinephrine, stimulate body repairs, and regulate sodium and potassium levels in the blood. The **islets of Langerhans**, located in the pancreas, secrete insulin and glucagon to regulate the level of blood sugar. In females, **ovaries** produce estrogen, which stimulates sexual development, and progesterone, which functions during pregnancy. In males, the **testes** secrete testosterone, which stimulates sexual development and sperm production.

Gland	Hormones	Disease
Adrenal Cortex	Aldosterone Cortisol Androgens	Addison's Disease Cushing's Disease
Adrenal Medulla	Epinephrine Norepinephrine	Anxiety Attacks Depression
Anterior Pituitary	Adrenocorticotropic hormone (ACTH) Follicle-stimulating hormone (FSH) Gonadotropic hormones Growth hormone (GH) Luteinizing hormone (LH) Prolactin Thyroid Stimulating Hormone (TSH)	Dwarfism Gigantism
Hypothalamus/ Posterior Pituitary	Inhibiting hormones (stop the release of other hormones) Antidiuretic hormone (ADH) Oxytocin Releasing hormones (trigger the release of other hormones)	Diabetes Insipidus
Kidneys	Calcitriol Erythropoietin	Hypertension
Ovaries	Estrogen Progesterone	Endometriosis Menometrorrhagia
Pancreas	Insulin Glucagon	Diabetes Mellitus
Parathyroid	Parathyroid hormone	Tetany Renal calculi
Pineal	Melatonin	Alzheimer's Disease
Testes	Testosterone	Gynecomastia Klinefelter Syndrome
Thymus	Thymic factor (TF) Thymosin Thymic humoral factor (THF) Thymopoietin	DiGeorge Syndrome

Gland	Hormones	Disease
Thyroid	Calcitonin Thyroxine (T4) Triiodothyronine (T3)	Cretinism Hypo/Hyperthyroidism Goiter Myxedema
Digestive tract	Gastrin Cholecystokinin Secretin Ghrelin Motilin	Gastritis Gastroesophageal reflux

MAJOR ENDOCRINE GLANDS

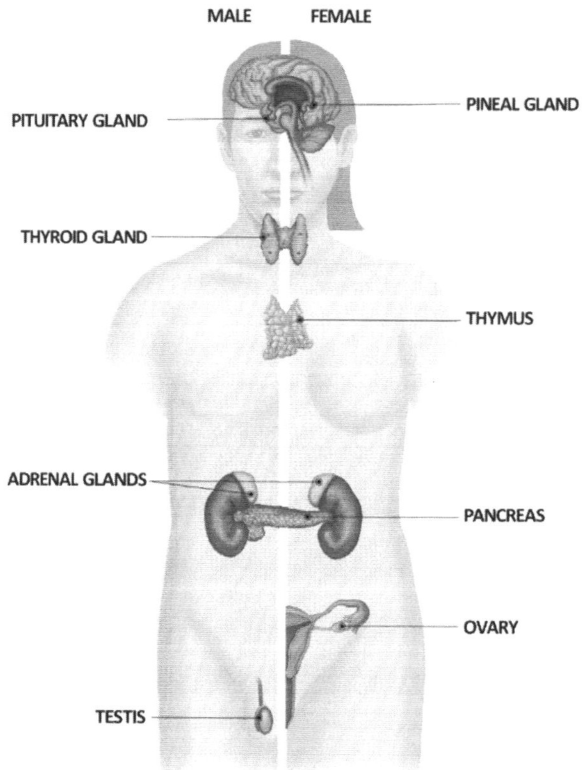

Review Video: Endocrine System
Visit mometrix.com/academy and enter code: 678939

IMMUNE AND LYMPHATIC SYSTEMS

IMMUNE SYSTEM

The **immune system** in animals defends the body against infection and disease. The immune system can be divided into two broad categories: innate immunity and adaptive immunity. **Innate immunity** includes the skin and mucous membranes, which provide a physical barrier to prevent pathogens from entering the body. Special chemicals including enzymes and proteins in mucus, tears, sweat, and stomach juices destroy pathogens. Numerous white blood cells such as neutrophils and macrophages protect the body from invading pathogens. **Adaptive immunity** involves the body responding to a specific antigen. Typically, B lymphocytes or B cells produce antibodies against a specific antigen, and T lymphocytes or T cells take special roles as helpers, regulators, or killers. Some T cells function as memory cells.

Review Video: Immune System
Visit mometrix.com/academy and enter code: 622899

Lymphatic System

The **lymphatic system** is connected to the cardiovascular system through a network of capillaries. The lymphatic system filters out organisms that cause disease, controls the production of disease-fighting antibodies, and produces white blood cells. The lymphatic system also prevents body tissues from swelling by draining fluids from them. Two of the most important areas in this system are the right lymphatic duct and the thoracic duct. The **right lymphatic duct** moves the immunity-bolstering lymph fluid through the top half of the body, while the **thoracic duct** moves lymph throughout the lower half. The spleen, thymus, and lymph nodes all generate and store the chemicals which form lymph and which are essential to protecting the body from disease.

The **lymphatic system** consists of the **thymus**, **lymph nodes**, **bone marrow**, and **spleen**. They primarily serve to distribute filtered fluids throughout the body and to remove excess fluid and debris. **White blood cells** are a key element of the lymphatic system which serve to prevent disease and repair the body after infection to prevent further illness.

Integumentary System

The integumentary system includes skin, hair, nails, sense receptors, sweat glands, and oil glands. The **skin** acts as a sensory organ, provides an exterior barrier against disease, regulates body temperature through perspiration, manufactures chemicals and hormones, and provides a place for nerves from the nervous system and parts of the circulation system to travel through. Skin has three layers: epidermis, dermis, and subcutaneous. The **epidermis** is the thin, outermost, waterproof layer. The **dermis** has the sweat glands, oil glands, and hair follicles. The **subcutaneous layer** has connective tissue. Also, this layer has **adipose** (i.e., fat) tissue, nerves, arteries, and veins.

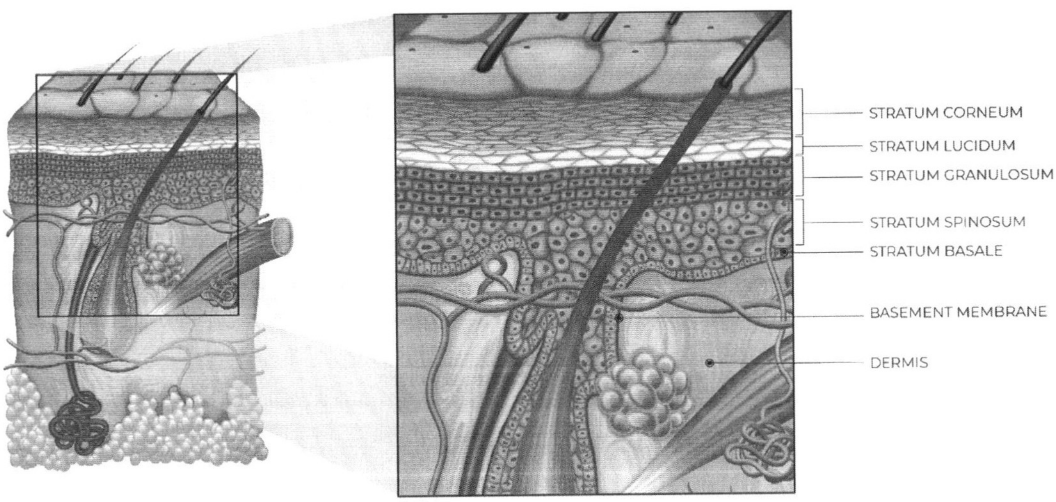

Review Video: Integumentary System
Visit mometrix.com/academy and enter code: 655980

Muscular System

The **muscular system** works in concert with the **skeletal system** to move the body and perform such core functions as cardiac activity. Key elements include:

- **Smooth muscle tissues** are involuntary muscles that are found in the walls of internal organs such as the stomach, intestines, and blood vessels. Smooth muscle tissue, or **visceral tissue,** is nonstriated. Smooth muscle cells are shorter and wider than skeletal muscle fibers. Smooth muscle tissue is also found in sphincters or valves that control the movement of material through openings throughout the body.
- **Cardiac muscle** tissue is involuntary muscle that is found only in the heart. Like skeletal muscle cells, cardiac muscle cells are also striated.
- **Skeletal muscles** are voluntary muscles that work in pairs to move parts of the skeleton. Skeletal muscles are composed of **muscle fibers** (cells) that are bound together in parallel bundles. Skeletal muscles are also known as **striated muscle** due to their striped histological appearance under a microscope.

Only skeletal muscle interacts with the skeleton to move the body. When they contract, the muscles transmit force to the attached bones. Working together, the muscles and bones act as a system of levers that move around the joints.

Review Video: Muscular System
Visit mometrix.com/academy and enter code: 967216

Major Muscles

The human body has more than 650 skeletal muscles that account for approximately half of a person's weight. Starting with the head and face, the temporalis and masseter move the mandible (lower jaw bone). The orbicularis oculi closes the eye. The orbicularis oris draws the lips together. The sternocleidomastoids move the head. The trapezius moves the shoulder, and the pectoralis major, deltoid, and latissimus dorsi move the upper arm. The biceps brachii and the triceps brachii move the lower arm. The rectus abdominis, external oblique, and erector spinae move the trunk. The external and internal obliques elevate and depress the ribs. The gluteus maximus moves the upper leg. The quadriceps femoris, hamstrings, and sartorius move the lower leg. The gastrocnemius and the soleus extend the foot.

Skeletal Muscle Contraction

Skeletal muscles consist of numerous muscle fibers. Each muscle fiber contains a bundle of myofibrils, which are composed of multiple repeating contractile units called sarcomeres. **Myofibrils** contain two protein microfilaments: a thick filament and a thin filament. The **thick filament** is composed of the protein myosin. The **thin filament** is composed of the protein actin. The dark bands (striations) in skeletal muscles are formed when thick and thin filaments overlap. Light bands occur where the thin filament is overlapped. Skeletal muscle contraction occurs when the thin filaments slide over the thick filaments shortening the sarcomere. When an action potential (electrical signal) reaches a muscle fiber, calcium ions are released. According to the sliding filament model of muscle contraction, these calcium ions bind to the myosin and actin, which assists in the binding of the myosin heads of the thick filaments to the actin molecules of the thin filaments. Adenosine triphosphate released from glucose provides the energy necessary for the contraction.

Skeletal System

The skeletal system serves many functions including providing structural support, movement, and protection; producing blood cells; and storing substances such as fat and minerals. The **axial skeleton** transfers the weight from the upper body to the lower appendages. Bones provide attachment points for muscles. The cranium protects the brain. The vertebrae protect the spinal cord. The rib cage protects the heart and lungs. The pelvis protects the reproductive organs. **Joints** include hinge joints, ball-and-socket joints, pivot joints, ellipsoid joints, gliding joints, and saddle joints. The **red marrow** manufactures red and white blood cells. All bone marrow is red at birth, but adults have approximately one-half red bone marrow and one-half yellow bone marrow. Yellow bone marrow stores fat.

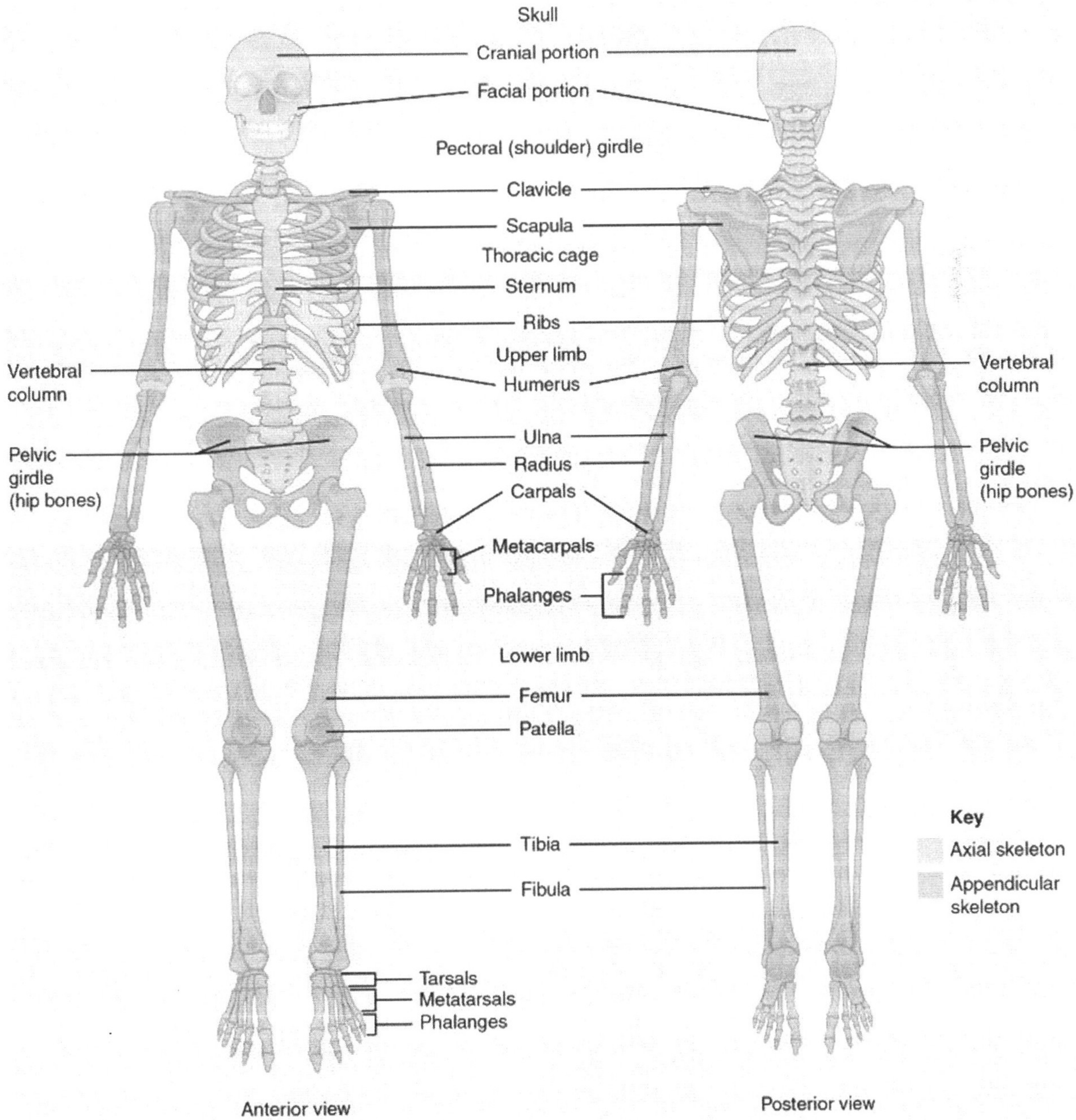

Structure of Axial Skeleton and Appendicular Skeleton

The **human skeletal system**, which consists of 206 bones along with numerous tendons, ligaments, and cartilage, is divided into the axial skeleton and the appendicular skeleton.

The **axial skeleton** consists of 80 bones and includes the vertebral column, rib cage, sternum, skull, and hyoid bone. The **vertebral column** consists of 33 vertebrae classified as cervical vertebrae, thoracic vertebrae, lumbar vertebrae, and sacral vertebrae. The **rib cage** includes 12 paired ribs, 10 pairs of true ribs and two pairs of floating ribs, and the **sternum**, which consists of the manubrium, corpus sterni, and xiphoid process. The **skull** includes the cranium and facial bones. The **ossicles** are bones in the middle ear. The **hyoid bone** provides an attachment point for the tongue muscles. The axial skeleton protects vital organs including the brain, heart, and lungs.

The **appendicular skeleton** consists of 126 bones including the pectoral girdle, pelvic girdle, and appendages. The **pectoral girdle** consists of the scapulae (shoulder blades) and clavicles (collarbones). The **pelvic girdle** attaches to the sacrum at the sacroiliac joint. The upper appendages (arms) include the humerus, radius, ulna, carpals, metacarpals, and phalanges. The lower appendages (legs) include the femur, patella, fibula, tibia, tarsals, metatarsals, and phalanges.

The axial skeleton and the appendicular skeleton:

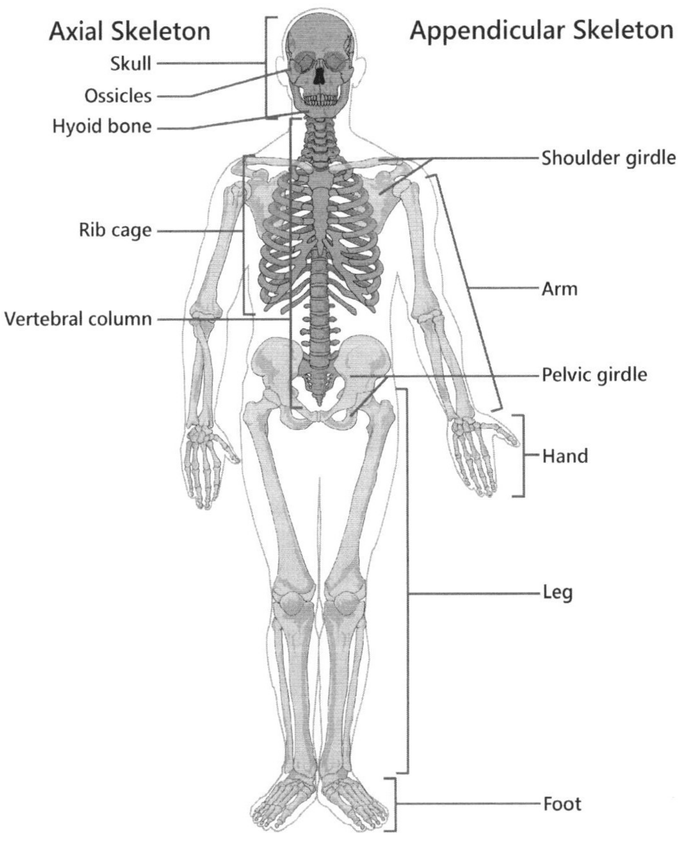

Review Video: Skeletal System
Visit mometrix.com/academy and enter code: 256447

Nervous System

The human **nervous system** consists of the **central nervous system** (i.e., brain and spinal cord) and the **peripheral nervous system** (i.e., nerves). They deliver voluntary and involuntary messages throughout the body. Core functions, such as digestion and respiration, are controlled by the brain via messages sent through the peripheral nervous system. The brain also receives external cues to regulate temperature and activate certain muscle groups.

Review Video: Function of the Nervous System
Visit mometrix.com/academy and enter code: 708428

The Eyes

The eyes are a sensory organ and therefore belong to the nervous system. The main **parts of the eye** and their functions are as follows:

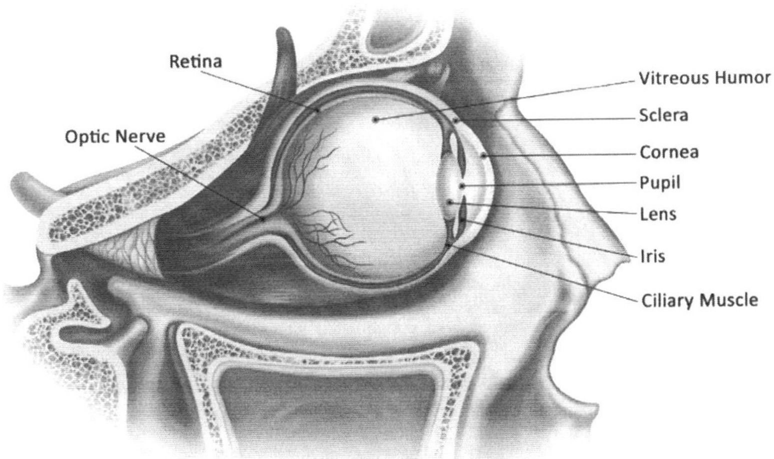

- **Aqueous humor** is watery fluid that maintains eye pressure.
- The **bony orbit** is the socket protecting the eye.
- **Cranial nerves** that help with the function of the eye such as movement or vision include:
    - The optic nerve (cranial nerve II)
    - Oculomotor (III)
    - Trochlear (IV)
    - Trigeminal (V)
    - Abducens (VI)
    - Vagus (X) nerves
- **Eyelashes and lids** protect the eye and sweep out particles.
- **Extrinsic muscles** focus the eye.
- The **lacrimal glands** are tear ducts to moisten the eye.
- The **lens** refracts light.
- The **optic disc** is the blind spot.
- The **pupil** regulates light entry.

- The **retina** has rods for black and white imaging and cones for color imaging, and helps trigger the optic nerve to send impulses to the brain.
- The **macula** is at the retinal center that is very sensitive to light. The black spot in the center is called the fovea which provides the sharpest vision.
- The **choroid** is a black layer behind the retina that absorbs light and nourishes the retina.
- The **cornea** is the window at the front of the eye that helps with focus.
- The **iris** regulates light entry.
- The **sclera** is tough, white fibrous connective tissue holding nerves and vessels that acts as protection for the eye.
- The **suspensory ligament** connects the lens to the ciliary muscles of the iris.
- The **vitreous humor** is jelly that maintains the eye's shape and refracts images.

Reproductive System

The **reproductive system** consists of the prostate, testicle, penis, and scrotum in males and ovaries, uterus, vagina, fallopian tubes, and mammary glands in females. The primary function is the creation of human life. **Sperm** is produced by the testes and is delivered to the ovary-produced **eggs** in the fallopian tubes for fertilization. The uterus then serves as the home for the developing fetus. **Mammary glands** secrete nutrients for the newborn child.

Male Reproductive System

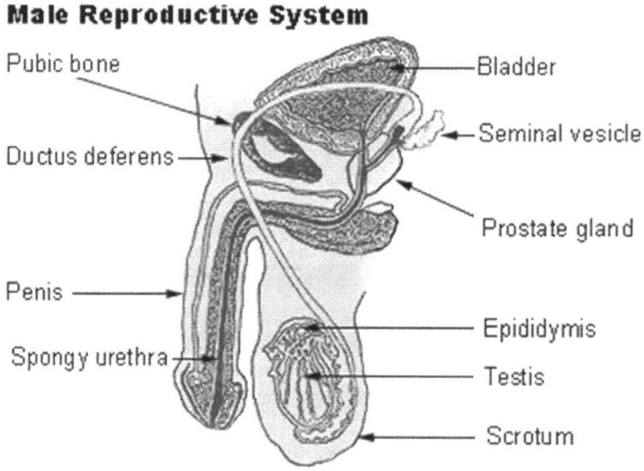

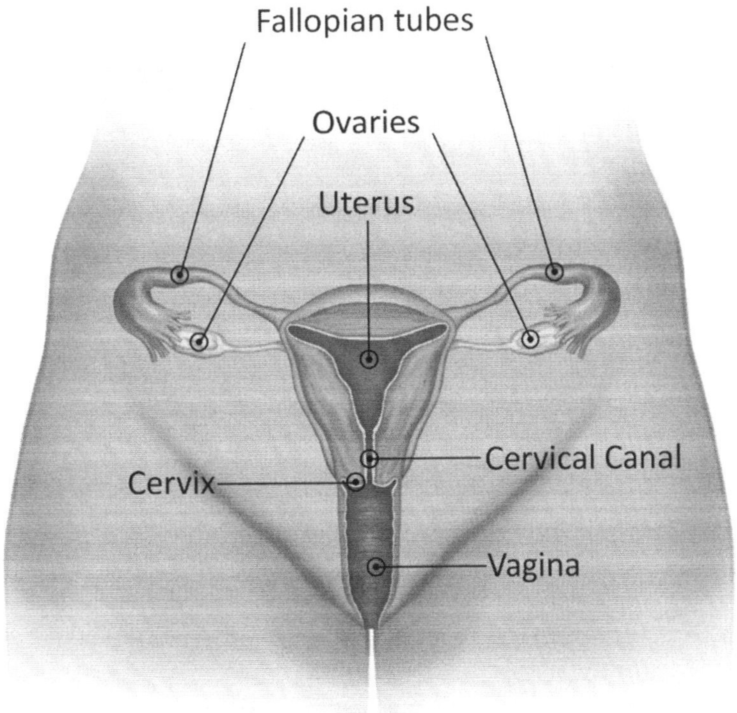

Review Video: Reproductive Systems
Visit mometrix.com/academy and enter code: 505450

Interconnectedness of Body Systems

Respiratory and Circulatory Systems Working Together

Body systems work in concert with each other to respond to increasing and decreasing demands on the body and regulate **homeostasis**, the manner in which the human body regulates itself based on internal and external conditions in order to maintain a physiological balance. For example, the heart pumps blood through the **circulatory system** to distribute oxygenated blood throughout the body to meet physiological demands at any given time. Blood becomes oxygenated in the lungs (**respiratory system**) after excess **carbon dioxide** is released from the body through respiration. Inspiration of **oxygen** into the lungs allows the blood to become oxygen-rich so as to be distributed throughout the body. When physiological demands of the body increase (e.g., quickly climbing stairs), inspiration of oxygen increases and the heart pumps faster in order to more efficiently increase the delivery of oxygenated blood throughout the body. When the intense physical activity subsides, breathing slows and the heart returns to a normal resting heart rate.

Impact of Diet and Exercise on the Circulatory System

The delivery of **oxygenated blood** throughout the body can be accomplished more efficiently with a pattern of consistent exercise and good dietary habits. **Aerobic** activity strengthens the heart by increasing the oxygen carrying capacity of the red blood cells (**hemoglobin**) while also lowering resting blood pressure. In addition, aerobic exercise helps increase high density lipoproteins (HDL) (i.e., "good cholesterol") and decrease low density lipoproteins (i.e., "bad cholesterol"), which helps keep the arteries (**circulatory system**) clear. Consistent and adequate physical activity also helps regulate blood sugars, which can reduce the likelihood of developing Type II diabetes. A high fiber, low fat diet also directly contributes to lower blood sugar levels, cholesterol management, and helps maintain healthy bowels (**digestive system**). Combining regular aerobic physical activity with a high fiber, low fat diet is one of the most effective methods to improve one's cardiovascular health, maintain a healthy weight, and increase personal longevity.

Factors that Affect Health and Development

Heredity, Environment, and Behavior

Heredity, environment, and behavior contribute to overall health:

- **Hereditary** factors are traits passed within a family that can impact one's health in both negative and positive ways. For example, a family history of heart disease and cancer can negatively impact risk of disease, and a family history of long life can positively affect longevity.
- Environment refers to the **physical environment** (e.g., polluted air and water, unsafe home, etc.) and the social environment (e.g., substance abuse in the home, partner abuse, etc.). Both can impact health.
- **Behavior** refers to **personal** choices that impact health. These behaviors include decisions on tobacco and alcohol use, drinking and driving, and dietary choices.

These elements interact to positively and negatively impact health. For example, a person with a family history of cancer (**hereditary factor**) should avoid excessive sun exposure, eat a high-fiber/low-fat diet, and receive more frequent cancer screenings (**behaviors**) than a person without the hereditary risk. As another example, one who is aware of a family history of heart disease (**hereditary factor**) and therefore chooses to eat a balanced, low-fat, high-protein diet and exercise (**behavior**) can reduce their risk. As a final example, a person with a family history of lung disease (**hereditary factor**) may decide to live in an area with reduced air pollution (**environment**) and choose not to smoke tobacco (**behaviors**).

Effect of Nutrition on Growth and Development

An adequate and **balanced diet** is a key element in proper growth and development. A balance of carbohydrates, proteins, fats, fiber, and minerals is necessary for the growth, development, functioning, and repair of the body. **Dietary deficiencies** of these nutritional building blocks can lead to health problems early in life with some that can extend into adulthood. For example, a diet consisting of whole grains with carbohydrates, fibers, and vitamins not only provides proper nutrition to growing bodies, but also provides energy allowing for increased exercise tolerance. A quality, balanced diet goes hand-in-hand with **physical activity** to maintain desired body weight and regulate blood sugars. Good dietary habits established early in life, when combined with physical activity, often extend into adulthood to maintain health as one ages.

Effect of Exercise on Growth and Development

Early development of bones and muscles are the foundation of proper growth. **Exercise** helps develop necessary bone mass and density, which can reduce the likelihood of osteoporosis and other bone diseases. Proper exercise also reduces the risk of heart disease and diabetes later in life. In addition to **disease prevention**, proper levels of exercise/physical activity increase coordination, balance, posture, and flexibility. It is recommended children aged 6–17 perform 60 minutes of aerobic exercise per day, combined with muscle strengthening exercises (e.g., pushups, rope climbing, etc.) and bone strengthening exercises (e.g., jumping, running, etc.) at least three times per week.

Effect of Sleep on Growth and Development

Proper sleep directly impacts growth, stress hormones, the immune system, respiration, and cardiovascular function. **Lack of sleep** is linked to obesity, heart disease, and increased infections later in life. **Adequate sleep** is linked to improved exercise outcomes because of the increased time given for muscle recovery. In addition, **growth hormones** which are critical to proper growth and development are released during sleep. It is recommended that:

- **Preschool children** (3–5 years) should sleep 10–13 hours during each 24-hour period.
- **Elementary school children** (6–12) should sleep 9–12 hours during each 24-hour period.
- **Teenagers** (13–18) should sleep 8–10 hours each 24-hour period.
- **Adults** (18–60) should sleep 7 or more hours each 24-hour period.

Key signs that one is receiving **enough sleep** include the ability to sleep through the night with minimal interruption, and awakening rested and alert.

Relationship Between Diet and Exercise

Personal health behaviors often have the greatest impact upon lifetime health, and many of these behaviors begin early in life. One of these key behaviors is eating a **balanced diet,** like one based on the **Healthy Plate Model**. A healthy diet combined with adequate, regular exercise have a cumulative effect on reducing obesity, the leading cause of **morbidity and mortality** (i.e., disease and death) in the U.S. It is recommended that one participate in at least 150 minutes of moderate physical activity or 75 minutes of vigorous activity each week. This should include a balance between **aerobic** exercise (i.e., activities that make a person breath hard and sweat), and **strengthening** exercises (i.e., activities that focus on increasing muscle mass and flexibility).

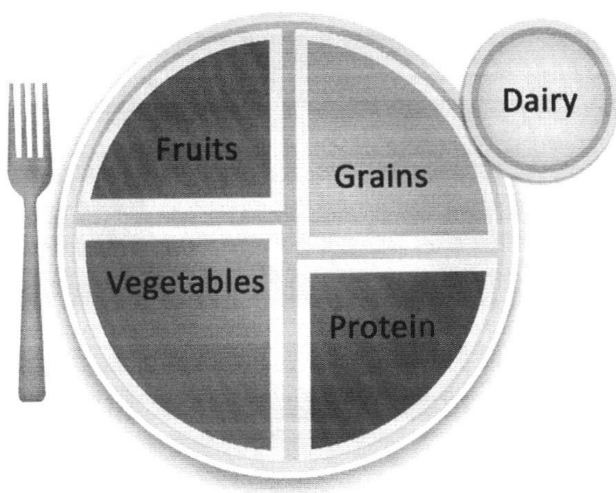

Common Changes Occurring in Puberty

The onset of **puberty** can occur as early as elementary school (8–12 years of age) or as late as high school (13–15 years of age) and can create a host of **physical and emotional** responses. Often these include changes in **personal hygiene** (e.g., increased showering due to body odor, use of feminine hygiene products in response to the start of the menstrual cycle). For females, puberty typically consists of beginning of the **menstrual cycle**, changes in body shape, breast tenderness, and hair growth. In males, puberty is characterized by acne, genital growth, hair growth, deepening of the voice, height and muscle growth, erections, and nocturnal emissions. Though the physical changes are the most obvious, the **emotional and social** impacts on personal health can be profound. Youth going through puberty often become more self-conscious, experience dramatic mood swings, develop a sexual interest in others, and experience changes in sleep patterns and energy levels. Given that sexuality is an uncomfortable topic for many parents, it is not uncommon for students to have little to no information about puberty. This creates further anxiety and confusion among many students.

Human Physical Development

Physical development is characterized by milestones for physical growth at various ages (i.e., newborn infant, 18-month-old toddler, etc.). Many milestones indicate the child is developing appropriate developmental tasks, including **fine and gross motor skills.**

- **Fine motor skills** refer to small movements in the hand, wrist, and fingers. Examples include grasping eating utensils and writing instruments.
- **Gross motor skills** involve the development of larger muscle groups that allow a developing infant to sit, crawl, and eventually walk. As the child ages, more complex tasks are accomplished through development of physical coordination and balance.

Much of physical growth and development is tied to the development and functioning of the various **body systems** (e.g., skeletal, neuromuscular, nervous system) used to regulate these behaviors.

Physical Development for Newborns to Six Months of Age

Developmental milestones are characterized by skills at least 75% of children can accomplish by a specific age. In the first **six months** of life a baby should exhibit specific **gross motor** physical developmental markers, such as using large muscle groups (e.g., arms, legs, neck, abdomen) to kick their feet when on their back, control head bobbing, lift their head when placed on their stomach, hold all of their body weight when supported in a standing position, and push up with the arms from a stomach position. **Fine motor skill** milestones include being able to hold objects placed in their hands, reaching for and grabbing objects, and drawing these objects closer to the body.

Physical Development for Children 6–12 Months of Age

By **9 months of age**, a child should be able to move into a sitting position unassisted and maintain that position without support, switch objects from one hand to the other, use their fingers to move food closer to the mouth, and be able to stop and pivot to pick up an object. A child may begin crawling at this age, though that may not occur until later. A **12-month-old** baby should be able to pull up on another object (e.g., chair) to stand unassisted, walk with support from other objects (e.g., furniture), drink from a cup with adult assistance, be able to point and poke with their fingers, and bang items together. They can also begin to feed themselves in a high chair, but often squeeze and squish food as they learn about texture and eating solid food.

Physical Development for Children 12–18 Months of Age

Children at this age are often known as **toddlers.** They advance from infancy towards greater independence in many functions. Children in the **12–18-month** range develop **gross motor** skills include unassisted standing, walking independently, squatting to pick up items, development of a gait for stiff running, crawling up stairs, and seating themselves on low-profile chairs. They often use their bodies to express their needs by shaking/nodding their heads, pointing, and grunting. **Fine motor** skills include pointing to pictures in a book, scribbling with a crayon, stacking items on top of each other, feeding themselves with more precision, and drinking from a cup with some spillage.

Physical Development for Children 18 Months to Three Years of Age

Children in this age group are known as older toddlers and demonstrate increased **gross** and **fine motor** skills. Children in this age group can usually run well, walk up and down stairs with minimal assistance, remove shirts and pants without assistance, stack multiple blocks on top of each other, and feed themselves with less assistance. In addition, it is common for children in this age range to help bathe themselves. They demonstrate improved skill in catching, throwing, and kicking balls. They may also be able to jump and land on a spot, turn pages in a book, ride a tricycle, and unscrew lids. These tasks are directly related to improved hand/eye coordination.

Physical Development for Children 3–5 Years of Age

Most children in this age group are very **physically active** and develop increased **independence**. Milestones include walking backwards easily, easily climbing up and down stairs, interchanging their feet without assistance, tumbling, skipping, hopping with balance, and easily catching a thrown ball. They can also stay balanced on one foot with their eyes closed. It is common for these children to show more skill using simple tools and eating utensils. They also use the toilet independently and feed themselves with minimal spills. Children demonstrate a **hand preference** and can hold crayons/writing instruments between the thumb and first two fingers. They can independently cut paper with scissors and can imitate a variety of shapes when drawing (e.g., triangles, squares, and circles).

Physical Development for Youth 6–12 Years of Age

Adolescents in this age group typically demonstrate increased muscle strength and dexterity as hand/eye coordination continues to be refined. The **gross motor** skills of increased large group muscle mass leads to skill development in sports and other physically-demanding activities. The **fine motor** skills of increased small muscle development leads to the ability to complete complex tasks such as typing on a computer, bowling, playing golf, solving multi-piece puzzles, and working closely with other small, detailed tasks. It is during this phase that involvement in team sports increases as physical abilities continuously improve with maturation. Increases in the **sex hormones** estrogen and testosterone during puberty is also responsible for much of the rapid growth of weight and muscle mass, leading to increased strength, endurance, and dexterity.

Physical Development for Adolescents 13–18 Years of Age

As **puberty** (a period of rapid physical development) heightens in the teenage years, the **sex hormones** testosterone and estrogen begin to play a more prominent role in physical development. In **males**, the voice deepens, genitals become larger, facial hair may begin to appear, muscle mass increases dramatically, sweat glands become more active, and acne develops. In **females**, acne becomes more common, breasts become larger, body hair increases, body fat increases, and the menstrual cycle begins. Due to the **idiosyncratic** (individualized) nature of the release of testosterone and estrogen, physical developments may come earlier or later for each individual teen. Hormones also often lead to dramatic mood swings, changes in temperament, and differing emotional responses.

Individual Variation in Patterns of Physical Development

Individual variations in developmental patterns are normal. **Physical changes** can be impacted by a variety of factors including environment, heredity, sex, exercise, nutrition, hormones, and familial influence.

The most common delay in physical development in infants is **motor delay** (i.e., rates in sitting, crawling, and walking independently). When there is no identifiable underlying cause for the delay, most children eventually "catch up" with their peer group. **Diseases** such as Down's Syndrome and Autism can result in mild to profound physical development variation. Along with a number of cognitive developmental issues, these diseases can create a spectrum of **developmental delays** that vary from person to person.

Cognitive Development

Human Cognitive Development

Cognitive development refers to the way children experience the world and make sense of it. The steps of cognitive development include **reasoning**, **intelligence**, **language**, and **memory**.

- **Reasoning** refers to thinking about things in a logical and rational manner.
- **Intelligence** refers to the ability to obtain, interpret, and apply knowledge and skills in common daily interactions.
- **Language** refers to the emergence of words and communication through symbols.
- **Memory** refers to the ability to encode, store, and retrieve information so that once novel concepts and situations become routine and recognizable.

Cognition involves recognizing familiar scenarios and reacting in an appropriate manner based on past behaviors. Age-appropriate cognitive development is characterized by children gaining knowledge through interactions with the world at-large and building upon stored knowledge

Piaget's Stages of Cognitive Development

Jean Piaget's **Theory of Cognitive Development** divides cognition into phases within approximate age ranges.

- **Sensorimotor Intelligence** (approximately birth to 2 years of age) is marked by the infant interacting with the world through movements and sensations, along with looking, reaching, grasping, and sucking.
- The **Preoperational Phase** (approximately 2–7 years of age) is marked by the use of language and pictures to represent objects. In addition, children in this phase are egocentric and only think of the world from their perspective. Preoperational children struggle **object constancy**, the concept that things exist even though they may not be visually apparent.
- The **Concrete Operational Stage** (approximately 7–11 years of age) is marked by the use of logical thinking and the development of reasoning ability.
- The **Formal Operational Stage** (approximately 12 years of age and older) is marked by the development and use of abstract thought, reasoning through hypothetical situations, and the development and refinement of moral, philosophical, ethical, and moral reasoning.

Review Video: Piaget's Cognitive Development Theory
Visit mometrix.com/academy and enter code: 100376

Individual Variation in Patterns of Cognitive Development

Cognitive development refers to how children perceive, think, and respond to different aspects of their world. **Cognitive delays** are conditions in which children lag significantly behind their peer group in cognitive development. Depending on the severity, these delays may be classified as intellectual disabilities or a cognitive/intellectual disorder. With appropriate therapy, many of these cognitive delays can be remediated. **Speech/language delays** are those in which the child is not developing an age-appropriate vocabulary and lags behind their peers in developing speech patterns, such as with pronunciation and grammar. Language and cognitive skills are linked in that stronger language skills often means stronger cognitive skills (i.e., language as a programming tool for cognition). Therefore, early, consistent therapy to remediate delayed language skills is essential for improving eventual cognitive function.

Social and Emotional Development

SOCIAL/EMOTIONAL DEVELOPMENT

Social/emotional development refers to a person's ability to experience, regulate, and express emotions, and to communicate and interact with others. It also includes the recognition of and adherence to social norms and mores. These skills develop as the child interacts with others, and lay the foundation for other, more advanced, cognitive skills like literacy and numeracy. Self-awareness, self-management, social awareness, relationship skills, and responsible decision-making are all components of social/emotional learning. **Empathy** is a key milestone in social/emotional development.

PATTERNS AND PROCESSES

Social/emotional development begins at birth when children **bond** with parents and other adults by understanding emotions through facial expressions and voice patterns. Infants are particularly sensitive to social and emotional stimulation. As the child ages, maintaining positive relationships with parents and other nurturing caregivers leads to increased social/emotional development. This development is characterized by:

- **Interactions and relationships with adults**: cooperative activities with caregivers
- **Interactions and relationships with peers**: cooperative activities with same-age children
- **Identity of self in relation to peers**: responding to own name, body parts, etc.
- **Recognition of ability**: understanding they make things happen
- **Expression of emotions**: using facial expressions and vocalization
- **Regulation of emotion**: exhibiting voluntary control over emotion
- **Development of empathy:** recognizing and experiencing the emotional states of others
- **Impulse control**: exhibiting voluntary control over behaviors
- **Social understanding:** relating to others' reactions and life experiences

INDIVIDUAL VARIATION AND RISK PATTERNS

Age-appropriate social and emotional development is impacted by several factors.

- **Family risk factors** include maternal depression or mental illness in the family, parental substance abuse, parental incarceration, family violence, poverty, and parental unemployment.
- **Environmental factors** include unsafe or unhealthy living conditions, low-quality childcare, and lack of resources in the community to support the child and their family.

These and other factors can result in developmental delays marked by changes in **temperament** (i.e., the way a child experiences and reacts to the world) and **behavior** (i.e., control of behavior in response to specific situations). Common signs of social/emotional delays are delayed empathy for others and difficulty making social/emotional connections with peers.

Prenatal Care

A Healthy Embryo and Fetus

Practices that promote **development** of a healthy embryo and fetus include early and consistent **prenatal care**, avoiding tobacco or alcohol use, taking vitamin supplements such as folic acid, following a healthy diet, exercising with the guidance of a physician, avoiding exposure to toxic substances, limiting caffeine intake, and maintaining a healthy weight.

Avoiding **maternal disease** can also improve fetal outcomes. Pregnant women should maintain all vaccinations and avoid contact with people carrying infectious diseases (e.g., measles, mumps). **Fetal development** can be measured through ultrasound and amniocentesis procedures.

Poor fetal development can lead to a lifetime of **physical, mental, and emotional challenges**. It is therefore important to detect pregnancy at its earliest stages in order to begin a medically supervised **prenatal program,** which can reduce the risk to the developing fetus.

Problems as a Result of Restricted Prenatal Growth

Poor prenatal growth is often referred to as **Intrauterine Growth Restriction** (IUG) and can impact the developing infant in a variety of ways. The key marker for IUG is when the developing fetus is not as big as expected given the **stage of pregnancy** (i.e., "gestational age"). The typical cause of IUG is a lack of proper nutrients to the developing fetus. **Low birth weight** (less than 5.5 pounds) is often tied to **prematurity** (birth before the 37th week of pregnancy) which can lead to trouble eating, difficulty gaining weight, and difficulty fighting infections. **Neurodevelopmental challenges** for IUG infants can include reduced responsiveness, delayed bonding with the mother, and lack of engagement with adult faces. Some IUG infants show increased cognitive and developmental delays later in life. The vast majority of IUG cases can be prevented by improved maternal diet, increased maternal sleep, and avoidance of alcohol and other drugs.

Personal Health Plans

Developing and Following a Personal Health Plan

Maintaining adequate nutrition, exercise, and an appropriate body weight are key parts of improving overall wellness. A **personal health plan** (PHP) is a personalized roadmap to achieve health and wellness goals. To develop a personal health plan, one should complete a **personal health inventory** to evaluate their overall health and find their starting point. For example, an individual can assess whether they are at a healthy weight by calculating their **body mass index** (BMI) and their **waist circumference**. Regularly reflecting on and assessing nutritional habits is a crucial component of developing a personal health plan. Keeping a food and beverage diary that tracks daily food and beverage consumption can help one identify their current intake patterns. An activity log can track physical activity throughout the day. Pedometers, fitness watches, or smartphone fitness applications can also be used to track activity levels. **SMART goals** (specific, measurable, attainable, realistic, and time-bound) can help an individual create actionable steps to achieve their health and wellness goals based on their personal health inventory. Finally, **new habits** can be reinforced and unhealthy behaviors replaced through regular **reflection and positive self-talk**.

Overview of Disease and Illness

Communicable Diseases

Diseases are divided into two types: communicable and noncommunicable. **Communicable diseases** are illnesses caused by infectious agents transmitted from an infected person or animal to other people or animals. They are caused by **pathogens** like bacteria, viruses, and fungi. Transmission can be **direct contact**, which occurs through contact with an infected person via blood or bodily fluids, touching (e.g. staphylococcus), kissing or sexual contact (e.g. gonorrhea, HIV), or contact with fecal or oral secretions (e.g. hepatitis A), or **indirect contact**, which occurs without human-to-human contact but through contact with contaminated surfaces or objects (e.g. Norwalk virus), food (e.g. salmonella, E. coli), water (e.g. cholera), insect bites (e.g. malaria, yellow fever, and plague), or air (e.g. tuberculosis, measles). Most communicable diseases are acute—which means the disease and symptoms appear over a short period of time—and occur seasonally.

Noncommunicable Diseases

Noncommunicable diseases (NCDs) are diseases that are not contagious or transmittable to other people. They contribute to far more deaths worldwide than communicable diseases—approximately 70% of all deaths. Unlike communicable diseases, NCDs are long-lasting, slow progressing **chronic illnesses** that are often a result of poor lifestyle choices (e.g., type 2 diabetes, emphysema, and cardiovascular disease) or genetic mutation (e.g., cystic fibrosis, sickle cell anemia, lupus, and cancer). They are not the result of a pathogen; rather, they result from multiple risk factors that are further divided into modifiable risk factors, environmental risk factors, and non-modifiable risk factors. **Modifiable risk factors** are personal behavior or lifestyle choices that can be reduced or controlled by intervention like diet, physical activity, smoking, and alcohol or drug use. **Environmental risk factors** result from the physical environment and contribute to health outcomes like pollution, radiation, noise, and climate change. **Non-modifiable risk factors** cannot be reduced or changed, like age, gender, family history, and race.

Review Video: Gene Mutation
Visit mometrix.com/academy and enter code: 955485

Viruses and How They Are Transmitted

A **virus** is a microscopic entity that uses living organisms like animals, plants, or bacteria to replicate. Viruses **reproduce** by attaching themselves to their host's cells and reprogramming them to make new copies of the virus, effectively spreading as they go. The most common virus **transmission** methods are through droplets generated from coughing and sneezing, fecal contamination of food or water, contact with skin rashes or lesions, contact with contaminated surfaces, and bites from an infected animal vector. Once infected, the virus can cause damage to one or multiple body systems.

Bacteria and How They Are Transmitted

Bacteria are single-cell microorganisms that can live inside and outside of the body. They are larger and more complex than viruses and can **reproduce** on their own. Although most bacteria are harmless and even beneficial, those that cause illness in humans are called pathogenic bacteria. **Pathogenic bacteria** are infectious but not always contagious, which means that they cause sickness when they enter the body but are not always spread from person to person. Bacteria are **classified** by their gram-negative or gram-positive status—the ability to produce an **endotoxin** that causes tissue damage or death— and their need for oxygen, genus, and shape (spheres, rods, and spirals). Similar to viruses, bacteria can be **transmitted** through coughing and sneezing (e.g., pertussis), contact with infected people (e.g., impetigo, chlamydia), animals or insects (e.g., Lyme disease), contact with contaminated surfaces (e.g., cellulitis), and food or water (e.g., salmonella).

Fungi and How They Are Transmitted

A **fungus** is an organism that feeds on **decaying organic matter**. Although fungi are often found outdoors in soil and plants, they can also be found on and inside of the body. Fungi **reproduces** through the spread of microscopic spores. When an individual inhales or touches fungal spores, they may contract a lung and skin infection. Fungal infections are rarely transmitted from one person to another. There are two types of fungal infections: opportunistic and primary.

- **Opportunistic fungal infections** spread aggressively, but typically only impact individuals with weak immune systems.
- **Primary fungal infections** can develop in individuals with functioning immune systems, but are slow to develop. and usually emerge once a person has inhaled fungal spores.

Fungal infections can be local or systemic.

- **Local** infections only affect one area of the body. For example, a local fungal infection may only show up on the nail that was infected–not any other part of the body. Common locales for local infections also include the skin, genitals, and mouth.
- **Systemic** infections can affect many areas of the body or multiple organs at one time.

Parasites and How They Are Transmitted

Parasites are organisms that live in or on their host and feed on their host while causing it harm. There are three main types of parasites that cause disease in humans: protozoa, helminths, and ectoparasites.

- **Protozoa** are rapidly reproducing microscopic single-celled organisms that invade the body's tissues to obtain nourishment. They are spread through a variety of ways, but are most often transmitted by contact with human feces (e.g., giardia, cryptosporidium).
- **Helminths** (worms) are macroscopic multi-celled organisms that live in and outside of the body and cause infection. They are transmitted by eggs spread through fecal contamination and are most common in tropical and subtropical regions. Examples of parasitic diseases include Guinea worm disease, Chagas disease, and trichomoniasis.
- **Ectoparasites** are large multi-celled organisms that live on or feed off of skin (e.g., ticks, mosquitos, fleas, lice). They are vectors of infectious viral and bacterial diseases like Lyme disease, typhus, encephalitis, malaria, etc.

Communicable Diseases

Risk Factors for Contracting Communicable Diseases

An individual's **risk** of contracting a **communicable disease** varies based on their overall health, vaccination status, personal hygiene, number of people they live and work with, socioeconomic status, and condition of their housing. Those who frequently come into contact with wildlife and other potential vectors (e.g., mosquitos) are at **higher risk** of contracting a communicable disease. Certain populations are at **higher risk** of becoming severely ill (i.e., hospitalization, ventilator, death) once they are infected. This includes individuals who are 65+ years old or under 2 years old, individuals experiencing health and social inequities (e.g., racial and ethnic minorities, low socioeconomic status), and people with medical conditions like cancer, chronic lung disease, diabetes, and heart conditions. Individuals living in communities with poor water and sanitation, insufficient public health surveillance, poor waste management, and inadequate government regulations regarding food and water safety are at higher risk of contracting a communicable disease. Communities with high exposure to climate-related catastrophes and few health professionals or medications are more susceptible to disease outbreak and inadequate disease management.

Methods for Treating Different Types of Communicable Diseases

- **Bacterial diseases** are treated with **antibiotics**, which kill bacteria or slow their development to allow for the immune system to respond.
- **Viral infections** can be prevented with **vaccines**. When given a vaccine which contains an agent (e.g., weakened forms of the microbe, proteins) that resembles the virus, the body mounts an **immune response** and produces **antibodies** that will terminate the active form of the virus in the future. If already infected with a virus, **antiviral medications** can be used to treat the infections. They do not destroy the pathogen, but inhibit further development of the virus.
- **Fungal infections** are treated with **antifungal medications** that attack the fungal cell membrane to either kill fungal cells or prevent them from reproducing.
- **Parasites** are treated with **antiparasitic drugs** that kill the parasite.

Preventative Measures Reducing Spread of Communicable Disease

The most effective way to **limit the spread** of many communicable diseases is through **quarantine** and **physical distancing**. **Vaccines** also prevent many infectious diseases. Keeping up to date on vaccinations, getting vaccinated before traveling, and getting the recommended vaccinations during childhood are important for reducing transmission. **Practicing good hygiene** (e.g., hand washing after using the bathroom, before and after eating, treating a wound, touching others' hands or an animal, or coughing/sneezing) can prevent the spread of bacteria, viruses, and parasites. **Safe food handling and preparation**, such as washing utensils and surfaces during food preparation, washing fruits and vegetables before eating, and cooking/storing food at proper temperatures, are also effective strategies for preventing the spread of many foodborne illnesses. **Cleaning surfaces** regularly with soap and water, especially the bathroom and kitchen, can reduce the spread of many diseases that are transmitted indirectly. Finally, **reducing stress** can prevent disease transmission as chronic stress can suppress the immune system and make a person more susceptible to infection.

Non-Communicable Diseases

Asthma

Asthma is a noncommunicable disease. While the exact **cause** of asthma is unknown, genetics, allergies, respiratory infections, and contact with allergens or environmental irritants are likely to contribute to the development of asthma. Those with asthma experience **recurring symptoms** like chest pain, chest tightness, and shortness of breath. Individuals with an **asthmatic parent** are more likely to develop asthma. A **childhood respiratory infection and allergies** can increase the risk of asthma. Working or living in **environments** in which one comes into contact with **irritants** like industrial or wood dust, chemical fumes, and solvents can lead to the development of asthma. Smoking, secondhand smoke, and air pollution can also lead to asthma. Additional **social factors** like poverty and poor access to health care can exacerbate asthma symptoms.

DIABETES

Diabetes is a noncommunicable disease that affects how the body uses a sugar called glucose. There are three types of diabetes: type 1 diabetes, type 2 diabetes, and gestational diabetes.

- **Type 1 diabetes** is caused by an autoimmune reaction which causes the body to destroy cells in the pancreas that make **insulin**. The pancreas is unable to produce insulin, and glucose is unable to move out of the blood and into the cells which results in **very high blood sugar levels**. **Risk factors** for type 1 diabetes include family history of diabetes and exposure to a viral infection that triggers the autoimmune disease.
- In **type 2 diabetes**, cells become **resistant** to insulin and sugar builds up in the blood. **Risk factors** for type 2 diabetes are being overweight or obese, family history of diabetes, physical inactivity, race and ethnicity, older age, gestational diabetes, abnormal cholesterol, and high blood pressure.
- **Gestational diabetes** is a pregnancy-induced condition in which the pancreas is unable to produce enough extra insulin to overcome the hormone-induced insulin resistance. This must be a new-onset condition that presents in the second or third trimester of pregnancy to be diagnosed.

CANCER

Cancer is a noncommunicable disease that occurs when there are **DNA mutations** within a cell that inhibit growth and replication. The new cancerous cells crowd out non-cancerous cells and damage body tissues. The most common **causes** and **risk factors** are related to environmental exposure, radiation exposure, infections, age, family history, and various lifestyle factors. Exposure to carcinogens, asbestos, and benzene in the home and workplace environment can lead to cancer. As people age, they are exposed to more **carcinogens** and the body loses its ability to find and destroy cancerous cells, which can lead to the development of cancer. **Radiation** from the sun or medical treatment, viral infections that affect the DNA or suppress the immune system (e.g., HIV, human papillomavirus), and **genetic susceptibility** can also cause cancer. **Major lifestyle risk factors** like tobacco use, alcohol use, physical inactivity, obesity, diets high in processed and red meats, sun exposure, and unsafe sex can increase the risk of cancer.

HEART DISEASE

Heart disease refers to numerous conditions that affect heart health (e.g., coronary artery disease, arrhythmias, congenital heart defects, heart valve disease, heart infection). The causes of heart disease depend on what kind of heart disease a person has. For example, **coronary artery disease** is caused by a buildup of plaque in arteries. **Heart infection**—also called endocarditis—is caused by bacteria, viruses, and parasites. **Cardiomyopathy**—the thickening of heart muscle—can be caused by damage from heart attacks, drugs, or genetics. **Risk factors** for heart disease include old age, sex, family history, smoking, poor diet, high blood pressure and cholesterol, diabetes, obesity and overweight status, physical inactivity, stress, and poor dental health.

METHODS FOR PREVENTING NONCOMMUNICABLE DISEASES

Primary disease prevention seeks to prevent disease or injury before it occurs through restricting exposure, modifying existing risk factors, and increasing resistance to disease before exposure. Examples of noncommunicable primary disease prevention include adjusting poor eating habits, tobacco cessation, exercising and weight loss, using legislation to ban substances associated with a disease or health condition (e.g., asbestos, lead paint), and implementing legislation to mandate safe and healthy practices (e.g., workplace health standards, restrictions on air pollution emissions, tobacco regulations).

Methods for Early Detection of Noncommunicable Diseases

Secondary prevention aims to reduce the impact of existing disease or injury through early disease detection and treatment and developing strategies to prevent reinjury or reoccurrence of disease. A common secondary prevention method is the implementation of regular **cancer screening tests** to detect early-stage disease (e.g., regular mammograms to detect breast cancer, colonoscopies to detect colorectal cancer, and pap smears to check for cervical cancer). Another method is **genetic counseling** to assess the likelihood of a person or their relative developing a genetic condition or disease and help them explore treatment options. Genetic counseling can be conducted before and during pregnancy to address concerns that can affect infant health (e.g., birth defects, genetic conditions, abnormal test results, maternal infections). It can also be used to address concerns about genetic disorders in childhood like abnormal newborn screening results, birth defects, or intellectual and developmental disabilities. Genetic counseling is often used in adulthood to assess symptoms of a condition or family history of a hereditary condition (e.g., hereditary breast and ovarian cancer, Huntington's disease, sickle cell disease, muscular dystrophy).

Immune Responses

Immune System Response to an Antigen

Many different organs, cells, and proteins make up the **immune system**. The immune system defends the body from **pathogens** and removes harmful substances from the body. When a foreign substance—called an **antigen**—enters the body and attaches to immune system cells, the immune system begins mounting a response. Examples of **common antigens** include bacteria, fungi, viruses, allergens, and pollutants. Once eliminated, the immune system stores information about the pathogen and how to eliminate it to maintain protection for future encounters.

Fevers

A **fever** is a temporary rise in body temperature above the **normal range**, which is within 1 degree above or below 98.6 degrees Fahrenheit. Although commonly thought to be bad for the body, a fever is an example of one of the many **helpful defense mechanisms** that the body employs to respond to disease. When the immune system identifies an antigen, it sends biochemical substances called **pyrogens** to a part of the brain called the **hypothalamus**. In response, the hypothalamus commands the body to produce and retain more heat. An elevated body temperature creates an **inhospitable environment** for pathogens like viruses to replicate or for temperature-sensitive bacteria to survive. Fevers also speed up and strengthen immune cell response by altering their surface proteins to improve their ability to reach the infection site. Since fevers help the immune system fight disease, it is not always necessary to suppress them. However, if a fever exceeds the safe temperature threshold or is accompanied by unusual behavior, medical attention should be sought.

Antibody Formation

Antibody formation is an example of a process that the immune system uses to respond to disease. **Antibodies**—also referred to as immunoglobulins—are proteins that the immune system manufactures when it identifies an antigen in the body. Antibodies are created by **white blood cells** called B lymphocytes or **B cells**. B cells bind to antigens and produce antibodies that are circulated throughout the body. The released antibodies ambush all antigens like the one that prompted the body to mount an immune response. The body continues to produce antibodies until it eliminates all detected antigens, but antibodies may remain in the body for up to several months.

The white blood cells of the immune system include the following:

WBC	Type	% of WBCs	Causes of Increase	Causes of Decrease
Basophils (black or purple)	Granulocyte	1%	Asthma, chronic myelocytic leukemia, Crohn's disease, dermatitis, estrogen, hemolytic anemia, Hodgkin's disease, hypothyroidism, polycythemia vera, and viruses	Allergies, corticosteroids, hyperthyroidism, pregnancy, and stress.
Eosinophils (orange-red, double-lobed nucleus)	Granulocyte	1–3%	Allergy, asthma, or parasitic infestation	Cushing's disease or glucocorticoids use
Lymphocytes (dark, large nucleus surrounded by thin cytoplasm rim)	Agranulocyte	15–40%	Antigens or chronic irritation	AIDS
Monocytes (lavender)	Agranulocyte	2–8%	Myeloproliferative process, like an inflammatory response or chronic myelomonocytic leukemia (CMML)	Hairy cell leukemia
Neutrophils (pink cytoplasm, dark nucleus)	Granulocyte	50–70%	Burns, kidney failure, heart attack, cancer, hemolytic anemia	Leukemia and abscess

Autoimmune Responses and the Immune System

Occasionally, the body mistakes its own cells as antigens during an immune response and attacks healthy, harmless cells in the body. This process is called an **autoimmune response**. When an individual has an **autoimmune disease**, their immune system is unable to distinguish between foreign cells and healthy cells and releases proteins called autoantibodies to attack parts of the body (e.g., the pancreas attacked in type 1 diabetes) or the whole body (e.g., lupus). The exact cause of autoimmune responses is unknown, but scientists theorize that family history, sex, diet, prior infections, and exposure to chemicals may contribute to developing an autoimmune disease. Examples of **common autoimmune diseases** are rheumatoid arthritis, psoriasis, ulcerative colitis, and psoriatic arthritis.

> **Review Video: Immune System**
> Visit mometrix.com/academy and enter code: 622899

Factors Influencing Disease Risk

Environmental Factors Affecting Health and Disease

Environmental factors have a significant impact on health and disease. In fact, 70–90% of chronic disease risk can be attributed to **environmental factors** like air, water, and soil pollution, exposure to harmful chemicals, metals, and nanomaterials, climate change and natural disasters, and ultraviolet radiation. Exposure can **disrupt bodily function** and cause health problems like respiratory diseases, cardiovascular diseases, and certain types of cancer. The health impacts of, and exposure to, the previously mentioned environmental factors can be exacerbated by an individual's **socioeconomic** and **biological characteristics**. This places people with low incomes, those living or working in heavily polluted or poorly environmentally-regulated areas, children, pregnant women, and immunocompromised individuals at increased risk of poor health and/or disease due to environmental factors.

Influence of Laws and Policies on Disease Prevention

Health laws and policies are important preventative measures to address health-related issues.

- **Health policies** are plans, decisions, and actions that achieve health goals. They can be implemented at the local, state, and national level or codified within a clinical environment.
- **Health laws** are legally binding regulations that can lead to consequences if not followed. Local, state, and national legislation are necessary for eliciting changes that reduce disease.

When legislation to address factors contributing to disease is enacted at each level, it can have a **profound impact** on disease prevention. For example, local smoke-free restaurant and business ordinances, state-wide tobacco tax increases, and a national program like the National Tobacco Control Program influence the ease with which individuals can acquire tobacco and consume it and limits broad exposure to harmful pollutants that tobacco contains.

Stages of Prevention and Intervention Along the Continuum of Care

The continuum of care includes all aspects of care that influence outcomes. The primary components are prevention, intervention, and recovery/maintenance during which the person is monitored for compliance.

Prevention	Intervention
May be aimed universally at the entire population, at selected groups, or at-risk individuals, and it usually involves long-term goals. Primary: Aims to prevent disease occurrence and may include educational campaigns (no smoking, use seatbelts), vaccinations. Secondary: Aims to identify and reduce impact (screening mammograms, BP checks). Tertiary: Aims to prevent/delay disease progression (support programs).	Usually aimed at specific groups or individuals and often involves specific treatments (such as surgery, chemotherapy, medications) to alleviate a problem or disorder. Goals may be long term, or they may be time limited with the aim to resolve the problem as quickly as possible.

Components of Nutrition

Nutrients the Human Body Needs to Function

There are 6 main nutrients that the body needs to function: water, carbohydrates, protein, fat, vitamins, and minerals.

- **Water** regulates the body's temperature, transports nutrients to cells, and removes waste products.
- When **carbohydrates** are digested, they are broken down into glucose which is used to fuel the brain, heart, kidneys, and nervous system. They come from grains, fruit, starchy vegetables, and dairy.
- **Protein**, which helps build and repair the body's tissues, is found in meat, seafood, eggs, dairy, and beans.
- **Fats** or lipids produce energy for the body, insulate and protect vital organs, and support cell function. They are often found in foods like meat, dairy, nuts, seeds, and oils.
- **Vitamins** and **minerals** can be found in many different food groups and carry out many tasks to keep the body functioning.

IMPORTANCE OF CALCIUM FOR BONE GROWTH

Calcium is a type of **mineral** that is most often associated with **bone and tooth health**. The body cannot make calcium, so it must consume calcium-rich foods like dairy milk and fortified plant-based milks (e.g., almond, oat, soy, rice milks), milk products like cheese and yogurt, canned fish with bones, leafy greens (e.g., broccoli, kale, mustard green, spinach), and legumes. Once digested, the body deposits the calcium in the **bones**, where 99.5% of the total calcium in the body resides. Thus, calcium is crucial for bone and tooth growth, development, and maintenance. Calcium is also an important mineral for muscle relaxation and contraction, blood clotting, blood pressure, and nerve functioning. Without enough calcium in the diet, the body will remove calcium from where it is stored in the bones, which can lead to **weak and fragile bones**.

IMPORTANCE OF IRON FOR RED BLOOD CELLS

Iron is a type of **mineral** that is primarily necessary for **transporting oxygen** around the body. It makes up a large part of **hemoglobin**, which is a substance in the red blood cells that carries oxygen from the lungs to the rest of the body. Iron is found in two forms: heme and non-heme. **Heme iron** comes from animal flesh (meat, poultry, seafood), while **non-heme iron** is found in plant-based sources like grains, seeds, legumes, leafy greens, and nuts. Without iron, the body is unable to make enough healthy oxygen-rich red blood cells to deliver oxygen to all parts of the body. This can cause fatigue and a weakened immune system. Individuals at **higher risk of iron deficiency** include menstruating or pregnant women, children, and kidney dialysis patients.

IMPORTANCE OF VITAMIN A FOR VISION

Vitamin A (also called retinol or retinoic acid) is a **fat-soluble vitamin** that can be found in many foods. Although both are organic substances that are made by plants or animals, **fat-soluble vitamins** do not dissolve in water, while **water-soluble vitamins** dissolve in water. The resulting effect is that fat-soluble vitamins are stored in the body's tissues; high and frequent intake can lead to accumulation of vitamins in body tissues that lead to toxicity. Vitamin A is crucial for **vision and eye health**. Specifically, it helps the eye see in low-light conditions, protects the cornea (the outermost layer of the eye), and lubricates the eye. Vitamin A assists in producing and distributing T-cells to protect the body from infection. There are two different sources for vitamin A: preformed vitamin A and provitamin A carotenoids. **Preformed vitamin A** can be found in fish, organ meats like liver, dairy products, and eggs. **Provitamin A carotenoids** are plant pigments that the body converts into vitamin A inside of the liver. They are highest in yellow, orange, and red fruits and vegetables.

Dietary Practices

Components of a Well-Balanced Diet

There are **6 essential nutrients** that the body needs to function properly: carbohydrates, protein, fat, vitamins, minerals, and water. Although **calorie requirements** differ by age, sex, activity levels, and weight goals, a well-balanced diet consists of meals that contain appropriately proportioned amounts of the six essential nutrients.

- **Carbohydrates** should make up most of the diet (60%), since they meet most of the body's energy needs.
- Because **protein** is vital to repairing cells and tissue, approximately 25% of daily calories should be derived from it.
- **Fats** are also a major source of energy and vitamins and should provide 15% of daily calories.
- Fruits and vegetables are important sources of **vitamins** and **minerals**.
- Drinking at least 8 cups of water per day can satisfy requirements for **water consumption**.

The best way to achieve a **well-balanced diet** is through A) minimizing consumption of refined simple carbohydrates (sucrose and glucose), saturated and trans fats, and salt, and B) eating a diet rich in foods like whole grains, lean protein, unsaturated fats, and fruits and vegetables.

Healthy vs. Unhealthy Dietary Practices

Healthy dietary practices include healthy weight management and regular eating patterns. These include meeting appropriate caloric and nutritional needs for health goals, drinking sufficient amounts of water, and avoiding foods that are high in calories from sugar, fat, and sodium. **Unhealthy dietary practices** are exemplified by frequent dieting or unhealthy weight management, obsessive or no exercise, and disordered eating (binge eating, purging, or restricting). **Fad diets**—diets that become popular for a short period of time and make unreasonable and unfounded claims for rapid weight loss—consist of many unhealthy dietary practices. They typically promote rapid weight loss, highly restrictive diets, and the consumption of nutritionally imbalanced foods. **Eating disorders** (e.g., anorexia nervosa, bulimia nervosa, binge eating, orthorexia) are also comprised of many unhealthy dietary practices like binge eating, skipping meals, avoiding specific foods, self-induced vomiting, laxative misuse, and use of diet pills. Dieting, especially fad dieting, is a significant predictor for developing an eating disorder. Understanding the progression of behaviors that lead to eating disorders or fad dieting is crucial in preventing them.

Influence of Diet on Personal Health

A **healthy diet** is important for maintaining physical, mental, and social wellbeing. Eating well-portioned nutritious whole foods can positively impact the body. For example, eating plenty of fruits and vegetables, whole grains, nuts, and lean meats is associated with improved blood pressure levels, inflammation, and insulin sensitivity. Eating the appropriate number of calories for a person's age and physical activity level can improve energy levels and sleep quality—both integral to weight management. Positive moods and mental clarity are associated with healthy eating patterns (i.e., eating when hungry and stopping with satisfied). Healthy dietary practices and good nutrition are also linked with positive social development and friendliness among children.

Contribution of Federal Food Guideline Tools

Federal food guideline tools were created to help people understand how to make healthier food choices throughout their lives. The USDA's **Food Pyramid** used a pyramid to show the types of food and suggested amounts people should eat to meet their daily nutritional goals. Foods like fruits, grains, and vegetables were placed near the base of the pyramid as they were recommended more often. Foods such as oils, fats, and sweets were atop the pyramid as they were meant to be limited each day. In 2011, the Food Pyramid was replaced by **MyPlate** as another visual representation of a plate to illustrate what constitutes a healthy meal. The plate is separated into four groups—fruits, vegetables, protein, and grains—with a small circle to the right of the plate to represent dairy. Unlike the food pyramid, fats and sugars are omitted from the MyPlate. Both of these tools show how eating balanced meals is important to sustaining a healthy diet.

Most recently, the guidelines were updated again with the introduction of realfood.gov's **New Pyramid**. Introduced as part of the 2025-2030 Dietary Guidelines for Americans, The New Pyramid shifts the focus from meal portions to the quality of foods people choose. It emphasizes the importance of real, whole, nutrient-dense foods in our diet. Foods such as dairy, protein, fruits, vegetables, whole grains, and healthy fats are among those it focuses on. It also encourages the avoidance or limiting of highly processed foods, refined carbohydrates, added sugars, excess sodium, unhealthy fats, and artificial ingredients. This change was put in place to encourage building meals around the foods that provide the most essential nutrients to support lifelong health.

Dietary Choices

Influence of Food Labels and Promotional Claims

Food labels are located on most packaged foods. The nutrition facts label is required to be on each food package to help buyers make quick and informed food choices. It breaks down the number of calories, carbohydrates, fiber, protein, and vitamins per serving of food, which makes it easier to read and evaluate nutritional information and compare the nutrition among similar foods. Although food labels contain key information about a food's serving size, nutritional information, and ingredients, they can be difficult to interpret without sufficient knowledge about nutrition. **Front-of-package labels (FOP)** include symbols or graphics that feature the product's favorable nutritional aspects (e.g., lower in calories) but omit less favorable aspects (e.g., high in saturated fats). These labels tend to **overrate** how healthy a product is and can **mislead** buyers if they do not also read the nutrition facts label. Additionally, promotional claims about a product's health benefits are often featured on the front of products. They highlight the health benefits of the food, but can also mislead buyers about the overall healthfulness of a product.

Factors Influencing Nutrition and Calorie Requirements

Nutritional and caloric requirements vary based on factors related to age, activity level, and pregnancy status. **Metabolism** decreases with age as the body's ability to digest and absorb nutrients slows down. As a result, overall energy requirements decrease throughout the lifespan. However, although older adults need fewer calories, they require similar or higher nutrient needs compared to younger adults because their nutrient absorption declines. Aging is also associated with **changes in physiology** that impact the ability to chew, swallow, and sense thirst or hunger. Nutritional requirements also differ based on the frequency, type, duration, and intensity of physical activity. Those who engage in **high levels of physical activity** require more carbohydrates, protein, and water than the average person to fuel the brain and muscles during exercise, build and repair muscles, and replenish fluids lost to sweat. **Pregnant individuals** require more calories and higher amounts of folic acid, iron, calcium, and vitamin D to promote healthy fetal development.

Factors Influencing Food Choices

There are many different factors that influence food choices.

- **Cultural background** can contribute to which foods you eat and how they are prepared. For example, individuals who adhere to Hinduism believe that the cow is a sacred animal, and they do not consume beef.
- **Family eating patterns** have a significant influence on food choices. During childhood, meals are prepared and eaten with family members. From these interactions, children observe eating behaviors, food selection patterns, and food preferences that shape their eating habits.
- **Peer behaviors** also have a sizable influence on food choices, especially as the degree to which parental influence on food choices diminishes with age. Children's desire to fit in with their peers contributes to the adoption of new food choices and preferences.
- **Food advertising** is intended to influence food choices through a variety of media, especially in children and adolescents. There are many advertising techniques that food and beverage companies use to influence food choices. These may include inflated claims about a product's health and nutrient content, appealing songs or catchphrases, celebrity endorsements, and promotional discounts. They may also use targeted techniques to attract children, such as free toys or prizes, cartoon characters, and colorful packaging.

Making Healthy Food Choices

Mindful eating is a strategy for making healthy food choices that consists of focusing on one's sensory awareness and the experience of eating. Practices include heeding **signs and signals** from the body (i.e., stomach growls or low energy) rather than eating to quell feelings of sadness or boredom, eating foods that make a person feel healthy and energized rather than those that are emotionally comforting, and avoiding eating while multitasking. Keeping a **daily food journal** is also an effective and motivating strategy for making healthy food choices. By writing down what one eats and their emotional state when they eat each meal, individuals are better able to understand their eating habits. Planning and preparing meals in **advance** is an effective way to make sure that meals are balanced and reflect healthy food choices. It eliminates impulsive eating patterns and promotes mindful eating.

Dieting, Exercising, and Maintaining a Healthy Weight

Physical activity and healthy eating are essential to achieving and maintaining a **healthy weight**. The amount and type of exercise needed depends in part on an **individual's health goals**. For example, one may participate in cardiovascular—also called **aerobic and endurance**—exercise to lose weight (e.g., running, swimming, biking), or **anaerobic exercise** to strengthen muscles and improve bone health (e.g., weightlifting). Healthy eating is a long-term strategy to achieve a healthy weight characterized by balance and moderation, while dieting consists of restricting or limiting calories or certain foods. Dieting often takes place in combination with exercise to reduce weight among obese and overweight people. An individual is able to maintain a healthy weight by eating diverse foods in the required quantity for their health goals and exercise practices.

Fitness and Exercise

Components of Fitness

There are 3 main components of **physical fitness**: flexibility, muscular strength and endurance, and cardiovascular fitness.

- **Cardiovascular fitness** improves the ability of the heart and lungs to deliver oxygen and fuel to the body during exercise. It also helps burn calories to achieve a healthy **body composition** (the total amount of fat mass compared to muscle and bone mass). Cardiovascular fitness is usually divided into two types: **moderate intensity** (50–70% of the maximum heart rate) and **vigorous intensity** (70–85% of the maximum heart rate). Examples of cardiovascular fitness include **aerobic** activities like brisk walking, running, bicycling, and swimming.
- **Muscle-strengthening activities** like lifting weights or exercises that use body weight for resistance help improve strength and endurance and are useful for achieving and maintaining a healthy body composition. Strength training tends to be **anaerobic**, as the muscles consume more oxygen than the replenishment rate.
- **Flexibility** exercises, like stretching and yoga, improve range of motion. Well-balanced exercises are comprised of activities that address all 3 components of fitness.

METHODS FOR ASSESSING FITNESS

Cardiovascular fitness is often assessed through a calculation of one's at-rest heart rate, their target heart rate zone, and a running or jogging test like the Cooper Test. The **target heart rate zone** is a guide for assessing the **intensity** of exercise for an individual's age. By measuring the number of heartbeats per minute during exercise, one can assess whether they need to increase or decrease the intensity of their workout. The **Cooper Test** assesses cardiovascular fitness level based on age and sex by measuring how far a person is able to run in 12 minutes. **Muscular** strength and endurance are often assessed through **pushup and sit-up tests**. These tests measure the number of pushups and sit-ups one is able to do in one minute. This amount is compared to the average number for individuals of the same age and sex. **Flexibility** is commonly assessed through the **sit-and-reach test**, which measures the distance a person is able to reach from a sitting position. The distance reached is used to determine the flexibility of their legs, hips, and lower back.

TYPES OF EXERCISE

There are 4 main types of exercise: endurance, flexibility, strength, and balance.

- **Endurance exercise** generally refers to aerobics. Aerobic exercise refers to exercises that actively oxygenate the involved muscles at a sustainable rate. **Aerobic exercise** is usually cardiovascular in nature as well, as the heart rate increases to sustain the increased need for oxygen.
- **Flexibility exercises** stretch the muscles and tendons to improve and maintain the body's limberness. Examples include yoga and Pilates.
- **Strengthening exercises** build up the muscles through the use of weight resistance and repetitive motion.
- **Balance** exercises like heel-toe-walking and standing on one foot focus on steadiness to maintain stability.

INFLUENCE ON DIFFERENT BODY SYSTEMS

- **Aerobic** exercises enhance **cardiovascular system** functioning to improve the condition of the heart, lungs, and circulatory system. They are beneficial for reducing the risk of heart disease and stroke, lowering blood pressure, and raising "good" HDL cholesterol.
- **Strength training** increases the amount of force that a person's muscles can resist, and stimulates bone growth, which is essential for musculoskeletal system functioning.
- **Flexibility** exercises also improve musculoskeletal health by stretching an individual's muscles to reduce risk of muscle damage and improve their range of motion.

- **Balance** exercises improve overall steadiness to prevent falls and age-related damage to muscles and joints. Types of flexibility and balance exercises, like yoga and tai chi that use meditation and breathing exercises to reduce stress, can also improve cardiovascular system health.

HEALTH BENEFITS OF PHYSICAL ACTIVITY

Regular physical activity provides numerous **health benefits** throughout the life span, especially weight control. In **childhood and adolescence**, regular physical activity improves cardiorespiratory fitness; strengthens bones; contributes to muscle development; lowers symptoms of anxiety and depression; improves cognition and brain development; and prevents heart disease, diabetes, obesity, and cancer later in life. In **adulthood and old age**, regular physical activity reduces the risk of heart disease and stroke, and developing type 2 diabetes, hypertension, and some cancers. In **older adults**, regular physical activity reduces the risk of falls or injuries from falls, and delays the loss of physical functioning and muscle mass related to old age. It is also associated with improved physical function, mental health, and overall quality of life in individuals managing existing chronic conditions like arthritis and type 2 diabetes.

MAINTAINING AND IMPROVING FITNESS

Assessing and recording an individual's baseline physical fitness is the first step in creating strategies to maintain and improve fitness. A person's results provide information on their **starting point** to use to measure their progress and establish fitness **goals**. Measure pulse rate, running distance, number of pushups or sit-ups, sit-and-reach distance, waist circumference, and/or body mass index (BMI) to assess baseline fitness. Create **SMART fitness goals** by creating goals that are specific, measurable, attainable, realistic, and time-bound (SMART) in order to create actionable steps to gauge one's progress and maintain motivation. Individuals should select fitness activities that engage all components of physical fitness (cardiovascular, strength, flexibility, and balance). All activities selected should be appropriate for fitness goals and physical capabilities. Individuals should monitor their progress by retaking the physical fitness assessments every few months and comparing them with the baseline. Exercise progress can be used to create new fitness objectives that reflect evolving healthy lifestyle goals.

Interrelationships Between Components of Health

PHYSICAL, MENTAL, EMOTIONAL, AND SOCIAL HEALTH

Overall health is a combination of physical, mental, emotional, and social health.

- **Physical health** refers to a person's exercise level, diet and sleep.
- **Mental health** refers to emotional, psychological, and social heath, as well as how an individual thinks, feels, acts, copes, and interacts with others or the world around them.
- **Emotional health** is a component of mental health; it refers to a person's ability to cope with emotions.
- **Social health** is another component of mental health which refers to the ways in which a person interacts or relates with others.

Each of these components of health are deeply intertwined and can influence each other. For example, an individual with chronic pain may experience sleep disturbances which lead to depression and associated symptoms of depression like social isolation, excessive or undereating, etc.

Influence of Child Abuse and Neglect

Child abuse and neglect can have a significant impact on an individual's short and long-term health. Injuries inflicted by abuse or neglect can contribute to poor **short-term** physical health outcomes. In the **long-term**, chronic abuse and neglect negatively affect **brain development**, which can lead to **cognitive delays** or **learning disorders**. Additionally, child maltreatment is associated with chronic pain, obesity and eating disorders, heart disease, and hypertension in adulthood. The impact of abuse and neglect on **mental health** can persist into adulthood. Child maltreatment is associated with post-traumatic stress disorder (PTSD), attention deficit hyperactivity disorder (ADHD), anxiety, depression, anti-social personality disorder, and borderline personality disorder. Child abuse and neglect can also influence **emotional and social health**, as children do not develop vital communication skills or coping mechanisms. As a result, they are prone to drug and alcohol abuse and tend to have difficulty maintaining healthy relationships. Since the components of overall health are interconnected, poor outcomes in one dimension can influence others and contribute to inferior overall health.

Influence of Substance Abuse on Overall Health

The effects of **substance abuse** are cumulative, and the impacts of substance abuse extend beyond individual health and wellbeing. When an individual begins to abuse illicit and licit substances, their physical, mental, and emotional health diminish. In the **short-term**, they are more likely to experience direct effects like injuries (e.g., car accidents, drug-related violence) and overdose. **Persistent use** increases the risk of cardiovascular disease, stroke, liver failure, HIV/AIDS, hepatitis B and C, lung disease, problems with memory and decision-making, and an array of mental disorders (e.g., depression, anxiety, mania, drug-induced psychosis). Substance abuse **strains social relationships** with peers and family members. Due to stigmatization and withdrawal, users often disengage from relationships with friends and family. These **direct consequences** of drug abuse are interrelated and can exacerbate poor health in other dimensions of overall health. **Indirect effects** of substance abuse include the impacts felt by those close to users. They can experience financial and emotional hardship as they witness their loved one struggle with substance abuse, which can result in poor physical, social, emotional, mental, and economic health among non-users.

Changes in Mental and Emotional Needs Throughout Life

Attachment Theory

Emotional attachment is characterized by feelings of closeness and affection and refers to the connections and bonds individuals form with others. According to **attachment theory**, emotional attachment patterns shift throughout the life span, with the first 3 years being the most formative for developing healthy emotional attachment. Children who have a responsive and dependable primary caregiver are far more likely to have healthy attachment patterns, good self-esteem and self-reliance, healthy romantic relationships, and trust in others more easily than those who experience early abuse, neglect, or abandonment. As people age, friends, romantic partners, and life experiences begin to influence attachment more than primary caregivers. Thus, interactions in personal relationships and negative life events can influence adult attachment. For example, bullying, death of a loved one, divorce, or domestic abuse can cause insecurity, anxiety, or avoidance in a person with secure attachment.

Decision-Making Throughout the Lifespan

Changes in decision-making can be attributed to brain development throughout the life span, life experiences, and changes in motivation. The **frontal lobe**—a part of the brain that controls personality characteristics, decision-making, and movement—develops throughout childhood and adolescence and typically reaches maturation at age 25. As **new brain connections** are formed, children and adolescents adopt new behaviors and make decisions characterized by overestimation of rewards, underestimation of possible risks, and egocentrism. **Social relationships** with peers and caregivers also influence decision-making for youth. The results of new behaviors and how decision-making is modeled creates brain circuits that are retained into adulthood. Behaviors that elicit positive feedback from others during development are also retained throughout adulthood. As frontal lobe development slows, decision making becomes more **stable**. Decision making—specifically, perceived risk and reward—becomes more **balanced**. As the brain ages, older adults are increasingly unable to hold on to multiple thoughts and struggle to make decisions that require consideration of many options. They become less concerned about bad outcomes that result from their decisions and more focused on the good outcomes.

Perception of Life and Death

As people age, their **perceptions of life and death** shift due to cognitive development, social influences, and personal experiences.

- **Infants** cannot comprehend death, yet they can be physically impacted by maternal separation. Infants separated from their mothers tend to lose weight, sleep less, display less energy, and no longer coo or smile.
- During **early childhood**, young children struggle to understand death. They believe death is temporary and/or reversible and may believe that the death resulted from their actions or misbehavior.
- In **middle and late childhood**, children begin to understand that death is permanent and universal. Throughout adolescence, teenagers begin to think abstractly about death and ponder existence. However, their lack of realistic understanding of life and death and perceived invincibility is evident by their risky behaviors.
- **Adults** begin to report increased anxiety and fear about death, peaking in middle adulthood.
- **Older adults** generally fear death less than younger adults. They often have fewer caregiving responsibilities and usually become more comfortable with death as they experience it more frequently with age.

Factors that Affect Mental and Emotional Health

Effect of Heredity on Mental and Emotional Health

Heredity—or genetics—can affect mental and emotional health. Although specific mental illness genes have not been identified by researchers, it is well known that if an individual has a biological family member with a diagnosed mental health disorder, they are at an **increased risk** of developing one. However, their inherited susceptibility to mental illness does not mean that they will inevitably develop one or that they will develop one with the same severity as their family member. **Mental illness** occurs from an interaction between genetic, social, and environmental factors. These factors can either trigger an illness in someone who is genetically susceptible or serve as protective factors. Hereditary factors include **single gene expression** which occurs when one gene activates and triggers a mental illness, and **epigenetic expression** which describes how a person's genes change in response to environmental stimuli. Some mental illnesses, like schizophrenia, anxiety, depression, bipolar disorder and addiction, have a **higher genetic predisposition** than others; however, the development of these illnesses results from a combination of environmental, social, and genetic factors.

Effect of Personal Experience on Mental and Emotional Health

Personal experiences during childhood and throughout adulthood can profoundly affect mental and emotional health. Individuals who **experience adverse childhood experiences (ACEs)**, such as abuse or neglect, violence, divorce, or caretaker mental illness, are at risk for developing depression, anxiety, substance abuse, and other poor health behaviors as they mature. Conversely, those who experience **positive childhood experiences (PCEs)** like healthy interactions with caregivers and other adults and household stability tend to have better coping skills and higher self-worth, self-efficacy, and optimism. Personal experiences in adolescence and adulthood can also affect mental and emotional health (e.g., separation or divorce, living with chronic illness, death or loss of a loved one, job transition, moving, substance abuse, and unhealthy relationships).

Effect of Environmental Factors on Mental and Emotional Health

While there are many **environmental factors** that contribute to mental health and wellbeing, an individual's **social and physical environment** can increase their susceptibility to mental illness. **Physical environmental factors** can influence a person's neurochemistry or cause distress. Examples of biology-altering environmental factors include food insecurity, poor housing conditions (e.g., living in a home with asbestos or lead), exposure to pollution in childhood, and parental substance abuse. Other examples include natural disasters, climate change-related events, and living in a community with unsafe drinking water. **Social environmental factors** refer to racial and ethnic, relational, and economic conditions that influence an individual's mental health and wellbeing. Examples include isolation, prejudice (e.g., racism, sexism, homophobia, xenophobia), experiencing war, community violence or crime, poverty, and social stigma.

Mental and Emotional Disorders

Anxiety

An **anxiety disorder** is mental health condition in which an individual experiences intense, excessive, and persistent worry. An anxiety disorder is different from regular nervousness because it—like other disorders—inhibits a person's ability to cope with everyday stressors and negatively impacts their social and occupational functioning. Anxiety may induce heart palpitations, chest pain and tightness, difficulty breathing, cold or sweaty hands, and muscle tension. Panic, fear, and unrest are common among those experiencing anxiety. Nightmares, sleep disturbances, and turbulent thoughts can also be caused by anxiety. **Chemical imbalances** resulting from severe or chronic stress, **environmental stressors**, and **heredity** are common risk factors for anxiety. Though there are multiple types of anxiety disorders, they differ in their characteristics and triggers. However, despite their differences, the symptoms of each are persistent and interfere with daily activities or relationships.

Depression

Depression is mental health condition that is characterized by persistent feelings of sadness and hopelessness. Depression may be short-term or long-term, known as **acute** or **chronic depression**, respectively. Individuals who are depressed **lose interest** in things they used to find enjoyable and may experience concurrent feelings of **worry or frustration**. Those with depression may experience trouble falling or staying asleep, chronic pain, memory loss, and difficulty thinking or concentrating. Factors like atypical chemical levels and faulty mood regulation due to injury or abnormal brain development can make a person prone to depression. An individual with a family history of depression can be more susceptible to depression. Life events (e.g., unemployment, domestic abuse, childhood neglect, chronic illness) and environmental factors (e.g., natural disasters, community violence, war) can incite and exacerbate depression.

Eating Disorders

An **eating disorder** refers to a condition in which an individual engages in persistent **unhealthy dietary behaviors** to alter their appearance or quell emotional distress. Since there are many types of eating disorders, the symptoms vary. However, those with eating disorders may exhibit inexplicable weight changes, mood swings, food rituals to eliminate food-related anxiety, and avoidance (e.g., isolating while eating, refusing to eat certain foods). Those with a **family history** of eating disorders, adverse childhood experiences, and a history of dieting are vulnerable to developing an eating disorder. **Major life changes** and **mental health disorders** like obsessive compulsive disorder (OCD), depression, and anxiety can increase susceptibility to developing an eating disorder or worsening an existing one. **Social pressure** to be thin and certain personality traits such as perfectionism or low self-esteem are additional causes of eating disorders.

Suicide

Suicide occurs when an individual self-inflicts a fatal injury with the intent to die. An individual who is considering or planning to commit suicide may withdraw, isolate, and increasingly talk about death. No single, specific cause leads to suicide. It often results from converging risk factors and stressors that cause **hopelessness** or **despair**. Individuals with existing mental health conditions, especially conditions that cause persistent feelings of hopelessness and despair like chronic illnesses, adverse childhood experiences, and traumatic brain injuries are at **higher risk of suicide**. Access to firearms and drugs, chronic relationship or financial stress, and upsetting or traumatic live events are risk factors for suicide. Witnessing or experiencing another person's suicide and previous suicide attempts can significantly increase the risk of suicidal ideation and suicide. **Protective factors** reduce the likelihood of a negative outcome. Examples of protective factors that reduce the risk of suicide include healthy relationships, accessible mental health care, and limited access to weapons or lethal drugs.

Obtaining Assistance for Mental and Emotional Problems

Seeking professional help is the best way to address an unmanageable mental health problem. Primary care doctors, physician assistants, and nurse practitioners can help refer individuals to a mental health provider or counsel them on alternative solutions or resources. Psychologists, therapists, and social workers are trained experts who provide counseling, psychological testing, and mental health education to improve coping skills. **Psychiatrists** prescribe medications to manage mental health symptoms. Another method for obtaining assistance for emotional problems is through **support groups**—spaces where individuals share their experiences, troubles, and coping strategies. These resources are accessible in-person or online and are facilitated by community organizations, churches, private institutions, hospitals or healthcare providers, etc. **Mental health services** are often available through community outpatient, inpatient, and residential treatment facilities, universities, teaching hospitals, churches, and non-profit organizations.

Causes, Effects, and Management of Stress

Stress

Stress develops as a reaction to an external situation or event or internal distress. Individuals may experience acute stress or chronic stress.

- **Acute stress** is short-lived and accompanies minor stressors like speaking in front a group of people or a traffic jam.

- **Chronic stress** is long-term and can lead to many health problems (e.g., high blood pressure, heart disease, chronic pain, depression).

Common **external causes** of stress include major life changes (e.g., moving, starting a new job, unemployment, death, divorce, imprisonment), work or academic pressure, relationship problems, financial difficulties, children and family problems, crowds, and noise. **Internal causes** of stress are factors that come from within an individual. Examples include negative self-talk, unrealistic expectations, shyness, low self-esteem, and uncertainty. Internal stressors can lead to **social anxiety** or the development of **irrational perceptions** that influence social interaction.

Effects of Stress on Individual and Family Health

The health impacts of stress can have positive or negative effects which differ depending on duration and severity of stress. **Acute stress** can keep a person alert and motivated, while no stress can lead to boredom or depression. **Brief, intermittent stressful events** produce stress hormones that improve brain performance and help a person adapt to cope with similar future situations. **Chronic stress**, however, causes chronically elevated levels of stress hormones that impair memory and increase risk of obesity, heart disease, and depression. **Physical effects** of stress include headaches, muscle and chest pain, fatigue, digestive issues, and sleep problems. Stress can lead to anxiety, restlessness, poor motivation and focus, irritability and anger, and sadness. Chronic stress can also influence an individual's behavior. Stress may lead them to over- or undereat, have angry outbursts, misuse alcohol or drugs, withdraw socially, and engage in less exercise. Stress does not only impact individuals; it can also impact **relationship and familial health**. Although each family reacts differently to stress, common effects include increased arguments or fighting, family discord (e.g., lasting disagreements and estrangement), missed commitments, poor productivity or behavior among children, and substance overuse.

Coping with and Managing Stress

The best way to manage stress to is engage in preventative strategies that promote wellness and stave off stress before it happens. **Preventative strategies** like eating a healthy and nutrient-dense diet, exercising, and sleeping regularly improve mood and foster relaxation. **Emotional regulation techniques** like relaxation techniques (e.g., yoga, meditation, deep breathing) can help a person calm down and refocus when stressed. **Reflection strategies** like regular check-ins about workload and emotional wellbeing can prevent stress and fatigue. Self-assessments are another kind of reflection strategy that guides users through identifying stress triggers and creating strategies to advocate for their needs. Creating and using mantras or encouraging phrases can be a helpful tool for modeling **positive self-talk** to students and increase confidence when faced with a stressful situation. Counseling with a mental health professional can help a person develop positive coping mechanisms to manage stress.

Managing Anxiety and Grief

Managing Anxiety

Psychotherapy and medication are often first-line treatments for anxiety; however, there are a number of **coping strategies** to manage anxiety. Strategies for reducing stress levels and anxiety generally include promoting overall health, avoiding stressors, and effectively processing existing stress.

Promoting overall health by following exercise routines, pursuing a balanced and healthy diet, and adopting healthy sleep patterns all play a role in promoting healthy stress levels and reducing anxiety. Meditation, stretching, and relaxation are also known to help with reducing stress levels and easing the symptoms of anxiety. Similarly, healthy and lasting relationships are key aspects of a healthy life and tend to help reduce stress.

Those suffering from excess stress and anxiety should avoid **stressors** and **promotors of stress**. Alcohol, recreational drugs, smoking, and caffeine can contribute to anxiety, as each of these acts to artificially alter mood. It also helps to **identify stressors** in life that can be avoided or altered, such as challenging and unhealthy relationships, work, and home environments. One method for identifying stressors is to keep a **stress journal** and look for patterns of what is correlated with anxiety over time.

MANAGING GRIEF

Grief is an emotional response to loss. It can result from death of a friend or loved one, divorce or breakup, job loss, miscarriage, loss of a friendship, etc. Common **reactions** to grief include denial, shock, despair, anger or guilt, sadness, vulnerability, physical pain, or apathy. The **grieving process** is unique to each person and takes time. Research suggests that individuals with adequate **social support** and **healthy habits** can recover from loss better than those without. **Maintaining physical health** is an important part of managing grief. Establishing and continuing in exercise, sleep, and eating routines can keep an individual productive and motivated. Limiting alcohol and drugs and eating nutritious foods can keep a person healthy and active. **Maintaining connection** with trusted confidants or others experiencing loss can help an individual cope with the loss and prevent isolation. **Visiting a physician or mental health professional** may be beneficial to address the fear, guilt, depression, or anxiety associated with loss. Trained professionals can help build resilience and develop coping and grief management strategies through evidence-based treatments.

SUICIDE PREVENTION

Like other mental health conditions, **preventative strategies** are most effective for suicide prevention. **Improvements** made to an individual's mental health care coverage and accessibility can make it easier to receive treatment from trained mental health professionals. **Limiting access** to lethal weapons and drugs can thwart attempts. Social emotional learning programs, mental health first aid training programs, and crisis intervention programs can help individuals experiencing suicidal ideation. These kinds of programs are typically hosted by community-based or religious organizations with the intention of improving social support and community connectedness to prevent isolation. **Health promoting activities** that foster physical, social, and emotional wellbeing can improve a person's mood, strengthen their support networks, and develop coping mechanisms to intercept suicidal thoughts or attempts. **Postvention strategies** are activities or treatment for individuals who have attempted suicide or experienced the suicide of someone they know. They are crucial strategies for minimizing repeated or imitative suicide risk.

Human Sexuality

SEXUAL ACTIVITY

Sexual activity refers to intimate relations or behavior through which a person expresses their sexuality; it can be **solitary** or between **two or more individuals**, and can be **penetrative** (e.g., anal, vaginal) or **non-penetrative** (e.g., oral, touching). Poor adherence to safe sex precautions and engagement in high-risk sexual behavior (e.g., unprotected sex, early sexual initiation, multiple partners) can result in consequences that may impact a person's physical or emotional wellbeing. **Physical consequences** of sexual activity are **unplanned pregnancy**—unintended or mistimed pregnancy that results from misuse or non-use of contraception—or **sexually transmitted infections (STI)**—infections that are transferred from an infected person to a non-infected person through semen, blood, or vaginal fluids. **Emotional consequences** like **sexual regret** are largely dependent on one's emotional wellbeing (e.g., existing depression, anxiety, or low self-esteem), assertiveness and refusal skills, sexual negotiation skills, perceived reputational damage, and knowing one's partner prior to sexual contact.

Abstaining from Sexual Activity

An individual who practices **abstinence** refrains from engaging in sexual activity; it is the **most effective way to avoid risks associated with sex.** Abstaining from sexual activity outside of a committed relationship prevents the risk of unintended pregnancy and minimizes one's risk of contracting a sexually transmitted disease. Remaining abstinent outside of a committed relationship can reduce stress or concern associated with sexual activity (e.g., fear of contracting STIs, pregnancy). It also reduces feelings of guilt, shame, or regret that can be associated with casual sex. Abstinence is associated with **improved emotional wellbeing** for those who harbor negative feelings or experiences involving sexual activity, or individuals for whom sexual activity is a source of **anxiety**. It can help an individual develop greater self-confidence and self-worth. Abstinence is often associated with better academic outcomes and improved focus on school or work. Choosing not to engage in sexual activity outside of a committed relationship can improve one's ability to develop and maintain non-sexual or non-romantic relationships.

Influence of Peer Pressure

Sexual decisions refer to one's choices about whether to participate in sexual activity, and with whom, when, or what kind of sexual activity they engage in. Decisions about sexual activity are **heavily influenced by indirect peer pressure and direct peer pressure**. Of the two, indirect peer pressure has a greater impact on one's decision to engage in sexual activity—especially among adolescents. Two examples of the impact of indirect peer pressure on decisions to have sex are **perceptions about peer sexual activity** and **peer approval**. An individual who believes that their peers are engaging in sexual activity may feel an indirect or unspoken pressure to have sex and is more likely to engage in sexual activity. Perceived peer approval (i.e., whether their friends would approve or disapprove of engaging in sexual activity) can also influence one's decision about sexual activity. Direct peer pressure or **sexual coercion**—nonphysical pressure imposed on a person (e.g., ridicule, lying, repeated requests or harassment)—can influence one's decision to engage in sexual activity.

Influence of Personal Values

An individual's personal values can guide their beliefs and decisions about sexual activity. **Sexual values**—personal beliefs regarding one's sexuality and sexual activity—are **not static** and are continually shaped by many factors. Family, friends, culture, media, personal experiences, and religion are the **most influential**. Those with **strong sexual values** are often more aware of acceptable or appropriate sexual behavior, which may make them better able to communicate their wants and needs to their partner, make decisions regarding their sexual activity or health, negotiate sex, assert themselves when their values are violated, or refuse unwanted sexual advances. Those whose behaviors and actions align with their personal values often have **improved self-confidence and sense of empowerment**. Strong sexual values may lead to more fulfilling and healthier relationships, especially if they are clearly communicated to one's partner. Those with poor or no sexual values may struggle to make decisions about if, when, where, how, and with whom they engage in sexual activity. This can put them in a dangerous situation or result in emotional distress, abuse, or unintended consequences like pregnancy or STIs.

Influence of Media

Media refers to the various channels through which information and messages are communicated (e.g., television, newspaper, music, photographs, videos, social networking websites or apps). Media serves as a **primary source of information** regarding sex and sexual activity for many; however, **inaccurate information** and **unhealthy portrayals** about sexuality and sexual activity relayed through media can negatively influence sexual decisions. This can significantly impact one's **perception** about healthy relationships, consent, potential consequences of sexual activity, sexual or gender stereotypes, sexual objectification, and sexual violence. The content and messages about sexual activity can also influence an individual's **ideas about sexual norms**. For example, suppose a television show depicts popular male characters making inappropriate comments or unwanted sexual advances directed at passive female characters without consequence. In that case, viewers may develop a warped view of acceptable sexual behavior. Unbiased and realistic portrayals of sexual activity and comprehensive sex education are **protective factors** that counteract the effects of negative media messages.

Making Responsible Decisions

An individual can make responsible decisions about sexual activity through abstaining from or limiting substance use, media literacy, comprehensive sex education, positive and healthy relationships with peers, and parent-child communication. Substance use can impact one's decision-making and place them at risk of many adverse outcomes (e.g., sexual abuse or rape, pregnancy, STIs). **Abstaining from or limiting substance use** can help an individual think and act clearly as they make decisions about their sexual activity or health. **Improving one's media literacy** can make them better prepared to identify biased or inaccurate information about sexual activity and relationships. Additionally, **comprehensive sex education** increases a person's knowledge of sexual health and improves their ability to protect and advocate for themselves when making decisions about sexual activity. **Positive and healthy relationships with peers** can reduce pressure to initiate sexual activity and secure peer guidance and support for making responsible decisions regarding their sexual health. **Open communication between parents and children** about sex and reproductive health can promote healthy sexual behaviors and prevent negative sexual health outcomes.

Healthy Skills for Dating Relationships

Expressing Affection

Affection can produce mutual feelings of trust and security between two people in a relationship. However, expressing or displaying affection inappropriately can cause **discomfort**. Affection can be expressed through physical touch, words of affirmation, gifts, quality time, and acts of service. **Physical touch** can be sexual or non-sexual (e.g., holding hands, hugging). Expressing physical affection appropriately requires **consent**—mutually agreed-upon and respected **boundaries** related to physical contact or sexual activity. In a caring relationship, the type of and degree to which different kinds of affection are expressed should be appropriate for the needs and wants of both partners. Affection should never be **forced or coercive**. It is important that the individual receiving affection honestly and clearly express whether they like or dislike of the action. Open and honest communication can **prevent inappropriate displays of affection** and ensure both parties feel fulfilled and comfortable.

Refusing Sexual Advances

An individual can refuse a sexual advance by clearly and **directly saying "no"** to the person making the advance. Ambiguous or passive responses to advances can lead to **misunderstanding** between the two involved. It could also contribute to future advances or an unsafe situation. One should **avoid explaining their refusal** or **implying that certain circumstances contributed to their decision** (e.g., relationship status, other people around, too busy) as that may signal that the person making the advance should try again or use other strategies to convince them. Using **body language** and **maintaining personal space** are nonverbal gestures that reinforce an individual's refusal. **Avoiding isolation** or **preventing unsafe situations** (e.g., substance use, accepting drugs or alcohol from strangers) can make it easier for one to refuse sexual advances. If there are more people around, the perpetrator is less likely to make unwanted sexual advances. Additionally, stating one's discomfort around others when sexual advances are made can add **social pressure** to comply and group accountability when one's refusal is not respected. **Separating oneself, avoiding conversation, and limiting interaction** with the individual making sexual advances can help prevent further contact.

Dating Relationships

Each person's role within a dating relationship depends on their partner's needs. For example, a person whose partner is experiencing emotional distress may fill the role of confidant, while one whose partner is struggling to meet their financial commitments may fill the role of supporter. One's role also requires fulfilling the three components of love as determined by Robert Sternberg's **Triangular Theory of Love: intimacy, passion**, and **commitment**. It is one's responsibility is to act in a way that fosters connectedness, excitement, and loyalty. These components can be fulfilled through **identifying and asserting one's boundaries, respecting their partner's boundaries, demonstrating empathy, sharing responsibility, communicating clearly and honestly**, and **compromising when necessary**. Setting and respecting boundaries cultivates loyalty and strengthens a pair's connection. Demonstrating **empathy** can increase intimacy and passion between two people. Sharing responsibility with one's partner can show commitment and nurture the bond between both people. **Communication** strengthens mutual understanding, which can foster connectedness. **Compromising** shows one's commitment to and support of the other's wellbeing, which can bolster the connection between two people.

Legal and Ethical Implications of Unacceptable Behaviors

Legal and Ethical Implications of Sexual Harassment

Sexual harassment refers to unwanted sexual advances, explicit or implicit requests for sexual favors, or verbal or physical sexual transgressions (e.g., sexual jokes or comments, unwanted touch). Committing sexual harassment is **implicitly unethical** and can result in **emotional damage**, such as emotional distress (e.g., fear, humiliation, anxiety, depression) among victims and fear of damage to their interpersonal relationships, reputation, or security—especially if committed by a person with **authority**. It can create a **hostile environment** for all involved. The legal implications of sexual harassment depend largely on the context in which it occurs. Most employers have internal disciplinary policies for **addressing sexual harassment**. For example, employers can demote or terminate harassers. Victims can also file charges with government and state agencies (e.g., the Equal Employment Opportunity Commission) to ensure that their employer adequately disciplines the harasser. In school settings, students are protected by **Title IX provisions** which prohibit sexual harassment; many school districts have clearly outlined consequences for sexual harassment. Victims of sexual harassment can sue harassers in civil court, but most acts of sexual harassment are not criminally punishable until they become sexual assault.

Legal and Ethical Implications of Acquaintance Rape

Rape is forceful or nonconsensual sexual intercourse. **Force** refers to the exertion of physical or coercive tactics to overcome a person, and **consent** refers to clear, informed, reversible, and enthusiastic assent to sexual activity. **Acquaintance rape** describes nonconsensual penetrative sex that occurs between a perpetrator and victim who know each other. Although rape is often committed by an attacker whom the victim knows, acquaintance rape is far **less likely to be reported** than rape involving strangers. Victims may experience emotional distress, embarrassment, or self-blame. They may fear not being believed by others who know both the rapist and the victim. Since victims may have a **preexisting personal bond** with their attacker, they may avoid reporting their experience to keep their attacker safe or prevent conflict among their mutual connections. As with other forms of rape, victims may be subject to **secondary victimization**—implying that a victim is partially or entirely responsible for the outcome (also known as **victim blaming**), which can affect emotional wellbeing and reporting. Rape is a criminal offense, and the severity of the punishment depends on the victim's age and the use of violence or substances to override consent.

Legal and Ethical Implications of Statutory Rape

Statutory rape is sexual intercourse between an adult and a person under the **age of consent**—the age at which an individual is competent to consent to sexual activity. It can refer to chronological age or mental age. Statutory rape is considered rape because a minor is **legally incapable of consenting** to sexual activity, thus the sexual act is deemed **coercive**. Consequences of statutory rape may include poor emotional wellbeing among victims (e.g., depression, low self-esteem, anxiety), loss of sense of security and safety, and disrupted capacity to form healthy, trusting interpersonal relationships. Statutory rape laws are intended to protect victims from overt abuses of power and authority. It is a criminal offense; however, criminal punishments for statutory rape vary from state to state since each state defines age of consent differently. The victim and perpetrator's age and the act committed determine the severity of the punishment. For example, nonforcible sexual activity that occurs between two partners—one 18 and the other 17—will carry a far lesser sentence than rape of an individual under the age of 13 by an adult in a position of authority.

Legal and Ethical Implications of Sexual Abuse

Sexual abuse describes any coercive or forceful sexual activity by one person upon another that occurs **without consent**; it includes but is not limited to groping or unwanted touching, rape and attempted rape, refusing condoms or access to contraception, threat or pressure by one person to engage in sexual activity, sexual contact with someone incapable of consent (e.g., unconscious or on drugs/drugged), and purposeful transmission or nondisclosure of STIs. The trauma that results from sexual abuse can lead to a number of **adverse mental health outcomes** like depression, anxiety, and PTSD. Those who experience sexual abuse are far more likely to develop substance abuse and attachment issues. Children who experience sexual abuse are twice as likely to experience intimate partner violence and sexual abuse in adulthood. As with other forms of sexual assault, victims may experience **secondary victimization** by their peers or institutions whom they confide in. Since sexual abuse is broadly defined, the legal implications of sexual abuse vary. Acts such as rape and child sexual abuse carry severe criminal punishment, while unwanted touching or nonconsensual sharing of personal sexual images have few, if any, legal ramifications.

Review Video: Ethical and Professional Standards
Visit mometrix.com/academy and enter code: 391843

Sexually Transmitted Diseases

Chlamydia

Chlamydia is a bacterial sexually transmitted disease. It can be **spread** through penetrative sex (e.g., vaginal, anal), oral sex, and transmitted to an infant during birth. Typically, those with chlamydia experience **no or mild symptoms**; however, symptoms can include painful urination and sex, abdominal pain, abnormal discharge, and bleeding between menses. **Rectal infections** may cause soreness, anal discharge, or bleeding. **Antibiotics** are used to treat chlamydia. If chlamydia is untreated, the bacteria can ascend into a woman's reproductive organs (e.g., uterus, fallopian tubes) and cause **pelvic inflammatory disease** (PID) and accompanying infertility. Women with chlamydia are at higher risk of scarring in their fallopian tubes and **ectopic pregnancies**—a pregnancy that occurs outside of the uterus (i.e., in the fallopian tube, abdomen, ovary, or cervix). Using condoms and dental dams and having few sexual partners can **reduce one's risk** of contracting chlamydia, but the most effective way to prevent transmission is through abstinence. Sexually active individuals should get regularly tested for STIs.

Gonorrhea

Gonorrhea is a bacterial sexually transmitted disease that can be **treated** with antibiotics. It is **spread** through semen and vaginal fluids during penetrative and oral sex. Pregnant women may also pass gonorrhea to their infants during childbirth. Similar to chlamydia, gonorrhea can present **without symptoms**. In fact, most women have no symptoms at all or have mild symptoms that are often mistaken for a bladder or yeast infection. Those who do have symptoms may experience painful urination, abnormal discharge, and bleeding between periods. **Rectal infections** can cause discharge, pain or soreness, and itching. If untreated, gonorrhea can spread to a woman's reproductive organs and cause PID. This may result in infertility, ectopic pregnancy, or chronic pain. A person with gonorrhea is at **higher risk** of contracting or spreading HIV (Human Immunodeficiency Virus), since having an STI like gonorrhea, herpes, or syphilis alters one's genital, rectal, and oral cell lining—making it easier for the virus to infect its host. The best way to prevent and minimize risk of gonorrhea is through abstinence, condom use, and regular STI testing.

HIV

Human Immunodeficiency Virus (HIV) is a sexually transmitted virus that has **no cure**. The virus infects and destroys white blood cells called **helper T cells** and severely limits the immune system's ability to fight disease. There are three stages of infection: acute HIV infection, chronic HIV infection, and AIDS. **Acquired Immune Deficiency Syndrome (AIDS)** refers to the final and most severe stage of HIV. AIDS occurs when the body no longer has enough T cells to fight off illness effectively, usually ending in death due to illnesses that the body could have otherwise fought off. The virus remains contagious throughout each stage. HIV is transmitted through certain bodily fluids—blood, semen, vaginal fluids, breast milk, and anal mucous. One can **contract** HIV through penetrative sex, shared needles, pregnancy/childbirth, breastfeeding, or contact with infected fluids via open cuts or sores. HIV can be managed through **antiretroviral therapy** (ART), which reduces the viral load, slowing the progression and minimizing risk of transmission. HIV prevention includes abstinence, condom use, regular STI testing, and **pre-exposure prophylaxis** (PrEP) or **post-exposure prophylaxis** (PEP). PrEP and PEP induce antibody production to prevent transmission and reduce risk of transmission after exposure, respectively.

Contraception

Methods of Contraception

Contraception refers to various methods aimed at preventing **conception**—the fertilization of an egg by sperm. **Long-acting reversible contraception** (LARC) include hormonal or copper intrauterine devices (IUDs) and arm implants. Hormonal IUDs and implants release **progestin**—synthetic progesterone that prevents egg release and fertilization by thickening cervical mucous and thinning the uterine lining—into the bloodstream. Copper IUDs inhibit sperm movement to prevent entry into the uterus. **Hormonal contraception** refers to shots, patches, oral tablets, and rings used to prevent pregnancy; they include progestin-only or combined hormonal contraception (i.e., containing both estrogen and progestin). Both prevent fertilization by thickening cervical mucous and thinning the uterine wall to make it more challenging for sperm to travel to the egg and implant. **Barrier methods** like male and female condoms, diaphragms, sponges, and spermicides block and kill sperm. Permanent contraception refers to **tubal ligation**—closing the fallopian tubes to prevent fertilization—and **vasectomies**—blocking the supply of sperm to semen. **Abstinence** and natural methods (e.g., **fertility awareness-based methods or FAM, withdrawal,** and **breastfeeding**) can also be used to prevent pregnancy.

Hormonal Contraceptives

Combined hormonal contraceptives can make periods lighter and shorter, reduce risk of uterine or ovarian cancer, reduce acne, and minimize period symptoms caused by fibroids and endometriosis. **Progestin-only hormonal contraceptives** can reduce or stop menstrual bleeding and unlike combined hormonal contraceptives do not increase the risk of heart disease, blood clots, or high blood pressure. They are best for those who are sensitive to estrogen. Most hormonal contraceptives ease menstrual symptom and duration. No hormonal contraceptive protects against STIs. **Oral tablets** are 91% effective. They must be taken at the same time every day, so they may be troublesome for forgetful people. **Implants**—small rods inserted in the arm—are 99% effective. They last about three years and are removed easily. **Injections** are given every three months, so they are a good option for those who prefer a long-acting contraception. They are 94% effective, but they may cause weight gain and bone loss. **Vaginal rings and patches** last approximately one month and are 91% effective. Similar to implants and injections, rings and patches do not interrupt sex but can be less effective if not put in/on correctly. Patches may cause skin irritation and are visible.

Long-Acting Reversible Contraception and Barrier Methods

LARCs can remain in one's uterus for up to twelve years and can be easily taken out. They do not impact fertility once removed and can be used as a form of emergency contraception. They are 99.2–99.9% effective, depending on the type. Hormonal IUDs can reduce menstrual bleeding and symptoms (e.g., cramps, anemia), but they may result in **secondary amenorrhea**—the absence of a previously regular period. **Copper IUDs** contain no hormones and cause no amenorrhea. Although very rare, LARCs may cause PID or ectopic pregnancy, and most people experience temporary pain during insertion. LARCs do not protect against STIs. In general, **barrier methods** are less effective at preventing pregnancy than LARCs or hormonal contraception; however, some can prevent STIs (e.g., condoms) and do not affect menstruation. Most require no prescription and are an effective alternative for breastfeeding women and those who are sensitive to hormonal contraceptives. However, barrier methods are only effective at preventing pregnancy if correctly used each time. Some can cause **genital irritation** (e.g., spermicide, sponge, latex condoms) or **toxic shock syndrome** (e.g., cervical cap, diaphragm, sponge). The effectiveness of barrier methods ranges from 73% to 86%.

Natural Methods and Permanent Contraception

Fertility-based awareness methods (FAM) refers to tracking the number of days that one is fertile or infertile to prevent pregnancy. FAMs are no-cost and involve no devices or medications to prevent pregnancy. However, they do not protect against STIs and are only 76–88% effective. **Withdrawal**—otherwise known as the pull-out method—describes the removal of the penis from the vagina before ejaculation. It is typically 78% effective at preventing pregnancy but does not protect against STIs. Exclusive **breastfeeding** prevents ovulation and induces lactational amenorrhea. It can be just as effective as hormonal contraceptives (~98%) but does not protect against STIs and requires that one breastfeeds every 4–5 hours to be effective. **Abstinence** is 100% effective at preventing pregnancy and STIs. **Permanent contraception** (e.g., sterilization via tubal ligation and vasectomy) are surgical procedures that prevent pregnancy. **Sterilization** is 99% effective at preventing pregnancy and is hormone-free. However, sterilization is expensive, invasive, irreversible, and not protective against STIs.

Chapter Quiz

Ready to see how well you retained what you just read? Scan the QR code to go directly to the chapter quiz interface for this study guide. If you're using a computer, simply visit the online resources page at **mometrix.com/resources719/oaehealth** and click the Chapter Quizzes link.

Avoiding and Preventing Health Risks

Legal and Illegal Drugs

Categorization of Drugs

Drugs are substances that produce a psychological or physiological effect in the user. Drugs can be **categorized** by their effects as depressants, stimulants, hallucinogens, inhalants, and opioids.

- **Depressants** slow down or depress parts of the central nervous system (CNS), which can have a sedative and relaxing effect on users. Examples include alcohol, cannabis, and barbiturates.
- **Stimulants** activate the CNS, increasing users' heart rates and blood pressure and improving their alertness. Examples include cocaine, caffeine, methamphetamine, and Adderall. Nicotine, a compound found in tobacco, is considered both a depressant and stimulant.
- **Hallucinogens** affect an individual's perception of reality; they can influence sensory experiences and mood. Examples include LSD and psilocybin. Inhalants are drugs—often everyday household items—that cause brief euphoria when inhaled. Examples include aerosol sprays, gasoline, and nitrous oxide.
- **Opioids/opiates** are highly addictive drugs—also referred to as **narcotics**—that are used to treat pain and incite feelings of euphoria. The term "opiates" is often used interchangeably with "opioids," but opiates (e.g., opium, morphine, heroin) refers to drugs extracted from plants while opioids (e.g., oxycodone, fentanyl) are often synthetic.

The category that a drug is placed in has no influence on its legality nor how it is ingested.

Legal vs. Illegal Drugs

Legal drugs are lawfully prescribed and used, whereas possessing, selling, and using **illegal drugs** is considered unlawful and carries strict penalties depending on the drug class. For example, possession of drugs that are **highly addictive** and carry a higher potential for abuse like opioids carry a much heavier criminal penalty than possession of alcohol by an underage individual. Additionally, possession and use of some drugs without authorization (i.e., a prescription) is illegal, as is use of some drugs in public or unauthorized spaces. A drug's legality does not make it any less addictive or harmful to the individual ingesting it. For example, legal substances like alcohol and tobacco can be very addictive and have a high risk of harm. Some drugs are legal for those with a prescription but illegal for those without, such as some stimulants (e.g., Ritalin), steroids, some opioids (e.g., morphine, oxycodone), and some depressants (e.g., Xanax). **Common illegal drugs** are stimulants like cocaine, depressants like cannabis, narcotics/opiates like heroin, and hallucinogens like LSD. **Over-the-counter drugs** and herbal supplements are legal and mostly accessible to all yet can carry a high risk of harm if overconsumed (e.g., Aspirin) or unregulated (herbal supplements).

Short-Term Effects of Drugs

Short-term effects of the appropriate use of prescribed drugs can alleviate health ailments, but their **misuse** (e.g., exceeding recommended doses, unauthorized use) can result in serious complications. Effects can also differ by the type of drug that an individual takes. **Short-term physical effects** of **depressants and opioids** are feelings of drowsiness, lethargy, hypoventilation, and potential unconsciousness. **Stimulants** may cause increased blood pressure and heart rate. The altered perception of reality that **hallucinogen** users experience may increase their risk of serious bodily harm. **Short-term psychological effects** vary. **Stimulant and hallucinogen** abuse can cause hyperfocus, irritability, or paranoia. Some drugs—specifically, those that induce feelings of euphoria—produce a neurochemical reaction that releases excessive amounts of dopamine from the brain. **Dopamine depletion** can lead to depression and emotional numbness following drug use. Misuse or abuse of drugs can alter one's mental state, which can result in erratic behavior or poor decision-making and **social effects**. Their behavior may deter those around users and **alienate** them from their friends and family. The emotional impacts paired with undesirable physical sensations from hangovers or withdrawals can prompt an individual to use drugs again to ease the symptoms.

Long-Term Effects of Drugs

Chronic use of drugs can increase their addictive potential and cause internal organ damage. **Long-term physical effects** of **stimulants** include cardiovascular disease and dopamine depletion. Long term physical effects of **depressants** include chronic fatigue and respiratory distress. Depressant withdrawal—specifically, alcohol and benzodiazepine withdrawal—following heavy abuse is especially dangerous, as it can lead to seizures, hallucinations, delirium tremens, and even death. Beyond opioids' high addiction potential, long-term effects of **opioids** include brain and liver damage. The ingestion method can also have long-term effects. Drugs that are inhaled (e.g., tobacco, cannabis) can cause respiratory complications and cancer. Drugs that are **snorted** can cause permanent damage to the nose, and drugs that are **injected** can cause collapsed veins and heart and blood vessel infections. **Hallucinogens** can cause **psychological effects** like persistent psychosis and disturbing flashbacks that can impact a person's emotional wellbeing. Long-term psychological effects of persistent **stimulant** use include dopamine depletion-induced depression, poor emotional and impulse regulation, memory loss, and paranoia. Since addicted drug users tend to be more irritable, secretive, and prone to isolation, their social relationships often become strained. Other long-term **social effects** include failed role obligations and estrangement from family members or friends.

Long-Term Effects of Drugs on Pregnant Women and Adolescents

Drug use during **pregnancy** can impact the **short and long-term health** of both the mother and the fetus. Illicit drug use can result in **miscarriage** and **stillbirth**. It may also result in birth defects, sudden infant death syndrome (SIDS), or a number of developmental disabilities. Mothers who use **intravenous drugs** are at **higher risk** of developing HIV and other bloodborne diseases, which can be passed along to their fetus. Fetuses exposed to **alcohol** during pregnancy are at **higher risk** of birth defects, cognitive developmental disabilities, and emotional/behavioral problems. Mothers who **smoke** while pregnant may expose the fetus to hazardous chemicals and **raise the risk** of preterm birth or stillbirth. **Drug use** during pregnancy can also cause **infant withdrawal**, which can lead to serious health complications for the infant. Substance use during adolescence can increase users' risk of chronic mental health problems (e.g., depression, personality disorder, suicide), memory loss, proclivity to commit crimes, and developmental delays. Use of drugs during adolescence can also have significant impacts on relationships. Friends and families may struggle to support their loved one, which can place a strain on relationships.

Addiction

Addiction often results from chronic and frequent drug abuse; as one's **tolerance** for a drug increases, their physical and psychological **dependence** often grows. **Physical addiction** refers to one's **physiological need** to maintain the homeostatic function they have developed through repeated use. With chronic use, the body grows **accustomed** the presence of the substance and adapts its functions to accommodate. Chronic exposure to drugs can cause **neurophysiological and neurochemical changes** that affect the basal ganglia, extended amygdala, and prefrontal cortex. These changes impact one's ability to feel pleasure and make it more difficult to stop using or practice sound decision making. **Psychological addiction** refers to an individual's **drive** to use substances despite their negative consequences to biological, emotional, and psychosocial health. It often includes an accompanying impairment of judgment and insight. **Physical and psychological addiction are often interrelated**. A person's psychological addiction to a drug can be caused by their physical dependency, and their physical addiction can be reinforced or strengthened by a mental craving.

Chemical Dependency

Factors that contribute to **chemical dependency** are an individual's environment, genetics, mental health, and the manner of their drug use. Chemical dependency is strongly influenced by social environment, specifically **spheres of social influence** (e.g., peers, family). Peer and family drug practices and attitudes can impact an individual's decision to try to continue to use drugs. Another aspect of an individual's environment that contributes to chemical dependency is emotional turmoil from one's career. Those in **high-stress jobs** (e.g., military, medicine) may use drugs frequently to ease the anxiety and stress that can accompany their careers. According to a 2012 study in the journal *Nature*, **genetic heritability** of addiction ranges from 42% to 79%, depending on type of drug and gender. **Mental health** disorders often contribute and co-occur with chemical dependency. Substance use may be used to cope with symptoms of psychiatric illness, and the dopamine rush from stimulants or dulling effect of depressants may ease emotional disturbances caused by mental illness. An individual's **drug of choice** can influence chemical dependency. Drugs with high addictive potential, like opioids, can lead to dependency much faster than other types of drugs.

Drug Use and Intervention

Factors Influencing Use and Abuse of Legal and Illegal Drugs

Home

- **Early exposure** to drugs by caregivers can make an individual more familiar with drugs, their effects, and how to procure them.
- **Regular use by caregivers** or others whom the individual looks up to or admires may imply that drug use is acceptable or condoned behavior.
- **Presence of drugs** and easy accessibility to drugs in the home can increase one's risk of experimenting or regularly using drugs.
- **Poor caregiver involvement** and supervision can increase the risk of early drug use and addiction.
- **Family history of addiction** can increase one's risk of developing a substance abuse disorder.
- **Early use of drugs** can alter an individual's brain development to make them more prone to drug addiction.
- The **quality of an individual's relationships** with family members can be both a risk and protective factor. Those who grow up in hostile or abusive environments and/or have poor relationships with their family members are more likely to develop drug addiction.

School and Community

An individual's **peers** at school and in the community can **significantly influence** their decisions to try or regularly use drugs. Pressure from peers and peers' favorable attitudes towards drugs may lead to **early initiation** of drug use and sustained use. The **accessibility and availability** of drugs in one's community can also impact their decision to use drugs. Although no causal relationship exists between poverty and drug use, those who experience **poverty** are more likely to develop drug addiction. One explanation for this is that individuals living in impoverished communities may have greater exposure to drugs than those living in wealthier areas. Since **educational attainment** is a protective factor for drug abuse, under-resourced schools with little academic support for students may fail to adequately intervene. Bullying and gang activity are also risk factors for drug use, so schools without sufficient drug, gang, or bullying policies and intervention programs could influence one's drug use/abuse.

Preventing the Use and Abuse of Legal and Illegal Drugs

The most effective strategy for preventing the use and abuse of drugs is **abstinence**. An individual with well-developed **refusal skills** may be better prepared to refrain from trying drugs, especially when confronted with peer pressure. **Establishing healthy relationships with non-users** and developing a strong and supportive network can prevent individuals from using or abusing drugs. A strong **knowledge of the effects of drugs, addiction risk factors** (family history, mental illness), and **how substance abuse develops** may prevent drug use and abuse. Those with mental illness can prevent drug use/abuse by **seeking mental health care**. Mental health professionals can work with patients to develop healthy **coping skills** and provide guidance or assistance in identifying drug use prevention resources. Since stress can be a contributor to drug use or abuse, developing **stress management skills** can help prevent drug use. Since drug abuse can develop from a growing tolerance and overuse of prescribed medications, maintaining **one's physical health** is also important for preventing drug use.

Promoting Individual Responsible Drug Use

Responsible drug use describes use that **minimizes harm** for the individual and others. **Designated driver programs** promote the use of sober drivers to safely shuttle intoxicated passengers home. Typically, the designated driver **abstains from drinking** at a social event in order to drive themselves and their friends safely. For illicit drugs, individuals can **check the purity and strength** of the drugs they intend to ingest to make sure it is not unexpectedly laced or cut with anything. This can help prevent unknown effects or overdose. Users can also **avoid mixing drugs** to avoid unknown or hazardous interactions. Harm reduction strategies are often implemented at the organizational and community-wide levels to prevent the spread of disease and encourage safe, responsible drug use. An example is **supervised injection sites** which gives users a safe location to inject drugs with sterile supplies without fear of injury or arrest. Users may also carry medication like Naloxone when using drugs to reverse opioid overdoses.

Intervention and Treatment Methods for Drug Abuse

Addiction is considered a mental health disorder, so intervention and treatment often require the assistance and case management of a licensed professional. **Counseling and therapy** can prevent the escalation of drug use to abuse. **Behavioral interventions** can improve a user's **motivation** to change their behavior and grants them the skills necessary to increase their self-efficacy. Therapists or counselors can help identify any **underlying mental health disorders** or **abnormal thought patterns** that preceded the drug use or addiction. Counseling may consist of individual, family, or group sessions, and different styles of therapy may be used (e.g., cognitive behavior therapy, dialectical behavior therapy, motivational interviewing). Treatment is multifaceted and tailored for each person. Those with mild or moderate drug addiction may be able to seek treatment in **outpatient settings** (e.g., addiction specialist office, support group meetings), while those with severe addiction may require **inpatient** treatment (e.g., hospital, rehabilitation centers). **Supervised withdrawal** is used to safely treat those with moderate to severe addiction. It describes the administering of medications to prevent severe, life-threatening symptoms of withdrawal. **Peer support groups** (e.g., Alcoholics Anonymous, Narcotics Anonymous, Self-

Management and Recovery Training or SMART) may be used as both and intervention and treatment strategy.

Confronting or Helping with Another Person's Substance Abuse

Discussing one's concerns with a **substance use specialist**, medical professional, or counselor can help identify the most appropriate strategy for **confronting** another person's substance abuse. Seeking **mental health care** may also be helpful for the friend or loved one of a user, because one person's addiction can greatly impact others. A person who is experiencing substance abuse may **fail to recognize** their behaviors. **Sharing one's observations** and information about the signs and symptoms of abuse in a non-confrontational and considerate manner may be a helpful intervention strategy. It is important to provide those struggling with substance abuse with encouragement, reassurance, and praise. **Positive reinforcement** is key to sustaining motivation. Since those struggling with addiction are often exposed to unsafe conditions or environments, **developing a safety plan** with the user can be helpful for maintaining their physical health and safety. The safety plan can also consist of a list of identified individuals who can offer support if the user experiences temptation.

Drug Use/Abuse and Health and Safety Problems

Since drugs may alter one's physical and psychological states, they can lead to a myriad of health and safety problems. The **loss of judgment and sound decision making** associated with drug use may result in non-use of contraception, which can lead to **unplanned pregnancies**. Poor decision making, slowed reaction time, the and propensity for risk taking that accompany drug use may result in **motor vehicle crashes** or other injuries. Some drugs, specifically depressants and opioids, can cause lethargy, numbness, or unconsciousness. This can cause life-threatening or fatal injuries. For example, if the user is operating heavy machinery, they may fall asleep and lose control of their vehicle or device. If the user is swimming, they may become too tired, fall unconscious, and drown. Use of drugs by injection can expose users to **diseases** like HIV and Hepatitis C, which are transmitted through exposure to blood of an infected person.

Promoting Drug-Avoidance Programs in the School and Community

Assertiveness, Refusal Skills, and Peer Pressure

Although they may be reluctant, those who experience **peer pressure** are more likely to use drugs. The **desire to fit in or bond** with others and **avoid perceived embarrassment** may make it more difficult to say no. Therefore, **strong refusal skills** are crucial for building the confidence to advocate for oneself when faced with peer pressure. An individual who practices refusal skills may feel more comfortable expressing their feelings about substance use and resist insistent peers. Refusal skills can be practiced in different ways: saying no, using humor to deflect, suggesting another activity, showing concern, leaving the conversation, etc. **Assertiveness** is an effective strategy for clearly and respectfully communicating one's disinterest in using drugs and standing their ground when pressured. An assertive individual would maintain their refusal in a respectful and dignified way and use both verbal and body language to communicate to others. They may make sure that they are not judgmental of their peers' choices and refrain from being overly critical or disparaging.

School-Based Efforts to Address Health Risk Behaviors

Health risk behaviors refer to factors that increase an individual's predisposition to poor health outcomes and raises a person's risk of harm or injury (e.g., tobacco and drug use, unprotected sex). Poor academic performance and lack of involvement in school activities can lead to health risk behaviors like drug use. Therefore, school-based efforts (e.g., tutoring, participation in after school activities, clubs, and leadership opportunities) to **address academic performance and commitment** can reduce the risk of drug use. Since unhealthy relationships and isolation can place an individual at risk of drug use/abuse, school-based efforts to improve the culture and connectedness among students and **educate students** about healthy relationships can be powerful intervention strategies. This can include anti-bullying and harassment initiatives or curriculum, opportunities for school bonding (e.g., school events, extracurricular activities), and positive behavioral incentive programs. Schools may also use **peer or adult mentorship programs** to connect students to a support network. Educational opportunities that speak to the dangers, pressures, and effects of drug use may help shift students' attitudes towards drug use.

Community-Based Efforts to Address Health Risk Behaviors

Community-based efforts to address health risk behaviors related to drug use can be achieved through education, messaging, and resource identification. **Educational campaigns** that discuss the factors which contribute to drug abuse, the short and long-term effects of drug use, and resources for treatment can confront drug use at the community level. Educating community members on how to successfully navigate peer pressure and temptations through social skill development classes may help address drug use. A **community-wide anti-drug messaging campaign** can help **shift local norms** regarding drug use. If a community cohesively works together to change how drug use is perceived, they may be able to change attitudes and behaviors among users or potential users. It is important that **anti-drug messaging maintains respectful and non-judgmental** language to ensure that recipients do not experience shame or embarrassment. **Free programs** that occur during times when drug use risk is high (e.g., after school) can be powerful interventions since they decrease accessibility during key timeframes. A readily accessible **compilation of resources** for drug users/abusers with information on where individuals can seek assistance or treatment may catalyze an individual's decision to stop using.

Promoting Student Participation

The most effective way to improve student participation in school-based and community-based efforts is to **include students in planning, implementing, and evaluating** efforts. If included, they are more likely to produce initiatives that reflect current student attitudes toward drugs. Their role may lead to more appropriate and effective efforts. Their stakeholder status is also likely to encourage their participation in the program and their promotion of the efforts to their peers. Providing opportunities for **student feedback** is important for ensuring participation. If students feel that their voices and opinions are **valued**, they may be **more likely to feel involved**. Participation in school and community-based efforts is more likely if **tactics that elicit fear or shame in recipients are not used**. Efforts that are accessible to **students** and their families and **provide incentives** are more likely to gain participation among students. For example, a program that occurs from the end of the school day to 6 p.m., provides a bussing option to students' homes, and provides food to students and their families will have greater participation than one that lets out at 4 p.m. with no food or transportation.

Health Hazards and Factors that Contribute to Safety Concerns

Biological and Chemical Hazards to Health and Safety

Biological hazards (e.g., viruses, bacteria) and chemical hazards (e.g., non-biological substances like acids) can be found in the home, school, and community. **Biological hazards** like bacteria and viruses are **transmitted** through contaminated objects, droplets, or contact and can spread disease among the residents of a school, home, or community. Poor or dated building infrastructure may contribute to **exposure** to various molds or materials like asbestos and lead, which can cause moderate to severe **allergic reactions** and the development or exacerbation of **asthma**. The risk of exposure to biological hazards increases in communities with high population density and high contact potential with wild animals or insects (e.g., ticks, bats, rodents). **Chemical hazards** may arise from use of **cleaning supplies**, **chemical agents** used in science labs, **mishandling of medications**, **lead exposure** from contaminated pipes or paint, **rodent control supplies** (e.g., superwarfarin), or **carbon monoxide** leaks. If ingested or inhaled, chemical hazards can cause serious health problems.

Environmental and Equipment Hazards to Health and Safety

Environmental hazards refer to natural conditions that cause adverse health effects and can impact the health and safety of a home, school, or community. These include **extreme weather** events like earthquakes, hurricanes, heat waves, freezes, blizzards, and floods. Environmental hazards can also result from **pollution** (e.g., oil spills, sewage leaks). **Equipment hazards** result from misuse or malfunctioning of a machine or device. Fires, electric shock, or drowning are unfortunate outcomes of equipment hazards. Fires may be caused by heat generating appliances (e.g., ovens, dryers) or electronics used for an extended amount of time, cooking mishaps (e.g., oil fires), faulty electrical wires, unattended candles or fires, and smoking. **Improper use of pool equipment or poor supervision** at pools and in bathtubs can lead to drownings, especially among those who are unable to swim or those who are incapacitated in or near water.

Avoiding and Preventing Unintentional Injuries

Driving an Automobile

Unintentional injuries refer to those that are not deliberate and are typically accidental. They can often be prevented by adherence to safety rules and precautions.

- **Following all traffic laws** pertaining to automobile safety can prevent unintentional injuries.
- **Staying alert and cautious** while driving can ensure that other drivers, bicyclists, or pedestrians who may not be attentive remain safe and free from injury.
- Proper and consistent **use of seatbelts and car seats** can protect all passengers from car accident-related injuries or fatalities.
- Practicing safe driving measures (e.g., maintaining a **safe speed**, keeping a **safe distance between cars**) and abstaining from erratic driving behavior can prevent unintentional injuries while driving an automobile. Additionally, avoiding alcohol or substance use before and while driving can prevent injury or death.
- **Limiting distracted driving**—any activity that limits the driver's focus and attention (e.g., texting or talking on the phone, eating or drinking, using a music player or navigation device)—can help keep all passengers safe from unintentional injury.

Bicycling

Similar to drivers, it is imperative that all bicyclists **adhere to local traffic laws** to prevent unintentional injury or fatality. Individuals should:

- Use hand signals, hand bells, or electronic devices to **signal their intention** to turn, pass, or brake.
- **Bike in a predictable manner** (e.g., no weaving or abrupt stops).
- **Avoid substance use** while biking.

- Since bicycles are often harder for automobile drivers to see, it is important that riders **exercise caution** on shared roads and **stay alert**. To stay alert, bicyclists should refrain from using cellular or navigation devices and listening to music. Staying alert while riding can also prevent injury that may occur from objects in the road, stationary objects, potholes, uneven surfaces, etc., that can cause a rider to lose control of their bicycle.
- **Using traffic lanes designated for bicycles** or sidewalks can prevent injury that may occur from sharing lanes with motor vehicles.
- **Wear protective gear** (e.g., helmets, protective glasses) and reflective gear to protect themselves and maximize their visibility while on the road.
- Bicycles should be appropriate for the rider's height and weight, and should receive regular maintenance to prevent unintentional injury.

Swimming

Prior to entering the water, it is important that one **learns how to swim** and/or properly wears a well-fitted **floatation device**. Individuals should:

- **Swim in supervised areas** patrolled by a lifeguard, and swim with or around another person whenever possible.
- **Obey all rules and safety regulations** and always make sure that it is safe to swim. Regardless of the location, swimmers should prepare to exit the water if thunder or lightning occurs. When at a natural body of water, swimmers should avoid swimming in fast-moving water or choppy waves. They should also practice caution when walking in the water as there may be submerged objects.
- **Entering water feet first** will protect swimmers from head or neck injuries associated with diving.
- **Refrain from alcohol or substance use** and swimming after eating to prevent drowning.
- Learn **resuscitation techniques** to prevent unintentional injury or death from drowning.

Fatigue

Fatigue refers to drowsiness or tiredness; it can significantly impair one's motor functioning, concentration, and psychological health. It can result from reduced sleep duration and quality, strenuous or stressful work conditions, and long or demanding work hours. Those who are fatigued **may experience** mood changes, communication and processing delays, irritability, reduced concentration, diminished memory, and impaired decision making. Each of these traits can **increase the risk of injury** as a person may exhibit irrational behavior and make poor or uncharacteristic choices. Fatigue is associated with **greater accident and injury rates** in fields like health care, emergency response, military, education, and manufacturing. Fatigue is also associated with **higher risk** of motor vehicle accidents, job error, poor productivity, and illness.

Use of Alcohol and Drugs

An individual who engages in **risk-taking behavior** makes potentially harmful or hazardous choices that can endanger themselves or others. Examples of risk-taking behavior include substance use, dangerous or impaired driving, or unsafe sex. Those who make risky behaviors often make **impulsive**, thrill-seeking choices that place them at **high risk** of sustaining injury or injuring others. Use of alcohol and drugs **impairs** a person's **decision-making abilities** and **psychomotor functioning**, which can cause an individual to engage in risk-taking behavior and have poor control over their physical motions. Research shows that as alcohol consumption increases, an individual's function and inhibitions decrease while their tendency toward risky behavior increases. For example, an inebriated person may lack the ability to recognize how impaired they are and become increasingly confident that they can return home safely. While driving, they will likely experience delayed reaction time, poor concentration, and an inclination to drive erratically. Their behaviors increase their risk of self-injury or injury to others.

Personal Responsibility in Avoiding Risky Behaviors

Personal Responsibility in Preventing Injury

Although **unintentional injuries** may occur due to others' poor or risky choices, individuals should act responsibly to minimize and prevent the risk of injury. One should always try to understand and respect the **safety rules and expectations** of their school, workplace, or other environment. In doing so, they can **maximize safety** for all and prevent potential hazards that result from non-adherence. Each person has a right to **opt out** of unsafe or risky behavior, and it is the responsibility of all to ensure that everyone involved has the ability to **communicate their concerns or refusal**. Maintaining effective communication with others can ensure that all feel confident and comfortable to speak up when they feel their safety is threatened. An individual should **utilize refusal skills** to establish boundaries or guidelines for what they will or will not do in order to maintain safety. **Peer pressure** is a powerful and coercive force, yet individuals should **always reject participation** in unsafe behavior—despite its real or perceived consequences—and maintain common sense to avoid situations that could result in unintentional injury. **Awareness of personal risk** is important for preventing injury. This involves being alert and aware of one's surroundings and being mindful of situations that may put others at risk.

Risky behaviors	Harmful behaviors
Critical—Public or private criticism, purposefully humiliating the person.	Aggressive/Abusive—Any type of hitting, shoving, pushing, or physical violence.
Irresponsible/Immature—Constant problems (social, financial) and discord.	Controlling/Possessive—Attempts to control another person's life and to isolate the person from others.
Noncommunicative—Difficulty expressing feelings and being open with others.	Volatility—Unpredictable bouts of anger and rage.
Self-centered—thinks only in terms of personal needs.	Manipulative—Pressuring someone to do something or using guilt or threats to get one's way.

Safe and Unsafe Behaviors

The **leading cause of death** for individuals under the age of 44 in the United States is unintentional injury. **Infants** are extremely curious but have little to no concept of danger and lack motor functioning. Thus, they are at higher risk of choking or falling and need constant supervision from a caregiver. From ages 4–9, **young children** begin to learn about the concept of danger from others or past experience and improve their self-control, yet they still **lack a mature ability** to recognize dangerous situations and employ strategies to prevent injury. They also begin to **gain confidence**, which makes them more likely to engage in risky behavior without the knowledge of their own limitations. During **adolescence**, teenagers begin to exhibit risk-taking behavior due to **peer pressure** and **lack a clear sense of mortality**. They are at far more **risk for injury**, and their behavior can have **lasting implications** for their adult health (e.g., adolescent substance abuse and increased risk of cancer, addiction, or permanent injury).

Recognizing and Avoiding Potentially Dangerous Situations

Maintaining personal safety requires that one recognize and avoid **potentially dangerous situations**. A potentially dangerous situation is any event or experience in which a hazardous or harmful outcome is possible, and the individual(s) involved feel uncomfortable or unsafe. A person can protect themselves from potentially dangerous situations by **avoiding areas where criminal activity often occurs** or those who engage in criminal activity. **Maintaining situational awareness**—the awareness of the physical and social happenings around a person—at all times can ensure that an individual **recognizes possible threats to safety** before they happen and takes actions to prevent them. Avoiding situations or crowds in which others begin to act aggressively or erratically can prevent a potentially dangerous situation from occurring.

Preventing and Responding to Dating Violence

Dating violence refers to physical, emotional, or sexual abuse within a romantic relationship. An important first step to preventing dating violence is to **understand the characteristics of healthy/unhealthy relationships** and the early warning signs of intimate partner violence (e.g., excessive communication, jealous or controlling behavior, gaslighting). **Learning and practicing skills** like communicating effectively, managing emotions, and refusing behaviors that make one feel uncomfortable can reduce the risk of dating violence. Developing **positive relationship-building skills** and **self-respect** during childhood and adolescence can prevent the victimization or perpetration of dating violence. **Assertiveness and boundary setting** are effective strategies to respond to dating violence. Both encourage an individual to **advocate** for their needs and **respectfully decline** any unwanted activity or behavior. Educating communities on **bystander intervention** can help individuals identify intimate partner violence and empower others to take action to support those affected.

Preventing and Responding to Gang Violence

Gang violence refers to any violence—physical, emotional, sexual—committed by members of a gang (e.g., assault, rape, intimidation). Violence may be directed **internally** (e.g., initiation) or toward other gangs and innocent bystanders. The most effective way for a person to prevent gang violence is to **remove oneself from the threat of violence**. If possible, one should **avoid locations** where gangs have a strong presence and **avoid association** with gang members. They should **avoid engaging in criminal activity and exhibiting aggressive behavior** when in public or online that may incite violence. Establishing healthy relationships with others who are not affiliated with a gang or do not commit criminal acts can prevent an individual's exposure to gang violence. If inadvertently exposed to gang violence, one should respond by **leaving the situation** or **alerting emergency responders** or law enforcement. At the organizational and community-level, **early and collaborative intervention** by community groups, school staff, law enforcement, parents, and local government is necessary to address risk factors for gang initiation and violence.

Preventing and Responding to Hate Crimes

A **hate crime** is any violent act or criminal offense directed at a person because of their identity (e.g., race, ethnicity, religious affiliation, gender, sexuality, or disability). **Federal legislation** like the Matthew Shepard and James Byrd, Jr. Hate Crimes Prevention Act and the Emmett Till Antilynching Act dictate that individuals who commit hate crimes may be liable to prosecution. Additionally, **state and local legislation** exists as a preventative and protective measure against hate crimes. If an individual experiences or witnesses a hate crime, it is important to **alert emergency responders and law enforcement** immediately. Victims and witnesses should respond with **caution** as offenders may exhibit violent behavior; however, it is important for bystanders to **de-escalate** the situation and support victims of hate crimes. **Education on hate**

crimes and its impacts and **critical-thinking skills** are important preventative measures to address hate crimes. Those who are able to identify hate crimes and assess discriminatory speech, material, or actions may be better able to prevent and respond to it. Improving **media literacy** is also an important strategy for preventing hate crimes since they increasingly happen online.

Emergency Response Planning

Home Safety Plans

A **home safety plan** is a set of procedures and preventative measures intended to lower the risk of danger at home. Home safety plans can **minimize injuries or fatalities** and **provide a sense of security** among those who live in the home. When revisited and practiced routinely, home safety plans can **alleviate the confusion or chaos** that often accompanies breaches to home safety. A home safety plan typically includes an emergency contact list and a detailed checklist of what to do if an emergency happens. An **emergency contact list** may include numbers of caregivers, family members or friends, neighbors, and emergency responders; it is intended to improve communication in case of a safety concern. Home safety plans may also include a **detailed checklist** of what to do in response to an emergency or safety concern (e.g., fire, tornados, burglary, unknown visitors, injury, power outage). Home safety plans can also include a **list of important information** or tools located in the home. This list can include information regarding when to replace the batteries in smoke/carbon monoxide detectors, how to check home alarm systems, and the location of fire extinguishers and stockpiles of emergency supplies (e.g., extra food, water, first aid kit).

Emergency Response Plans

Emergency response plans include a set of procedures for unexpected threats to health and safety. It is similar to a home safety plan but includes **detailed information regarding emergency response and recovery**. Emergency response plans typically include an emergency contact list, a list of external emergency resources, responsibilities for each household member, evacuation plans, and important information about where to locate emergency supplies. An **emergency contact list** can include contact information for caregivers or other family members, friends, neighbors, and emergency response teams. It can also include a **list of resources** an individual can access in case of an emergency (e.g., natural disaster shelters). Emergency response plans can also include a **list of instructions** for responding to various emergencies (e.g., fires, sudden weather event, intruder). Emergency plans may also include **designated roles and responsibilities** necessary to ensure the safety of all (e.g., who will contact first responders, administer first aid, acquire the emergency supplies). Emergency response plans often include **evacuation plans**—diagrams of the safest and quickest exit routes—and emergency supplies information. The location and contents of emergency supplies (e.g., first aid kit, food, water, clothing) is often listed in an emergency response plan.

CPR

Cardiopulmonary Resuscitation (CPR) is a first aid procedure that is performed when an individual's heart stops beating—also known as **cardiac arrest**. CPR consists of chest compressions that restore blood flow to the rest of the body, and rescue breaths that allow the blood that is being circulated to be oxygenated. If administered correctly, a person's **chance of survival is 2–3 times higher** when they receive CPR. If a mouth mask is not available to provide rescue breaths for ventilation, mouth-to-mouth breaths are not recommended and instead, only chest compressions should be administered. This prevents the risk for infection. Regardless of the mode of CPR being administered, an AED should also be utilized to determine the heart rhythm, whether a shock may restore spontaneous circulation based on that rhythm, and (if a shock is warranted) deliver that shock. Considerations for these interventions include the following:

- **Hands only CPR** is the recommended method for the general public. Those performing hands only CPR should push hard and quickly on the person's chest—usually at a rate of 100–120 compressions per minute. The depth of the compression varies depending on the depth of the victim's chest.
- **CPR with mouth-to-mouth breaths** should be done at the ratio of 30 chest compressions and 2 breaths that result in chest rise, with compressions always starting first. Pulse checks should occur every 2 minutes for no longer than 10 seconds.
- Portable machines called automatic external defibrillators (AEDs) monitor heart activity and can administer an electric shock to the heart to force it to beat again when deemed necessary. This technology can be used by anyone, as it clearly directs each step of the process audibly, to include applying the chest pads, pausing CPR for rhythm checks, and either resuming CPR or clearing the patient for a shock, then resuming CPR.

Conscious Choking

A **conscious choking** person may be awake or reactive yet is unable to breathe, cough, or speak due to a foreign object lodged in their throat. Their skin and lips may begin to flush and turn blue. It is vital that first aid be administered immediately, since an **obstructed airway** can prevent oxygen from reaching the brain. If a person is no longer able to speak, cry, laugh, or cough forcefully, the rescuer can use the "five-and-five" method or the Heimlich maneuver to clear their airway. The **"five-and-five" method** consists of 5 back blows between the victim's shoulder blades with the palm of the hand and 5 abdominal thrusts. Back blows and abdominal thrusts should be repeated until the object is dislodged. The **Heimlich maneuver** is performed by a person standing behind the victim, administering quick abdominal thrusts with a closed fist, until the object is dislodged. Those providing **choking first aid to infants** should administer thrusts with two fingers on the breastbone in a seated position and with the infant resting on their forearm. If at any point the victim becomes **unconscious**, the rescuer should begin performing CPR immediately until help arrives.

Family Structures and Roles within a Family

Diverse Family Structures

Contemporary families are not limited to the traditional nuclear definition of two or more biologically related individuals. Family living arrangements have **changed drastically** in the last few decades due to **demographic shifts** (e.g., life expectancy), fewer marriages, increases in the number of divorces and remarriages, postponed childbearing, increases in childrearing outside of traditional nuclear marriages, and rises in singlehood. Today, families are far more **diverse** than they used to be, and the **definition** of family has shifted significantly. The dimensions of family diversity can differ by race and ethnicity, socioeconomic status, gender, sexual orientation, family structure, and family process. Families may be related by birth, chosen, or made circumstantially through adoption, guardianship, or marriage. The **family process**, or interpersonal dynamics (e.g., support, decision-making, communication) between family members, varies based on family demographics, societal and cultural influences, family history, and family structure. Families can be connected through shared identities or experiences, cultures, or emotional commitment. Families may also be connected through **reciprocal relationships**, which refers to mutually beneficial and complementary actions. They may provide emotional and economic support, discipline, and affection.

Influence of Family Structure and Dynamics

Family structure and dynamics can have a profound impact on social relationships with others and individuals' overall health. It is through their observations of relationships among parents, siblings, extended family members, caregivers, etc., that children first perceive acceptable social dynamics and healthy relationships. **Sociological factors** like gender, age, sexuality, religion, economic status, race, and ethnicity can influence the practices and dynamics within a family. The quality of interfamilial relationships is of specific importance as it can impact social and physical wellbeing. **Interpersonal stressors**, such as frequent arguments and overly critical or demanding family members, and external stressors, such as lack of time or economic hardship, can contribute poor mental and physical health. However, **social support** (e.g., giving advice, providing care) is a protective factor against many poor health outcomes like immune system dysfunction and depression. A **diverse family structure** may strengthen family members' social networks and access to social support. For example, a multigenerational household in which grandparents assist in fulfilling family functions can reduce internal and external stress on primary caregivers.

Factors Influencing Relationships Within Families

Relationships can be influenced by the composition of family members, family structure, roles and expectations, values, family events or hardship, family member personalities or traits, and past and present relationships. **Changes in family structures** (i.e., the combination of family members) can impact dynamics and roles within a family. Shared or conflicting behavioral, moral, and cultural **values** can influence the health of familial relationships. **Family hardship**, **events**, and **trauma** can negatively affect a family and its function. For example, financial hardship can induce stress among family members that strains relationships. Trauma can lead to emotional turmoil and lasting effects on future generations that influence family dynamics. **Family personality traits** and **past and present relationships** can influence how family members feel towards each other and how they interact. Each family member holds a unique role within the unit that influences how they interact and communicate with others. **Roles** can influence individual's self-concept and perceived importance within the family. They may also influence family members' expectations of the individual which could impact self-confidence, self-efficacy, and emotional health.

Individual Roles and Responsibilities Within a Family

The **Family Systems Theory** posits that each family member occupies a distinctive role and level of influence within the family unit. A person's **family role** refers to the authority they hold and responsibilities or expectations assigned to them. As an individual ages and family dynamics shift, their role within the family changes. Typically, family roles are intended to maintain function and satisfy needs; however, roles may have a positive or negative impact on the family. Equitably assigned and allocated roles ensure that family members are able to accomplish their responsibilities and avoid conflict within the family unit. Explicitly defined and fairly allocated roles can help families develop healthy family roles and responsibilities.

Promoting Healthy Interactions Among Family Members

Expressing Needs and Wants Appropriately

Families must **balance** the needs and wants of many different people, which can lead to **conflict**. Respectfully **communicating** one's needs and wants can help to nurture physical and emotional wellbeing and improve interpersonal relationships. **Expressing** needs and wants appropriately can demonstrate self-respect and respect for others. Practicing **assertiveness** can help a person communicate their thoughts and feelings in a positive way and advocate for themselves. Expressing needs also promotes mutual respect, trust, and intimacy within a person's relationships. Individuals who **withhold** their wants and needs can develop feelings of resentment, frustration, and abandonment. This can impact their emotional wellbeing and how they interact with others.

Practicing Self-Control

Self-control describes the ability of an individual to **manage** their emotions or impulses. An individual with too little or too much self-control may develop depression, anxiety, or isolation. Those with **too little self-control** may be quick to blame others and have difficulty controlling emotions, which can cause conflict in their relationships. Individuals with **too much self-control** may be rigid in their beliefs and opinions, overly focused on details, struggle to display feelings, and can be overbearing in relationships. These qualities can create **distance** in relationships and make resolving conflict difficult. **Practicing self-control** can help an individual control impulses and negative reactions that may cause emotional distress or physical harm. It is also helpful in managing thoughts, emotions, and actions in order to become more productive and achieve a greater goal. Employing self-control strategies can help an individual achieve positive outcomes and maintain healthy, respectful relationships with others.

Building Trust

Building trust among family members promotes healthy interactions and strengthens relationships. **Mistrust** may cause family members to limit their involvement and vulnerability. It can lead to fragmentation within the family unit and conflict. Boundaries, accountability, and communication are key components of building trust and promoting healthy interactions among family members.

- **Boundaries**—clear limitations and expectations—create a shared understanding of acceptable behavior among family members.
- Respected boundaries can prevent conflict, but **accountability** for overstepped boundaries is important for repairing trust and mitigating conflict.
- An important aspect of trust-building is establishing strong **communication** skills. The ability to express one's feelings, wants, and needs, and the openness of their family members to accept what they share, can build trust among the family.

Expressing Affection

Expressing **affection** and **positive attention** promotes healthy interactions among family members. **Receiving regular affection** is associated with improved overall social, emotional, and physical wellbeing. Parental warmth and affection are associated with improved brain development, higher self-esteem, improved educational performance, stronger family communication, and fewer psychological and behavioral challenges. Affectionate behaviors elevate levels of a hormone called **oxytocin** in the body, which encourages bonding and calms those giving and receiving affection. **Positive attention** between family members builds connection and strengthens individual self-confidence. Expressing and receiving affection and positive attention can create close bonds between family members. Benefits resulting from positive interactions between family members can extend beyond the immediate relationship. For example, healthy intrafamilial relationships can improve an individual's ability to navigate social situations, increase compassion, and make them better able to relate to others.

Setting Limits

Setting limits promotes healthy interactions among family members. **Limits**, or relational boundaries, are personal guidelines and rules that people set for themselves in relationships. These limits identify acceptable ways for others to behave around them and reasonable ways to respond when their boundaries are overstepped. An individual with **healthy boundaries** values their own feelings and opinions, refuses to compromise their values for others, appropriately shares personal information, communicates their personal wants and needs, and accepts when others decline their requests. Setting limits allows a person to practice **self-respect** and **communicate their needs** in relationships. The practice of establishing and respecting limits promotes healthy interactions because it enables family members to demonstrate trust and respect, avoid conflict that may arise from physical and emotional space intrusion, and share responsibility and power.

Effects of Family Problems on an Individual

Influence of Abuse

Abuse refers to repeated harmful or injurious actions. It can have a significant impact on an individual's physical, emotional, and social health, especially when it occurs within a family unit. Individuals who experience abuse may sustain **immediate physical injuries**, but abuse can also result in **long-lasting physical ailments**. Individuals who experience abuse during early childhood may experience **stunted brain development and function**. Individuals who experience abuse are at **higher risk** of diabetes, respiratory and cardiovascular illness, and diminished vision and functional capacity. Abused individuals frequently experience persistent isolation and fear which impact their **emotional and social health**. They are far more likely to experience memory problems, impaired self-control, and mental health conditions (e.g., depression, anxiety) than their non-abused peers. Their **impaired mental state** can result in educational and learning challenges, which can influence academic attainment and job readiness if unaddressed. The **social health** of abused individuals can also be affected; those who experience abuse are more likely to develop attachment disorders and poor social skills. This can impact an individual's ability to form positive relationships. Abuse can contribute to poor decision-making and coping skills which may result in unsafe sexual activities, substance misuse, crime or violence, and future perpetration or victimization of abuse.

Influence of Divorce

Divorce refers to the termination of a legally recognized marriage. It can **drastically impact** an individual's physical, emotional, and mental health. **Self-reported health** is much lower among divorced individuals, and they have a greater overall **mortality rate**. Divorced individuals are more likely to develop heart disease, diabetes, cancer, and mobility challenges (e.g., climbing stairs, walking). They tend to report higher amounts of anxiety, depression, isolation, and stress than the general population. The individual health effects are not solely limited to those receiving a legal separation or divorce. **Children of divorced caregivers** have a higher perceptibility to illness and increased injury rates. They are more likely to become divorced as adults than their peers. Children of divorce are at **higher risk** of experiencing depression, anxiety, poor academic performance, substance use/abuse, early sexual activity, poor social maturation, and premature mortality.

Influence of Death

Experiencing death can influence all dimensions of health. Those who experience the death of their family member may experience **diminished health outcomes** as they grieve the loss of their loved one. Specifically, grieving individuals report chronic fatigue, compromised immunity, chronic pain, digestive issues, and inflammation. Individuals experiencing the death of a loved one can develop sleep disturbances which may increase feelings of depression or anxiety. Levels of **cortisol**, a hormone associated with stress, are much higher following the loss of a loved one. High levels of cortisol for an extended amount of time can raise blood pressure and increase risk of heart disease. Grief from the death of a loved one can increase an individual's risk of developing anxiety, panic disorders, substance abuse, post-traumatic stress disorder, depression, and suicide. The death of a family member can have significant impacts on the interaction between living family members as their family structure shifts. Following the death, many note a loss of personal or relational identity and difficulty connecting to others. The loss of a family member may continue to cause poor emotional and physical health outcomes among the bereaved long after their death.

Nature of Conflict in Families

Family conflict refers to disagreements or opposition among family members. Compared to other forms of relationship conflict, family conflict tends to be **more intense and complex** because of the duration of the familial relationships and the **strong emotional attachments** that exist among family members. Therefore, the nature of family relationships can intensify conflict and make managing family conflict more challenging. Conflict may be verbal, physical, sexual, financial, or psychological. **Conflict style**—the tactics and routines families use when conflict arises—can influence the intensity, duration, and severity of family conflict.

Causes of Conflict in Families

There are many causes of family conflict.

- **Financial difficulties** can be a major source of family conflict. Inability to pay bills or afford food and uncertainty about economic security can cause stress among family members.
- **Unemployment** can also have the same effect.
- **Marital and relational challenges** like infidelity, separation, or divorce can trigger conflict among family members.
- **Child rearing** is a major stressor; disagreements about discipline, caregiver responsibilities, children's assertion of independence, and sibling rivalry or disputes can lead to contention and conflict.
- **Poor communication** about wants and needs, the distribution of responsibilities, unresolved issues, and the inability to express needs and wants can lead to misunderstanding, disconnection, and conflict.
- **Intrusive relatives or friends** can also lead to conflict as family members struggle to manage extramarital and familial dynamics.
- **Contrasting beliefs, opinions, and values** can lead to disagreement and resentment among family members.
- **Differences in gender and age** can cause behavior that seem unreasonable to the other party. Specifically, gender stereotypes or generational and cultural differences may fuel conflict between family members.

Consequences of Conflict in Families

Family conflict **impacts all family members involved** and influences **multiple dimensions of health**. Family conflict can contribute to mental health problems like anxiety and depression. Parental or caregiver conflict reduces children's **emotional security** and can lead to emotional dysregulation and poor reactions to future conflict. **Intergenerational conflict** can sever supportive ties that provide crucial aid and companionship to family members. **Physical health impacts** of conflict include digestive problems, heart disease, sleep disturbances, high blood pressure, immune system suppression, and premature aging. Children who are involved in conflict may adopt unhealthy or risky behaviors (e.g., substance use, unprotected sex) and may develop poor attachment styles and unhealthy interpersonal relationships. **Chronic and severe conflict** can exacerbate health problems as family members grow increasingly overwhelmed and exhausted. **Social health** can also be affected by family conflict. Conflict strains relationships which can lead to resentment among those involved and distrust of others. The dissolution of families due to conflict can result in a loss of social contact between family members. This can cause stress as the family adjusts to a shift in structure and loss of emotional and financial support.

Supporting Students with Family Problems

Helping Students Cope with Family Abuse and Neglect

Abuse refers to the intentional harm or coercion directed by one person toward another. **Neglect** refers to the failure of a caregiver to fulfill a child's basic needs in a manner that threatens a child's health and wellbeing. Abused and neglected victims are often **reluctant** to open up about their experiences, so **identifying indicators** of abuse and reporting it is crucial to preventing it. Educators who are aware of the appropriate behaviors exhibited by children at each developmental stage are more capable of recognizing conduct that indicates abuse and intervening quickly. **Structured classrooms** provide a safe space in which abused and neglected children can cope with unhealthy behaviors in the family. For example, **consistent classroom routines** and schedules can counteract a turbulent home life. At school, students are able to engage in productive coursework that fosters a sense of achievement and develop healthy relationships with others outside of their family. Classroom activities that promote **social emotional learning**—the process of developing problem-solving, interpersonal, and emotional management skills—can help students establish **positive coping mechanisms** and strengthen their ability to **self-advocate**.

Helping Students Cope with Family Alcoholism

Alcoholism refers to a compulsive and uncontrolled dependence on alcohol. Children of alcoholics (COA) may be exposed to unsafe physical conditions and are at risk of violence or abuse, neglect, and emotional distress. **Age-appropriate information** about alcoholism and its secondary risks can help COA comprehend addiction. Information can be shared during lessons or through a classroom library that contains relevant books or articles on addiction. A readily accessible classroom **list of school and community resources** or professional counselors can help educators connect students and their families to support. COA are at higher risk of emotional and behavior challenges. Therefore, **skill-building opportunities, collaborative learning projects, and social emotional learning activities** can help them develop necessary coping skills to navigate alcohol-related conflict and receive constructive attention from others. Educators who model consistency and positive communication can build the trust and self-confidence of COA that they may lack at home.

Helping Students Seek Help in Dealing with Family Problems

As **mandatory reporters**, educators are generally required by federal and state law to report suspected maltreatment, although some reporting laws vary from state to state. Once reported, Child Protective Services investigates and identifies services to prevent future maltreatment. **School protocols** and **staff development programs** are effective strategies for identifying and reporting suspected cases of maltreatment; they eliminate obstacles for reporting and quickly connect students with appropriate resources or referrals. **Wraparound initiatives** refer to comprehensive services aimed at meeting the needs of children and families to foster student wellbeing. Examples include mental and physical health care, food and nutrition services, and community education and training. Wraparound initiatives can connect students and families to mental health professionals who can deliver counseling and treatment. They are also helpful for providing financial relief and social supports that cause and/or worsen child maltreatment. Research suggests that students who participate in **school-based programs** that offer training in life skills, parenting, and problem-solving openly communicate about maltreatment and seek help more readily.

Healthy and Unhealthy Interpersonal Relationships

Healthy Relationships

Regardless of the kind of relationship, four characteristics that are necessary for all healthy relationships are mutual respect, boundary setting, open communication, and trust.

- **Mutual respect** is expressed when an individual values and affirms another's feelings and opinions—regardless of whether they are different.
- **Setting healthy boundaries** establishes expectations for how individuals in a relationship should be treated and holds them accountable if boundaries are violated.
- **Open communication** ensures that both parties feel that they can share their feelings honestly and without judgment or interruption. Open communication is achieved through consistent, intentional, and honest discussions between both parties.
- **Trust** refers to security and fidelity; a relationship in which both parties trust one another elicits openness and honesty.

Along with the four mentioned above, there are a few characteristics that are particularly important in intimate and familial relationships. **Equality**, **compatibility**, and **shared decision-making** are crucial for developing and maintaining strong **romantic relationships**. **Accountability**, **support**, and **showing appreciation** are especially important for **optimal family functioning and family cohesiveness**.

Unhealthy Relationships

Qualities of an **unhealthy relationship** include control, disrespect, dependence, and dishonesty.

- **Control** within a relationship refers to an unequal distribution of influence and displays of dominance by one party towards another. A controlling person may use **coercive or intimidating tactics** to exert power over another or isolate them from their friends or family. They might also exhibit hostile or antagonizing behavior or resort to violence and intimidation to maintain control.
- **Disrespect** refers to insulting or humiliating behavior that devalues one's thoughts, feelings, opinions, or identity. It can cause one to feel undervalued or underappreciated.
- Although healthy relationships require interdependence—shared and equitable dependence of two people on each other—the level of **dependence** may be unbalanced in unhealthy relationships. This can result in relationships that are unfulfilling, one-sided, and mutually destructive.
- **Dishonesty**—deceit or intentional withholding of information—can erode trust and mutual respect.

Together, these characteristics can contribute to unhealthy behaviors such as jealous and unfounded accusations, picking fights, lying or withholding information, stealing or destruction of property, threatening self-harm or suicide with the intent to control another person, and committing sexual or physical violence.

Building and Maintaining Healthy Interpersonal Relationships

Mutual respect is developed as both parties practice open communication, respect boundaries, show interest in the other's interests, show appreciation, and encourage one another. Building mutual respect can be accomplished through **consistent and reliable actions** (e.g., follow through with promises). **Healthy boundaries** are established through **open communication** about an individual's needs and expectations. This may be accomplished when both parties assert their limitations or ground rules for the relationship, communicate when a boundary is breached, and identify mutually agreed upon consequences for violated boundaries. Open communication can be accomplished when both parties are **transparent** about their thoughts, feelings, beliefs, etc., and participate in respectful discourse. It can also be achieved when both parties are **approachable** (e.g., inviting behavior and positive language) and **receptive to feedback**. **Trust** can be developed through transparency, vulnerability, and willingness to accept and apply criticism. Expressing one's feelings and demonstrating vulnerability can **improve intimacy and connection** between both people. Relationships are **not static**; they change as a person grows and develops. Therefore, to maintain a relationship it is important for one to **check in** with their partner, friend, coworker, etc., regularly to ensure that both feel **content**, **respected**, and **fulfilled**.

Peer Relationships

A **peer relationship** refers to an established interpersonal connection between two individuals who share a developmental (e.g., age) or situational identity (e.g., school, work). Peer relationships are often influenced by early interactions with caregivers or family members and can be positive or negative. Those in a **positive peer relationship** may encourage each other to make positive, healthy decisions, reinforce healthy behaviors, and support one another. Those in a **negative peer relationship** may pressure or encourage one another to make poor decisions and reinforce unhealthy choices. The interactions that occur within peer relationships can influence an individual's identity, attitude, and ethics. Social skills, in-group norms, and socially-acceptable behavior are **learned through observation and peer interaction**. Additionally, peer interactions and peer reactions to an individual's behavior can promote or discourage health and behavior choices. The quality of peer relationships, peer status (i.e., popularity), and fear of social rejection can impact the level of peer influence on an individual.

Peer Pressure

Peer pressure refers to the external influence that members of a person's reference groups have on their behavior or decision-making. It can be **direct** or **indirect** (e.g., a teenager is directly pressured to drink a shot of liquor by a peer vs. a teenager is tempted to drink when surrounded by peers who are drinking at a party), and **negative** or **positive**.

- **Negative peer pressure** is associated with poor health outcomes. Specifically, it can result in depression, poor self-confidence, increased anxiety and stress, and sleep disturbances. Depending on how hazardous the activity is, it may also increase an individual's risk of injury.
- **Positive peer pressure** can encourage healthy behaviors that result in improved social, mental, and physical wellbeing outcomes.

The effect of peer pressure is especially powerful among **adolescents**, who are more **vulnerable** to social desirability and reinforcement than adults.

Responding to Peer Pressure

Having a diverse set of **ready-to-use strategies** is important for responding to negative peer pressure. Those who **plan ahead** and **practice** their refusal skills are often far better at responding to peer pressure when it occurs. An example is confidently saying, "no," or explaining how one's pressuring actions or language makes another person feel. Other examples of responses may include the use of humor to deflect, an excuse to leave the situation, a change of subject, or the use of a secret code with another person to swiftly exit the situation. **Remaining calm and unwavering** in one's decision is important for resisting negative peer pressure or persuasion. A clear understanding of one's **values and morals** (i.e., right and wrong decisions) can make it easier to refuse peer pressure and to discern between a healthy and unhealthy choice. Maintaining healthy relationships with positive influences can prevent negative peer pressure and reinforce making constructive choices.

Group Relationships and Dynamics

Groups, Group Dynamics, and Social Support Networks

A **group** is an aggregate of individuals who work interdependently to accomplish a common goal or outcome. They share a **collective identity** and adhere to an explicitly or implicitly **defined structure**. Groups can be **primary**, meaning small and connection-based, **secondary**, meaning large and objective-based, or **reference**, which vary in size and influence an individual's beliefs and behaviors. Group cohesion is reliant upon the fulfillment of various roles and **group dynamics**, which refers to the interactions within groups. A **social support network** refers to an individual's friends, family, and peers who provide reciprocal support and guidance. While groups are centered around a common goal, they tend to be more open and fluid when compared to social support networks. Social support networks are usually made up of more stable relationships and do not typically change very quickly.

Health Consequences of Group Interactions

An **in-group** is a group an individual belongs to along with likeminded or similar individuals, and **out-group** is a group that one does not identify with. In-group members may feel acceptance and belonging; however, **in-group/out-group bias** can lead to in-group favoritism or out-group exclusion/discrimination. Out-group members may feel rejection and disdain towards in-group members. The **black sheep effect** describes instances when an in-group member displays divergent beliefs or norm-violating behavior. As a result, they may be judged or denied membership. The **group-subgroup interaction** describes how an individual can belong to two groups—a group and a subgroup—that both shape and reinforce an individual's beliefs and behavior. For example, an individual who belongs to a religious family and a religious club that share complementary values should experience reinforcement from both groups. Membership in compatible groups may minimize emotional turmoil or conflict that can arise from discordant group beliefs. Group **mutual exclusivity** describes an inability of one to belong to two or more groups with incompatible characteristics or values. For example, a person who belongs to an academic club and sports team may feel pressured to choose between them.

Social and Communication Skills

Demonstrating Tolerance, Empathy, Consideration, and Respect

Practicing tolerance, empathy, consideration, and respect can enhance a person's interactions and improve the health and wellbeing of their relationships.

- **Showing tolerance** to others is expressed by conveying **fairness** and **acceptance** of a person or their beliefs regardless of disagreement or personal grievances. Practicing tolerance in relationships ensures that both parties feel included and accepted, which can improve the connection between both people and promote mutual respect.
- **Empathy** refers to a person's ability to understand or experience another person's point of view. Showing empathy in relationships can build trust between two people. It can also provide reassurance and validation, improve communication, and create more effective solutions to conflict.

- **Being considerate** of others is expressed through kind and accommodating—sometimes anticipatory—actions. Like tolerance and empathy, consideration demonstrates a respect for others. It is a display of self-control and shows others that one values them.
- **Demonstrating respect** in a relationship shows the other person that an individual admires and values them. It is exhibited through positive language and actions, honesty, encouragement, and acceptance. Respect builds trust and security within a relationship.

RESPONDING APPROPRIATELY TO CRITICISM

Although receiving feedback is a crucial part of self-improvement and relationship building, **criticism** can sometimes be difficult to accept. **Responding appropriately to criticism** is a type of communication skill that can prevent or mitigate conflict and foster self-evaluation. A person who responds appropriately to criticism acknowledges the **intent** of the criticism (e.g., constructive, destructive), **accepts accountability** while asserting themselves when necessary, and **inquires** to **gain understanding** and develop an **improvement plan**. Responding appropriately to criticism establishes a pathway for **improved communication** between the two parties. If effectively and appropriately communicated, criticism presents an opportunity for both people involved to demonstrate mutual respect, understanding, and empathy.

LISTENING SKILLS

Listening skills are important social and communication skills that maintain healthy and bidirectional communication within a relationship. **Active listening** is a listening skill that refers to attentive, responsive, and reflective listening. It consists of **verbal and non-verbal cues** to show engagement and non-judgment (e.g., nodding, body language, eye contact, paraphrasing). If practiced, listening skills can improve one's **empathy** and **tolerance** of another person's perspective, which can encourage others to open up. It is also a useful skill when engaging in conversation with others, which can be beneficial in building relationships.

DISCUSSING PROBLEMS

Discussing problems in a relationship is an essential part of building and maintaining healthy communication. **Constructive problem solving** is achieved when issues are discussed early, talked about honestly and productively, and received by an engaged and empathetic listener. Discussing problems or conflicts provides clarity to both parties. It also reduces **rumination**—obsessive and negative thoughts or feelings about a particular situation—that can lead to emotional or social distress. Discussing problems with another person can also present **different perspectives** that aid in problem solving and promote healthy conflict resolution. Since it requires **vulnerability** and **empathy** from both parties, discussing problems can maintain and strengthen **trust** in existing relationships.

CONFLICT RESOLUTION SKILLS

Conflict refers to disagreement or incompatibility between individuals or groups. **Conflict resolution skills** are communication strategies that prevent relationship disputes or avoid escalation. Though the method varies depending on the type of relationship, most effective conflict resolution strategies are rooted in **healthy and effective communication, empathy, and self-awareness**. Developing conflict resolution skills can help individuals navigate conflicting and contrasting perspectives or volatile situations resulting from conflict. Utilizing conflict resolution can **strengthen relationships** once a disagreement has occurred and **prevent escalation** or future conflict. Conflict resolution can improve the quality of relationships by promoting **reciprocal respect** for others' perspectives and shared problem solving.

Assertiveness

Assertiveness is a communication strategy in which an individual firmly and clearly **communicates their needs** and **respectfully advocates** for themselves. Compared to other communication styles—passive, aggressive, and passive-aggressive—assertive communication is the **healthiest** and **most effective** form of communication. Assertiveness is important for improving situations involving **interpersonal interactions** because it promotes the integrity and rights of both people involved. Assertive communicators address conflict early on, engage in active listening, and set/respect boundaries. As a result, all those involved are able to express their feelings honestly and confidently before conflict arises or escalates. Since assertiveness improves self-advocacy and prevents conflict, it can **reduce individual and relationship stress**.

Refusal Skills

Refusal skills are communication strategies that help an individual confidently refuse when they are confronted with a decision and remain resolute when pressured. They are a crucial component of **resisting peer pressure** and **preventing risky or hazardous situations**. Refusal skills are especially important for avoiding substance use/misuse, preventing injury, and protecting personal space and privacy. Refusal skills allows individuals to identify, assert, and uphold their **personal boundaries**, which can aid in establishing and maintaining healthy communication with others. Refusal skills are important for anyone at any age, yet they are particularly essential for children and adolescents, those with low self-efficacy, and individuals with low self-confidence, since all can increase an individual's susceptibility to peer influence. During childhood and adolescence, youth begin to form an identity and cultivate their psychosocial skills; this makes them very susceptible to peer influence. During this time period, they are often exposed to new, potentially dangerous, or risky experiences and situations (e.g., drug use, sexual activity) that necessitate refusal skills. Individuals with **low self-esteem** or **low self-efficacy** may struggle to assert themselves or develop strategies for refusal.

Conflict Avoidance and Resolution

Conflict Resolution Styles

There are five conflict resolution styles.

- An individual with an **avoiding** conflict management style may **withdraw or circumvent** an issue to prevent conflict. They may ignore a problem or person until the dispute is resolved or repeatedly evade a conversation to avoid conflict.
- One with an **accommodating** style of conflict management may **yield** to the needs or desires of others to manage conflict. These individuals may allow others to make decisions for them that conflict with their needs in order to keep the peace.
- An individual with a **competing** style uses **firm**, **dominating**, and **uncooperative** conflict management—often at the expense of another person. They may be headstrong and unaccommodating to the needs or desires of others.
- An individual with a **compromising** conflict management style works together with others to find **middle ground** and to create a resolution that is **mutually accepted by all parties**. Often, all participants must make concessions to appease the other and not everyone is pleased with the solution.
- Similar to compromising style, a person who uses a **collaborative** style is cooperative. However, one with a collaborative style seeks to find an **innovative resolution** in which all who are involved are engaged throughout the process and are satisfied with the result.

Mediating and Resolving Conflict

Conflict resolution refers to the informal or formal process of resolving conflict between two parties. It involves identifying the source of the conflict, contributing factors, and triggers, and creating a resolution. It is important that all involved feel **motivated to express their honest feelings and perspectives** without judgment or retribution. Active listening and assertive communication throughout the process are necessary to ensure that all involved feel affirmed and fairly represented. Successful conflict resolution occurs when both parties create a solution that settles their dispute. Conflict resolution can be achieved through **mediation**—the use of a neutral third party to guide those involved to resolution. In this style of conflict resolution, participants engage in a structured and facilitated process to reach a mutually agreed upon solution. The mediator works with both parties to identify the problem and strengthen understanding of both parties' perspectives. They work with participants to determine a shared goal and strategize potential solutions needed to reach one. Often, both parties create a formal plan that includes steps for achieving resolution and accountability measures needed to end the dispute.

Avoiding Unsafe Situations

One must practice **situational awareness** at all times in order to avoid unsafe situations. This requires that an individual stays **alert** (e.g., abstaining from mind-altering substances, minimizing distractions) and pays attention to others' odd behavior (e.g., staring, loitering or stalking, persistent attempts at conversation, unwanted advances).

- **Avoiding isolation** can offer protection from unsafe situations and ensure that there are others around who can provide aid if an unsafe situation occurs.
- **Maintaining visibility** (e.g., staying in well-populated areas) can be a deterrent to crime and unsafe situations since perpetrators often seek out an isolated victim in a secluded area.
- **Maintaining communication** with others and sharing one's location or plans with a loved one can increase the likelihood of intervention before a situation occurs or provide quick assistance if necessary. A lack or sudden halt of communication can signal to others that something is wrong and that they should intervene.
- Valuable items in plain view make an individual a target for crime; **keeping valuables hidden** or left in a secure place can prevent unsafe situations.
- **Avoiding conflict** or deescalating disputes can prevent injurious or fatal confrontations.

Bullying, Ridicule, and Harassment

Bullying refers to deliberate acts of intimidation or harm by one individual against another. Bullying may be physical, verbal, social, or cyber. **Ridicule**—the act of mockery and humiliation—and **harassment**—threating or intimidating behavior—are examples of bullying. Cultivating **healthy and nurturing relationships** with others can prevent bullying; those engaged in healthy relationships are far less likely to be the subject of bullying, harassment, or ridicule. Having friends or **surrounding oneself with others** is a deterrent to bullies, as they frequently seek out those who are isolated or vulnerable. Individuals should **avoid conflict and unsafe situations** (e.g., isolation, no adult supervision, bullying "hot spots") that could put them at risk. When faced with bullying, ridicule, or harassment, an individual can respond by **confidently and assertively telling their bully or harasser to stop**. However, they should remain calm and refrain from using intimidation or any other behavior that could escalate the situation. If possible, one can **remove themselves** from the situation or ignore any negative behavior. An individual can also **tell an adult or authority figure** who can mediate the situation and prevent further conflict.

Influences on Health Decisions and Behaviors

Beliefs

An individual's **health beliefs** can impact his or her **desire to seek medical services** and can **predict** whether he or she engages in a certain health behavior. According to the Health Belief Model, six theoretical constructs interact to influence a person's health beliefs:

- **Perceived susceptibility** describes how vulnerable a person believes he or she is to a disease, condition, or other health problem.
- **Perceived severity** refers to an individual's perception of the severity of the illness if he or she doesn't seek treatment.
- **Perceived benefits** describe a person's perception of the effectiveness and advantages of the actions he or she must take to prevent or treat an illness.
- **Perceived barriers** refer to the obstacles one believes impede his or her ability to perform a health-promoting action.
- **Cues to action** describe external (e.g., health campaign or PSA on the dangers of smoking) or internal stimuli (e.g., a persistent cough that prompts one to go to the doctor) that provoke action.
- **Self-efficacy** is an individual's confidence in how capable he or she is to perform a health-promoting action.

Each of these constructs influence a person's understanding of disease risk, how important or easy it is to act, and whether he or she can maintain health behaviors.

Attitudes

A person's **health attitudes** are formed by the **perceived quality** of his or her health and his or her favorability toward various aspects of health. For example, a person with a **positive health attitude** may consider his or her health very important, so he or she might participate in health-enhancing behaviors like exercise. On the other hand, someone with a **negative health attitude** may refrain from engaging in behaviors that improve his or her health and well-being. Often, one's health attitudes are informed by one's **participation in health-enhancing practices** (e.g., a person who exercises frequently and eats nutritious foods will have positive health attitudes). Positive health attitudes may shift one's beliefs about his or her vulnerability to disease and his or her belief that health-promoting behaviors can be maintained. The beliefs and attitudes of others can greatly influence health attitudes.

Knowledge

Health knowledge refers to a person's comprehension of disease etiology, transmission, treatment, and risk. An individual is more likely to have **low health knowledge** if he or she has low educational attainment and is a non-native speaker, older, or belongs to a lower socioeconomic group. Individuals whose caregivers or peers have low health knowledge may be more likely to have low health knowledge as well. A person with a **high degree of health knowledge** is more likely to engage in health-promoting behaviors and disease-prevention practices. One's health knowledge can greatly influence one's **health literacy**, which is the ability of a person to find, comprehend, and appropriately apply health information. For example, people with **poor health literacy** may rely on false health information disseminated through social media websites to inform their decision to get a COVID-19 vaccine. They may also **lack the critical thinking skills** to adequately **assess the validity** of the health claims and information they consume. Poor health knowledge may impact their perceived susceptibility to the virus and thus influence them to make poor health decisions.

SKILLS

Health skills refer to the tools a person uses to maintain good health. The ability to identify and seek out **reliable health information** and the ability to **assess the external influences** (e.g., peers, media) that promote positive or negative health behavior are two important health skills. These skills help a person **make informed decisions** that reflect his or her personal beliefs and attitudes. **Goal setting** is another health skill that empowers an individual to achieve his or her health aspirations by setting reasonable targets and action. Through successful goal setting, a person gains the confidence necessary to make positive health decisions. **Advocacy and negotiation** are health skills that encourage healthy decisions and behaviors. A person who is skilled in health advocacy **feels comfortable asserting** his or her beliefs and opinions when making health decisions. For example, a person may advocate for himself or herself by remaining resolute when faced with pushback from physicians or contempt from peers. **Negotiation and refusal skills** empower a person to make decisions that result in improved health and well-being.

PEERS

Both **implicit and explicit social pressure** from peers can encourage or reinforce healthy decisions and behaviors. **Explicit social pressure** describes direct, often verbal pressure to engage in a certain health behavior, whereas implicit social pressure refers to unspoken pressure by peers or society (e.g., observing friends who participate in fad diets). An individual with **positive peer influence** is more likely to make safe and health-promoting decisions than a person with **negative peer influence**. For example, a person who surrounds himself or herself with physically active peers may be more likely to engage in regular exercise than a person whose peers are sedentary. He or she may receive verbal encouragement, feedback, or advice from those peers that inspires him or her to engage in healthy behaviors. By surrounding oneself with individuals who make healthy decisions, a person may also observe the positive effects of exercise on a friend's health or identify achievable actions he or she can adopt to improve his or her health. Peers may also **expose a person to new experiences** (e.g., playing a new sport, trying a new food) that influence them to make positive health decisions and implement positive health behaviors.

ROLE MODELS

A **role model** is a person who can exhibit desirable attributes and shape the decisions or behaviors of others. The role model may lead by example or influence others' health choices through advice, guidance, or encouragement. Role models may also **influence a person's perception and attitude** toward health behaviors. For example, a person with a role model who maintains a healthy relationship with food, consumes nutritious foods, and encourages his or her mentee to maintain a healthy diet is likely to mirror those health behaviors. A **positive role model** may serve as an example of how health-promoting decisions and behaviors lead to good outcomes. Research indicates that adolescents with positive role models are **less likely** to make unsafe or risky choices (e.g., unsafe sex, drug use), receive higher grades in school, make healthier decisions about nutrition and exercise, and have higher self-esteem. The **benefits** of role models are **amplified** if a person has a **personal relationship** with his or her role model.

Informed Decision-Making Processes

MAKING DECISIONS ABOUT PRODUCTS OR SERVICES

A person seeking to make a decision about a health care product should first **compile relevant and credible health information regarding all possible products or services**. He or she should then **consider his or her personal values, health goals**, and the pros and cons of each option. Before making a final decision, the individual should **discuss the decision with a health care provider**

and/or family and friends. For example, a person who hopes to stop smoking cigarettes should first research all feasible smoking cessation aids (e.g., nicotine gum and/or patches, vaping, anti-craving prescription medication). Next, he or she should consider the pros and cons of each (e.g., cost, ease of access, addictive potential, side effects) and whether the product fits his or her goals (e.g., gradual cessation, reducing reliance on nicotine). Third, the person should discuss the potential decision with his or her physician and/or family and friends. Finally, the person should make a decision, implement the decision, and monitor his or her progress.

MAKING DECISIONS ABOUT A HEALTH BEHAVIOR

The **ABCDE decision-making rubric** can be used to make a decision about health behaviors. A decision about adopting a new health behavior is scored in five criteria: **a**ims, **b**enefits, **c**apacity, **d**ata-driven, and **e**ffectiveness.

- **Aims** refer to the extent to which the behavior aligns with a person's health goals.
- **Benefits** describe the number of potential benefits.
- **Capacity** is the extent of one's ability to adopt a new behavior.
- **Data-driven** describes the amount of credible research regarding the behavior.
- **Effectiveness** is how well the behavior will address the health problem.

The person would score the behavior on a scale. **The higher the final score, the better the decision**. For example, a person hoping to lose weight may opt to increase his or her exercise. The behavior aligns with the goal and has numerous benefits, so he or she may assign a 5 to aims and benefits. If the person lacks the time to exercise throughout the week and the funds to afford a gym membership, he or she might score capacity at 2. Exercise is well-researched and proven to reduce weight, so data-driven and effectiveness may be scored at 5. The final score is a 22, which indicates that this decision is achievable and well-thought-out.

ABCDE Decision-Making Rubric					
Aims	1	2	3	4	5
Benefits	1	2	3	4	5
Capacity	1	2	3	4	5
Data-Driven	1	2	3	4	5
Effectiveness	1	2	3	4	5
Composite Score Range	5 low	10	15 mid	20	25 high
Score:					

USING HEALTH INFORMATION FROM HEALTH PROFESSIONALS

Individuals making a decision about a health service, product, or behavior should **consult their health care provider first**. Providers can **advise patients** on the actual risks or benefits of health-related products, services, and behaviors. They can **provide factual and clear information** that aids in **informed decision-making**. However, health professionals' interpretations of the efficacy of a service, product, or behavior may differ, so it is important that consumers **seek a second opinion**. Consumers should **evaluate the similarities and differences** between the information they receive and **synthesize their findings**. Those making health-related decisions can use health information from health professionals to corroborate claims in advertisements for health services, products, or behaviors. For example, a person who is considering the ketogenic (keto) diet—a low-carbohydrate and high-fat diet—can consult his or her physician to determine if the diet is appropriate for his or her health goals and health status. He or she can use information from the provider to identify which health claims about the keto diet or keto products are trustworthy.

Using Health Information from Government Agencies

A person making a decision about a health service, product, or behavior can use health information from government agencies to make an informed decision. Health-related information from government sources (e.g., federal agencies, local health departments) is reliable and trustworthy. Resources provide credible health facts and statistics; accurate information on specific diseases, conditions, or treatments; advice on healthy behaviors; and helpful information on where to locate community health resources. Information from government agencies can be used **to prompt discussion about health concerns or treatment options with health care providers**. Government health resources are typically presented in plain and accessible language, which can **help consumers better comprehend information** from physicians and health claims. Comparing well-documented facts to claims can help a person **spot fraudulent or inaccurate health information**. For example, a diet pill advertisement may boast that its special ingredient will help consumers lose up to 20 pounds per week without any lifestyle changes. A person can compare information about fad diets and best practices from the USDA, NIH, FDA, or CDC to assess the validity of the product's alleged results.

Using Health Information from Private Nonprofit Agencies

A person making a decision about health services, products, and behaviors can use **health information from private nonprofit agencies** to inform his or her choices. Nonprofit agencies that synthesize credible source material to produce health information can be viewed as **credible**. They may also **conduct research** or **initiate advocacy** campaigns on health-related issues. Agencies that specialize in health-related issues often have in-depth information on a consumer's area of interest. They may have useful health materials or trainings that educate consumers about health topics and available resources for health care. For example, the **American Heart Association** (AHA) has wide-ranging materials on heart health, provides CPR training and courses on maintaining heart health, and publishes guidance on heart-healthy activities (e.g., recipes, fitness routines). Information from the AHA can be used to make decisions about adopting new behaviors, diet products, or heart health-related services (e.g., nutrition counseling, support groups).

Using Health Information from Internet Resources

A person making decisions about health services, products, and behaviors can use internet resources to **research health conditions and treatments** and **connect with health-related resources**. Reliable health-related websites can provide a plethora of information regarding common symptoms of specific illnesses and available treatment options and their outcomes. If used properly, the information can help individuals **discern between a benign and serious health problem**, which can save them time, money, and anxiety. However, the wide generalizability of health information can serve to increase health anxiety instead of relieving it. Reviews by consumers of various health products and services may **help a person identify health frauds or scams**. However, many internet sources promote products or claims that are biased or unsubstantiated by research. Therefore, a person should consult multiple resources and health experts before deciding. **Telehealth applications available through the internet can connect consumers to physicians** and health care professionals. Easy access to experts can provide quick confirmation of the validity of health information to make health decision-making less daunting.

Using Insights from Friends and Family Members

Since members of one's support system (e.g., family members, friends) are **familiar with the individual's personal goals, values, and barriers**, they can provide invaluable insights about health decisions. Due to their proximity to the individual, family members may be **more aware of the impact** that a health decision can have on a person's daily life or long-term health. Shared behavior alterations with family members and friends are often easier and more effective than when one adopts a new health behavior alone. **One's support system can provide motivation, accountability, and advice**. The family of a person seeking to lose weight may help him or her cook healthy meals or accompany him or her on daily walks. Their involvement may help a person feel more supported in his or her goal. Family-wide involvement may also be necessary for difficult health decisions. For example, a person with a substance use disorder may consult family about treatment options. Family involvement may reduce distress and treatment dropout.

Cultural Influences on Healthcare

Influence of Cultural Background

A person's **cultural background** can influence his or her decision-making when selecting a health care provider because it can influence one's understanding of the causes of a disease and the type of treatment one is seeking. Cultural influences can be difficult to pinpoint, but **they are related to geographic location, family history, religious values, language, and social interactions**. They can be subtle or strong but often still affect one's choices. Individuals with **stronger cultural values** often prefer to have a practitioner who **shares or is empathetic with their beliefs**. Practitioners should be careful to consider cultural backgrounds and values when dealing with a patient. Individuals pursuing health care services should be **encouraged** to consider and **disclose** their cultural values to receive the best care possible as **tailored to their beliefs**.

Types of Cultural Influence

Cultural influences **can both promote or discourage a person's reliance on health care services and products**. For instance, individuals on a sports team or within a health-conscious peer group may be more willing to take vitamins, purchase protective gear, exercise, and eat well. In some family dynamics, an individual might be **expected** to "push through" being sick, rather than visit a doctor, take medicine, and take time to recover. A patient holding **homeopathic or traditional religious-based health beliefs** may opt for alternative medical practitioners (e.g., acupuncturists, shamans) in addition to or in lieu of conventional providers. In some **traditional cultures**, individuals may believe that spirits or sorcery are the causes of illness instead of bacteria and viruses. As a result, these individuals may choose to forego conventional medicine for spiritual treatments. For example, one traditional practice originating in East and Southeast Asia is called **cupping**, which is the use of suction created from heated cups to draw negative forces out of the body.

Influence of Socioeconomic Status

Socioeconomic status can influence a person's likelihood of seeking health care services and the type of care that he or she receives. Individuals with **lower socioeconomic status (SES)** may be less likely to seek health care due to the cost of services. Those with low SES are more likely to be uninsured or underinsured, which can impact the providers they are able to see, the services that are or are not covered by their insurer, and the cost of their co-pay. A person with low financial security may lack the funds to select more efficient health products or higher-quality treatment options. Low or no-cost community resources (e.g., free clinics) and federal health insurance programs (e.g., Medicaid) can ease some of the financial restraints that impact the health and well-being of those with low SES. Research indicates that a person's SES is correlated with his or her **health literacy**, which is a person's ability to locate, comprehend, and apply health information properly. Individuals with low SES are more likely to have poorer health literacy, which may impact their medical decision-making and health care service selection.

Influence of Information Access

Access to health information can influence an individual's health attitudes and awareness of the health products, services, or providers available to him or her. **A person who has adequate access to accurate health information is better able to make informed health care decisions.** For example, a person with greater access to information about the causes of and management strategies for autoimmune diseases may be better able to make decisions regarding treatment options. He or she may also be able to identify more types of disease management options than those detailed by his or her provider or identify new health care practitioners to consult. With **greater access to health information**, a person may be better able to identify credible sources and recognize untrustworthy health claims. He or she may be more capable of selecting legitimate health care products and services than a person without adequate access to information. **Access to health information can be influenced by low health literacy or environmental barriers.** Individuals residing in rural areas and individuals with low socioeconomic statuses or low technology literacy may lack access to digital health information normally available through affordable or reliable internet.

Health Problem Solving and Decision Making

Using Problem-Solving Skills in Health-Related Contexts

Problem-solving is a process through which a person finds solutions to complex issues. It begins with **identifying and defining** the problem. This can be accomplished through a health care practitioner's diagnosis or a self-evaluation of one's health status. A person's health problem can be defined by determining the causes and contributing or mitigating factors. For example, a person may be diagnosed with prediabetes after a blood sugar test performed by his or her primary care physician. That person may work with the doctor to identify the lifestyle and environmental factors that led to the condition (e.g., family history, diet, physical inactivity). The next step in problem-solving is **generating potential solutions**. A person might make a list of treatment options and rank them based on preference, each solution's advantages and disadvantages, and the person's capacity to perform each solution. Once a treatment plan or solution is decided upon, it should be **implemented and evaluated**. The **measured outcomes** of a solution can determine whether it was effective in addressing the health problem and if the treatment plan should be revised.

Using Decision-Making Skills in Health-Related Contexts

The **DECIDE model** is a tool for making decisions regarding one's health, and it begins with **Defining the problem**. A person should consider his or her **health status** and each of the **determinants of health** (e.g., the social, economic, environmental, lifestyle, and genetic factors) when defining the problem. The second step is to **Establish the criteria**. One should contemplate what **outcomes** he or she hopes to achieve and avoid, and by determining such criteria, he or she will be able to **brainstorm possible solutions**. Third, one must **Consider the possible choices** using that criteria and **weigh the advantages and disadvantages** of each possible solution. He or she should also consider how each possible solution **aligns with his or her values**. Next, a person should **Identify the best solution**. The best solution may be one that aligns most with what he or she deems important or valuable or the one that is most practical to implement. The fifth step is to **Decide and act**, and the final step is to **Evaluate and monitor the solution**. A person should monitor one's health and continuously reflect on one's progress to assess how his or her choices impacted his or her health outcome(s). Doing so can also be helpful for the person as he or she prepares to make future health-related decisions.

DECIDE Model

Define the problem
Establish the criteria
Consider the possible choices
Identify the best solution
Develop and implement the solution
Evaluate the solution

Characteristics and Benefits of Risk Assessments

A **health risk assessment** (HRA) is an appraisal of an individual's health and risk factors. It can be performed by health care professionals to evaluate one's health status, determine health risks, and track health changes between doctor visits. It is also used in health research to assess population-level health data (e.g., health disparities). HRAs are used to identify one's **physiological and mental health status** and **assess the lifestyle and environmental factors** that increase or mitigate risk. Health status may be determined through **self-reported questionnaires** or through **biometric data**. Questions about one's personal medical history, family history, and lifestyle factors (e.g., smoking status, exercise and eating habits) can be used to identify risks. Qualitative data may be collected to **assess health beliefs and attitudes**, which can also be used to evaluate risk. Results from HRAs can be used to create **individualized feedback** and **tailor health plans** for reducing health risks and enhancing and maintaining health, **evaluate the efficacy** of health interventions, and **inform the type of programs** needed to address poor health outcomes.

Reducing Health Risks and Enhancing/Maintaining Health

Once health risks have been identified through a health risk assessment (HRA), an individual can use the findings to adopt health behaviors that **enhance and maintain health**. For example, a person whose HRA identifies a family history of breast cancer might conduct daily breast self-exams, schedule regular cancer screenings, and adopt lifestyle-related behaviors that mitigate the risk of cancer (e.g., weight control, abstaining from alcohol use, exercising). These behaviors can **prevent and detect cancer early** to improve and maintain health. **Biometric data findings** from HRAs can also be used to **adjust health habits**. For example, a person whose HRA determines he or she has high blood pressure can engage in daily exercise, eat nutritious and heart-healthy foods, practice stress-reducing activities (e.g., meditation, mindfulness), and quit smoking. These health risk-reducing behaviors can mitigate risk of complications due to high blood pressure and enhance overall physical, mental, and emotional health.

Planning, Decision-Making, and Goal-Setting Skills

The **DECIDE model** can be used to make decisions regarding one's health. A person with prediabetes seeking to make health behavior changes should **define the problem** first (e.g., poor diet, overweight). He or she should then consider what he or she would like to **achieve** (e.g., weight loss without a restrictive diet) and **brainstorm possible solutions** to accomplish the overall goal (e.g., changing eating patterns, abstaining from alcohol, exercise). Once he or she has identified and implemented the best solution, he or she should **monitor progress** (e.g., regular weigh-ins, A1C checks). **SMART goals** are specific, measurable, achievable, relevant, and time-bound and help an individual plan and successfully implement health goals. For example, a SMART goal for someone who seeks to lose 30 pounds could be to walk at least 30 minutes five days a week for six months. This goal includes a specific and appropriate exercise for weight loss, a measurement to assess progress (e.g., 30 pounds), and the method and rate of weight loss are achievable within the time frame. The SMART goal also has a **start date and deadline.**

> **Review Video: SMART Goals**
> Visit mometrix.com/academy and enter code: 100378

Problem-Solving and Decision-Making Skills and Procedures

The root causes of a person's, family's, or community's poor health outcomes can be determined through the **problem-solving process**. A person with **strong problem-solving and decision-making skills** may develop a more thorough and appropriate plan for enhancing his or her personal health than one who does not. The ability to identify and evaluate health problems, brainstorm solutions, and implement health behavior changes will better prepare a person to effectively manage his or her health. A **collective** (e.g., family, community) **approach** to problem-solving and decision-making can often be an effective way to solve a complex health problem properly and efficiently. The **diversity** of opinions, experiences, and assets of a larger group of people may **reveal novel ideas and improve the efficacy** of the solution. To **enhance collective health**, it is important that the opinions, beliefs, and values of all involved are regarded fairly. All affected by the health decision must be included in the problem-solving and decision-making process.

Seeking Advice and Guidance

Health Care Professionals

Health care professionals are well-versed in **disease etiology**, and they are often the **primary point of contact** for disease diagnosis, treatment, and prevention. Although they generally have a deeper understanding of medical science than the average person, their expertise is often limited to their **specialty**. Primary care providers hold a broad knowledge of medicine, yet they **lack the ability** to diagnose and/or treat a person with advanced health needs. **Specialists** are trained in a specific field of medicine (e.g., neurology, oncology, psychiatry) and can perform **specialized care**. Since health care professionals may have **differing interpretations** of an individual's health or treatment options, a person making an important health care decision should **seek a second opinion**. Asking for a second opinion can **corroborate the accuracy** of the initial findings and **confirm** the most appropriate treatment options. It can also equip a patient with the skills and knowledge to make informed decisions.

Family Members

While health care professionals provide indispensable medical expertise to patients, a person might hold a **family member's advice** and recommendations in **higher regard** than a physician's. Family members are often more attuned to a person's health beliefs, attitudes, and goals, so they can provide appropriate and responsive advice. They may also be more aware of the social and environmental factors that contribute to an individual's health outcomes or decisions because of their shared experiences. Family members may **see each other far more often** than a health care provider, so they are **more likely to notice changes** in a person's health and **suggest actions**. The close ties and personal relationships that a person shares with their family members may make them **more likely to disclose sensitive health information or health concerns**. Thus, family members are a **crucial component** of medical decision-making. However, a family member who is misinformed or holds inaccurate health beliefs may provide poor advice and guidance.

Developing Personal Plans for Maintaining and Enhancing Health

Benefits

A **personal health plan** details a person's health goals and the steps needed to achieve those goals. The plan is guided by an individual's personal health vision. Personal health plans often contain a **detailed account** of one's health objectives to achieve his or her goals, a timeline, and a list of benchmarks to track progress. Since personal health plans **contain clear and actionable goals**, they are useful tools for **maintaining accountability** and **sustaining momentum**. When a person **achieves the health goals** detailed by the plan, he or she may feel **empowered and motivated** to continue working. The framework that personal health plans provide enables a person to make better decisions regarding his or her health. Additionally, the practice of creating and adhering to a personal health plan requires **regular reflection**. A person who practices self-evaluation may be more equipped to **make better health decisions** and **advocate** for his or her health needs with others.

Procedures

The first step an individual should take to develop a personal health plan is **assessing his or her health status**. One's health status can be measured through assessments performed by health care professionals (e.g., biometric data collection) or through a self-evaluation of one's health habits. Second, one must **develop relevant and achievable goals** based on his or her health assessment findings. A person's current health status and/or health risks can inform whether one should seek to **maintain or enhance** aspects of his or her personal health. For example, a physically active person who is diagnosed with high cholesterol should create health goals that enhance one's eating behaviors and maintain one's exercise habits. Next, a person should **create a list of objectives** necessary to reach each goal and **establish a reasonable timeline** in which each objective can be accomplished. Once each objective is achieved, the person should **reflect on his or her progress**. Reflection is crucial to **understanding the barriers and mitigating factors** that impede or support a person in achieving his or her goals.

Chapter Quiz

Ready to see how well you retained what you just read? Scan the QR code to go directly to the chapter quiz interface for this study guide. If you're using a computer, simply visit the online resources page at **mometrix.com/resources719/oaehealth** and click the Chapter Quizzes link.

Health Education, Literacy, and Advocacy

Health Care Agencies, Programs, and Services

Primary Health Care

Primary health care describes the delivery of health services by entities that manage patients with acute and chronic conditions below a level of specialized care. **Primary care providers** (e.g., family doctors or general physicians, gynecologists, nurse practitioners) are often referred to as "gatekeepers" because they are often the first physician that individuals encounter in the health care system. Primary care providers may be the first physician visited when a person develops symptoms, and they are responsible for diagnosis, treatment, and management of illness or injury. They hold an **extensive breadth of medical knowledge** and frequently deliver patient education. Primary care providers may also **coordinate services** and **identify patient resources**. For example, if a patient requires specialized care or community resources (e.g., food assistance, reduced-cost medication), primary care providers may refer them to a specialist or a community organization who provides wraparound services. Primary health care can be delivered at physician's offices or through community agencies (e.g., community health centers and free clinics, health departments).

Preventative Health Care

Preventative health care seeks to prevent disease before it develops and reduce the impact of an illness once it occurs. It is typically divided into primary, secondary, and tertiary prevention.

- **Primary preventative health care** seeks to prevent the onset of illness or injury through legislation, education, and immunization. Lawmakers and government agencies may **implement legislation to reduce risk of injury** (e.g., tobacco tax, seat belt mandate) or **ban hazardous substances and working conditions** (e.g., lead ban). It can also include **interventions** like immunization and mandatory vaccination, health education/promotion, and nutritional fortification.
- **Secondary preventative health care** reduces the impact of disease or injury on an individual by identifying and administering disease treatment as soon as it is detected (e.g., cancer screening, preventative drug therapy).
- **Tertiary preventative health care** describes programs and services that **minimize complications or disability** that result from **chronic disease** and improve quality of life. Examples include diabetes management programs and cardiac rehabilitation. Secondary and tertiary preventative health care may take place within a medical setting but are **frequently implemented in the community** (e.g., community diabetes management classes, free STD testing at health departments, community cancer screenings).

Emergency Health Care

Emergency health care describes the rapid treatment of acute illness or injury and the prevention of serious complications from disease or death. Emergency health care is typically administered at emergency health care centers (e.g., hospitals, urgent care centers) by trained and licensed physicians. They are responsible for providing **immediate care** to individuals with **serious, sometimes fatal, conditions**. Emergency mental health care programs exist outside of the medical health care system, too. Many community organizations provide mental health first aid to intervene when an individual experiences a mental health crisis to reduce the risk of resultant harm. Federal and state entities and non-profit organizations (e.g., FEMA, DHHS, American Red Cross, Salvation

Army) may deploy emergency health practitioners and services when a community experiences a natural disaster or infectious disease outbreak. Their role is often to provide emergency aid and mitigate the damage caused by the emergency.

Community and National Health Care Needs and Goals

Community health care needs and goals are typically outlined in annual **community health assessments** (CHA). CHAs are often developed by state, local, or tribal government bodies to examine key health indicators within the communities they serve. Quantitative and qualitative data on risk factors, social determinants of health, and morbidity and mortality rates are collected and analyzed to identify health needs. Findings are paired with information on community assets, key partners, and essential services to establish health goals. National health care needs and goals are commonly identified through the US Department of Health and Human Services' (USDHHS) **Healthy People program**. Similar to local community health assessments, goals and objectives are identified through data collection, but needs and goals are redefined every ten years instead of annually. Both engage stakeholders and assets within their reach to address identified health needs.

Health-Related Social, Political, and Economic Issues

According the Bureau of Labor Statistics, medical costs have increased an average 2.1% annually over the past ten years. Over the same time period, the cost of commercial health insurance premiums rose 5.8% annually. **Rising medical costs** impact an individual's access to health care. Individuals may delay or avoid seeking care due to cost, which can have devastating impacts on their long-term health and wellbeing. **Uninsured and underinsured families**—who are often more likely to simultaneously experience poverty and poor health—are disproportionately affected by rising health care costs. Those who lack sufficient health care coverage are more likely to accumulate medical debt, delay or forgo treatment, utilize emergency health care instead of primary care services, or ration medical supplies and medication. Thus, health care delivery often transitions from primary care and prevention to late-stage treatment of injury and disease or emergency health care treatment.

Factors Influencing Cost, Availability, Accessibility, and Use of Health Care

Individual Factors

Social determinants of health (SDOH) describe the social and economic conditions that influence health outcomes (e.g., economic and housing stability, education, food access, the physical environment, social norms and attitudes, culture). Those with low **socioeconomic status**—one's economic position compared to others—have diminished access to health care and worse health outcomes than their peers. **Low financial security** may influence their decision to seek care and the type of care they receive. A person's **cultural background** and **health attitudes** can impact their perception of health, as well as their accessibility to and use of health care. The cultural background of one delivering care can impact **how well health information is communicated** and the **patient's treatment adherence**. One's cultural background can influence their **understanding** of the causes, severity, and treatment regimen of illness or injury and may also influence their health attitudes. For example, historically marginalized groups who have experienced medical maltreatment and discrimination are often more reluctant to use health care services. **Age** can influence health care use. For example, youth may lack access to care since their caregivers are responsible for their medical decisions. Older adults may use health care more frequently, yet their mobility can impact access.

Societal Factors

Economic trends can impact an individual's access to health care. During **economic recessions** or downturns, employers may revise coverage and benefits to reduce costs. Economic downturns are also associated with **increased unemployment**. One's loss of financial security and employee-sponsored insurance can influence their **accessibility to services and their willingness to seek care**. Widescale unemployment and changes in coverage associated with economic downturn can impact health care delivery. Inability to pay for services can lead hospitals to avoid clinical and technological upgrades or avoid hiring new health care professionals, which can diminish the health care quality. Medicare and Medicaid are federal insurance programs for seniors and disabled individuals and those with low income, respectively. Government policies like **Medicaid expansion** increase coverage and affordability of health care. **Price regulation** (e.g., price caps on prescription drugs and hospital service costs) enforced through government policy can reduce health care costs, improve affordability and accessibility of care, and increase use of health care services.

Sources of Health-Related Information

Validity of Health-Related Information

Assessing

Not all health-related information is **valid** or **trustworthy**. In some instances, the **primary source** of the information (e.g., research studies) may have **flawed study designs** that skew results. The **interpretations** of results by the authors or those citing the research may also be inaccurate. Both can impact the reliability of the information. If the author's intent is to shift the reader's opinion, the health-related information may also be biased. By assessing the validity of health-related information, **one can avoid making a decision based on inaccurate and/or unreliable claims**. An informed decision can **prevent unnecessary or harmful outcomes associated with invalid information**. For example, a person who consumes a weight-loss pill without researching its side effects, exploring its reviews, or without consulting a health care provider may suffer serious health consequences. He or she may also lose money purchasing an ineffective product and may become disheartened if intended results are not achieved.

Health Professionals

Health professionals receive rigorous medical training and education through which they acquire a wealth of knowledge about health. They are required to demonstrate their **proficiency** through competency-based exams and certifications from accredited organizations. Thus, health-related information from health professionals can be considered **valid**. Health professionals' level of education and specialty can **impact their knowledge** of the subject matter and their level of expertise. For example, a gastroenterologist is a far more reliable expert on stomach and digestive diseases than a nurse. Health professionals' **personal gains or biases** may also **cloud their judgement**, which can **impact the validity** of the health-related information or guidance they provide. Therefore, it is important for health care consumers to **practice good judgment** when considering their physician's advice (i.e., one should seek a second opinion). A person can **access health information** from health professionals through regular visits with his or her primary care provider and published educational materials (e.g., pamphlets, flyers) that are accessible in his or her doctor's office.

Government Agencies as a Source of Health Information

Government agencies (e.g., Centers for Disease Control and Prevention, National Institutes of Health) have a vested interest in the health of the nation. A **healthier population** can improve a nation's economic productivity and produce a more educated and larger workforce. Since they serve the public, **government agencies have a responsibility to release accurate and valid information**. Those who conduct government health research are often beholden to rigorous requirements throughout the research process that ensure the credibility of their findings. A person can access health information from government agencies through federal and state government websites. Most **government websites** end in ".gov." Examples of government agency websites include www.CDC.gov, www.NIH.gov, www.medicaid.gov, and https://www.dshs.texas.gov/. Government agencies often release health information that employs plain language (i.e., clear and easy to comprehend writing) to ensure that their constituents can understand it. They may use infographics, pamphlets, videos, social media, or written text to present health information.

Health-Specific Government Agencies Providing Valid Health Information

- The **Centers for Disease Control and Prevention** (CDC) is a federal agency that monitors communicable diseases, conducts health research, and produces health guidance materials.
- The **National Institutes of Health** (NIH) and the **US Department of Health and Human Services** (HHS) are federal agencies that conduct health and biomedical research. The HHS also provides many social services and publishes resources about disease prevention, public safety, and emergency preparedness.
- The **Food and Drug Administration** (FDA) and the **Substance Abuse and Mental Health Services Administration** (SAMHSA) are two agencies within the HHS. The FDA primarily enforces federal food and drug regulations, but it also conducts research and development. SAMHSA produces health materials related to mental illness and substance abuse, increases substance abuse and mental health awareness, and improves health care delivery.
- The **Centers for Medicare and Medicaid Services** (CMS) is another HHS agency that administers health insurance to low-income Americans and those over 65 and ensures regulatory compliance.
- The **US Public Health Service** (PHS) consists of nine HHS public health-related agencies that provide rapid response to public health crises and deliver health education.
- The **World Health Organization** (WHO) is an international agency within the United Nations that conducts health research, provides health guidance and standards, and organizes global public health emergency responses.

Private Nonprofit Agencies

Nonprofit agencies are often reliable sources of health-related information. They are more likely to use **scientifically valid and current research** to substantiate their health claims. They are also more likely to use **quality control measures** to ensure that the information they release is **trustworthy**. For example, an organization may exclusively use peer-reviewed journal articles or federal health information to support its claims. It might also use an editor or fact-checker to ensure the accuracy of its health information. However, since agencies are governed by a board of directors and trustees, **conflicts of interest can arise**. Similarly, although **private organizations** may use credible health research, their interpretation can be presented in a **biased** way. Furthering their mission or organizational interests may be the motive behind the information that they publish rather than presenting unbiased and factual information. Therefore, individuals should seek out information published by organizations that **openly state their mission** and **employ neutral references**. Nonprofit health information can be found on agency websites (usually those that end in ".org") or in books, pamphlets, articles, or social media.

Internet Resources

Health-related information from internet sources is generally the **least valid type of information**. While online, a person reviewing health information should use **caution** unless the resource is sponsored by government agencies, academic institutions, or credible nonprofit organizations (e.g., scientific associations, medical societies). Internet sources not affiliated with a credible agency or organization **may lack quality control measures** (e.g., fact-checking employees, editors) that ensure the reliability of the information. Many credible agencies use the internet to **improve the**

reach and accessibility of their published health information. However, health information may be presented **inaccurately or in a biased manner** by others as it is reshared through secondary websites or social media. Therefore, when reviewing health information posted on a website, it is vital that a person research the data source to ensure the validity of the site's claims. Government, academic, and nonprofit organization websites can be identified by their URL ending (e.g., **".gov," ".edu," or ".org."**). Websites with valid health-related information will have **clearly identifiable authors and contact information**. They may also include information on the last updated or published date and links to the information source.

Valid Health-Related Information and Products

When seeking valid health-related information and products, one should first **consider the sponsor** (e.g., government, nonprofit, academic institution, private company) of the information **and the author(s)**. The entity funding the health research or the creation of health materials may have secondary reasons for publishing the information. For example, a pharmaceutical company that releases a pamphlet on a disease may be interested in selling its product in addition to educating the public. Thus, one should examine the **purpose of the information** (e.g., inform, sell a product, shift opinion) since it can impact the trustworthiness of the resource. The goal or mission of the sponsor can suggest the purpose. The person consuming the health-related information should also consider the expertise and credibility of the author and the **publication date** because current material may be more accurate. **Transparent references and cited sources** listed throughout the resource often indicate that the information is valid. The **quality of the references** used to inform the health material (e.g., peer-reviewed research) can also indicate its validity.

Best Practices for Making Informed Health Decisions

When a person makes an informed health decision, he or she is aware of all possible choices and understands the outcomes of treatment. A person making an informed health decision should first obtain health information from multiple sources. Seeking information from **multiple sources** can help a person better understand his or her health condition and all available choices. Once he or she has acquired valid health information, the person should **synthesize all information gathered**. This entails evaluating the validity of the sources, determining the similarities and differences between the health information collected, and finding connections between the information to form insights. Although factual information is a crucial part of the decision-making process, individual values and health goals can influence a person's ultimate decision. For example, two individuals with the same cancer diagnosis who receive the same information from their doctors may have different health philosophies that impact their treatment. One may opt to pursue chemotherapy to prevent metastasis, while the other may reject it due to religious beliefs. Both are valid health decisions. Therefore, when making a final decision, one should **consider if it aligns with his or her values and health goals**. The person should then **consult his or her health provider** to confirm his or her understanding and discuss next steps.

Valid vs. Invalid Sources

Valid health information is factual, unbiased, and almost always based on research. Findings that form **valid health information** can be generated through **rigorous studies** performed by **experts**. Studies whose methodologies, analyses, and findings are **peer-reviewed** by experts in the field and whose authors perform **reliability and validity testing** can be considered **valid health information**. Examples of valid health information include government websites or medical journals. Although health information from secondary sources (e.g., newspaper articles) is an interpretation of data, materials that include neutral claims about health topics and use multiple primary sources to substantiate their claims are often more valid than those that do not. **Invalid health information** may be **inaccurate or biased**. Information regarding side effects or risks associated with a treatment option or medication may be omitted from invalid health information materials to influence perception. Invalid health information may also be used to purposely shift public opinion about controversial health topics. Common sources of invalid health information can include advertisements by pharmaceutical or medical product companies or personal testimonies.

Evaluating the Validity of Health Information

The first step in evaluating the validity of health information is **assessing the credibility and relevance of the source**. **Credibility** can be measured by the author's credentials, the use of peer-reviewed, scientifically sound source material, and date of publication. For example, a research article on COVID-19 written by a group of virologists that is published in a peer-reviewed journal is often far more credible than a blog post written by a member of the public. The next step is **assessing for partiality**. The purpose of the sponsoring agency or author in writing the health information can indicate partiality. For example, a federal agency whose mission is to inform the public about measles, mumps, and rubella (MMR) vaccines is a more valid source of health information about the benefits and risks of vaccination than an anti-vaccination association whose motivation is to prevent vaccination mandates. Health materials that use **sensational language** or **omit key pieces of information** from their sources may be **biased**. One should then **review other health materials to substantiate the information**. If the information is consistent with other credible sources, it is likely valid.

Identifying Fraudulent Health Information and Quackery

Fraudulent health information and quackery both refer to inaccurate and dishonest claims about medicine or medical practices. Such claims come from companies or individuals who allege medical expertise and intentionally deceive others to promote a service or product. Health frauds and quackery can **delay proper treatment**, which can exacerbate health problems. Products or services that **claim to be the sole cure** for a medical problem or **claim to cure many different health ailments** are often a form of **health fraud**. Other examples include products that use exotic ingredients, products that lack an endorsement by federal regulating agencies (e.g., Food and Drug Administration), and products or services with **unlikely or too-good-to-be-true health testimonials**. Celebrity and other **nonexpert endorsements** may also indicate health fraud and quackery. A person who suspects fraudulent health information or quackery should consult a credible health source or a medical professional.

Advertising and Marketing Methods Used to Influence Consumers

Health-related **marketing and advertising methods** use logos, pathos, and ethos appeals to influence consumers.

- **Logos** refers to an appeal to **reason or logic** and employs scientific facts or statistics. For example, a commercial for a weight-loss medication may advertise that the product is "clinically proven" to cause 60 percent more weight loss than other diet pills. Logical appeals are generally seen as the **most trustworthy** as they should be **based on verifiable facts**. Even without being based on true evidence, the **appeal to logic** may still be effective, which is one reason that customers should **consider truthfulness** when considering a product.
- **Pathos** is a technique that appeals to the consumers' **emotions or senses**. For example, a commercial for depression medication that depicts depression's impact on a person's life, relationships, and emotional well-being can elicit an emotional response. Advertisers may use a variety of film techniques (e.g., lighting, music, B-roll) to evoke a stronger emotion.

- **Ethos** refers to an appeal to **credibility**. Advertisements that appeal to ethos often include **credible experts to influence consumers**. For example, a commercial for an energy drink that features an endorsement from a doctor, and an athlete may imply that the drink is safe and effective.

Marketing Claims Used to Influence Behavior

Health-related claims about health care products and services can **elicit trust** if the claims are backed up by scientific research. The use of factual evidence and statistics in marketing advertisements reassures the consumer that the product or service is safe and proven to work. Claims about health care products and services can also **create an emotional response** that prompts a consumer to act. Consumers may form an attachment to the product or service or feel **compelled to adopt new health behaviors**. Emotional appeals may also **produce a fearful response** among consumers, which can lead to product or service avoidance. Health-related claims about health care services and products that use **bandwagon tactics** (i.e., a person performs a health behavior because others are doing it) use **social pressure** to influence behavior. Claims may imply that the product or service is used and well-liked by many, which can motivate a person to conform.

Health Care Systems and Services

Hospitals

The **primary role of hospitals** is to provide patients with medical care and support. Hospitals provide **emergency or trauma health care to patrons and host a range of specialized services** (e.g., radiology, oncology, psychiatry, gynecology). At a hospital, an individual may also receive such medical treatments and procedures as a surgery, an MRI or X-ray, radiation, or dialysis, among many others. Depending on the level of care needed, patients may stay overnight or for longer durations. In addition to providing patient care, **some hospitals provide training to medical residents and conduct health research.** Hospital staff often assist patients in identifying community resources to maintain good health after discharge. Hospitals are quickly becoming hubs for wraparound services and primary care. Individuals experiencing rising inaccessibility to health care (e.g., uninsured or underinsured, low proximity to primary care providers, reduced capacity of practitioners to provide timely care) are increasingly relying on hospitals and emergency medicine practitioners for primary care.

Clinics

Clinics are health care facilities that provide routine outpatient care. At clinics, **primary care providers conduct health checkups, provide immunizations, and treat mild to moderate illnesses.** Clinics rarely allow overnight stays, and appointments with medical practitioners can be booked ahead of time. Patients may also have the option of walk-in appointments; however, clinic hours are usually limited to the standard workday. Whereas hospitals generally provide disease treatment, at clinics, physicians may provide preventative health care services (e.g., blood pressure measurements, cancer screenings, vaccinations, or health counseling). **Clinics may also refer to specialized care locations at which medical practitioners perform outpatient care.** For example, a psychiatrist may conduct diagnostic tests, psychiatric treatment, and therapy at an outpatient psychiatry clinic. Some clinics—often referred to as free clinics—provide reduced or free services to the public. These clinics are managed by volunteer physicians, nurses, and administrative staff to serve community members experiencing financial hardship.

Health Care Professionals

Health care professionals are individuals who are licensed to perform medical services. Examples include primary care doctors, physician's assistants, dieticians, pharmacists, registered nurses, and specialty care physicians (e.g., pediatricians, obstetricians, dermatologists). The role of a health care professional varies by specialty, yet overall, these professionals are responsible for **disease prevention, diagnosis, and treatment**. Health care professionals engage in **disease prevention** through health education and health counseling. For example, a primary care doctor whose patient was recently diagnosed with high cholesterol may explain the risks associated with the condition and assess modifiable lifestyle factors. The physician may also assist with drafting a personalized plan of action to prevent the onset of diseases like heart disease and stroke. Other health care professionals, like dieticians and pharmacists, also provide disease treatment. For example, a dietician may provide medical nutrition therapy for a person with Crohn's disease to manage nutrient loss, while a pharmacist may supply immunosuppressants to control symptoms.

Benefits of Regular Medical Checkups

Medical checkups are annual comprehensive exams performed by a primary care provider. A medical checkup is a valuable preventative and diagnostic tool that can **delay the onset of disease, treat diseases early, and improve or prolong well-being**. It typically consists of a physical exam, a review of one's medical history, blood tests, and health counseling. Regular medical checkups can **reduce one's risk of developing an illness and can lead to the early detection of a disease**. Identifying a disease early can increase the success of treatment and reduce the risk of health complications. Patients with **existing health conditions** can be **monitored regularly** to track disease progression and adjust treatment strategies if needed. **Long-term benefits** of regular medical checkups include a longer lifespan, lower health care costs, and greater health knowledge.

Benefits of Regular Dental Checkups

Dental checkups are biannual exams conducted by a dentist and a dental hygienist. They typically consist of a **dental cleaning** (e.g., plaque and tartar removal, polishing) and an **oral exam**. Fluoride application and dental X-rays may also take place to prevent tooth decay, identify cavities or potential cavities, and monitor tooth migration. The dentist will also evaluate a patient's head and neck, soft tissue (e.g., tongue, cheeks), and gums to **identify possible oral health problems or diseases** like mouth cancer. Regular dental checkups can **prevent the onset or exacerbation of tooth decay or gum disease**. Both, if left untreated, can result in costly medical bills, infection, and tooth loss. The dentist can provide information on how to maintain proper dental hygiene and refer patients to other providers (e.g., orthodontists, prosthodontists, oral surgeons) for specialized care.

Advertising and Marketing in Healthcare

Advertising and Marketing Techniques Used

Testimonials and statistics are commonly used promotion techniques for health products and health services. **Health testimonials** utilize an endorsement by a celebrity or a trusted individual (e.g., health care professional, current user of the health product or service) to convince the consumer to purchase the product or service. **Statistics** are used to appeal to a person's logic. People often trust numbers and research—even if the statistics are inaccurate or unclear. Advertisements may also utilize a **personal appeal** that is intended to evoke an **emotional response** (e.g., joy, sadness, fear) that inspires the consumer to select or purchase the health product or service. For example, many hospitals and health care-related organizations released advertisements that urged the public to get vaccinated during the COVID-19 pandemic. They used strong emotional imagery, such as footage of vaccinated individuals reuniting with their family members after a substantial social distancing period or speeches from nurses and doctors describing their experiences, to **evoke empathy**. Most advertisements will use a combination of multiple techniques to enhance the consumer response and increase the likelihood that the public will purchase a product or service.

Determining If Advertising Claims Are Accurate

A consumer can **determine the accuracy** of an advertised service or product by **evaluating the legitimacy of its claims**. A review of a product's claims can be conducted through conversations with trusted peers or through independent research (e.g., examining consumer reviews, exploring available research about the product's or service's efficacy, reviewing similar products). For instance, a person seeking a personal trainer to lose weight might consult some fitness-related groups, or he or she may consult a health provider, friends, or family to determine the best service for his or her health goals or to identify possible trainers. **Feedback from trusted sources** can help someone determine if a trainer's advertised services are accurate and trustworthy. **Consumer reviews** often provide a spectrum of responses about various aspects of a health product, service, or provider. Consumers can assess desirable or undesirable attributes of a health care product by reviewing similar health products, and doing so may **reveal inconsistent advertising claims** if a product promises results not achievable by similar products. Reviewing research about different health care goods can help **identify trustworthy products** and **reveal the legitimacy of claims**.

Determining If Advertising Claims Are Misleading or Deceptive

Consumers should **avoid products or services that claim to be a cure-all or quick fix**. Very few products can be used to cure a wide range of diseases or treat illnesses in a short period of time. Products or services that list a suspiciously long list of ailments they treat or promise unreasonable desirable outcomes (e.g., "lose 15 pounds in two weeks," "eliminate type 2 diabetes") are likely **misleading or deceptive**. Testimonials can also be used to make misleading or deceptive claims about a health product or service since they are difficult to dispute. **Endorsements from credible health care professionals** are often more trustworthy than a testimonial from a single product user. A person should **pay attention to websites or advertisements with sensational titles and quotes that have been shortened** (e.g., "this product helped me lose weight ...") as these may be used to garner attention and misrepresent the truth. **Reviewing the statistics cited and/or any graphs or diagrams** depicted in the health product advertisement can help a person determine whether a claim is accurate or misleading.

Evaluating Health-Related Products

Evaluating and Selecting Health-Related Products, Treatments, and Services

Criteria

When evaluating and selecting health-related products, treatments, and services, one should consider the following criteria: cost, insurance coverage, quality, and legitimacy.

- **Cost and insurance coverage** can often be prohibitive factors when selecting a health product, treatment, or service. **A review of one's budget and the funds necessary** to sustain the intended health outcomes can help one determine if the product or service is a good choice. **A review of one's health insurance coverage** is also necessary to determine affordability, as some products, treatments, or services may not be covered.

- The **quality of a product** can reveal its **effectiveness** for treating a health condition or attaining a health goal. An **evaluation of the product's formula** can imply adequate quality. Oftentimes, **approval from a federal regulatory agency** like the Food and Drug Administration (FDA) is a good indicator of a product's reliability.
- The **legitimacy of a product** can be determined by **identifying the credentials and authority** of the seller and product. A **credible seller** is licensed by a legitimate certifying entity, such as the National Association of Boards of Pharmacy (NABP). Reviews or ratings from other consumer protection organizations, like the Better Business Bureau (BBB), can reveal the legitimacy of health-related businesses.

Skills

The following skills are important to use when **evaluating and selecting health-related products, treatments, and services**: health literacy, financial literacy, and negotiation skills.

- The Centers for Disease Control and Prevention describes **health literacy** as one's ability to locate, comprehend, and utilize health information and services. Health literacy is helpful for those evaluating and selecting health-related products, treatments, and services because those with high health literacy are **better at locating credible information and discerning between accurate and misleading claims**. They are also often **better at making informed health decisions** and **advocating for their health needs and goals**.
- Since cost is a significant factor when selecting a health product or service, high **financial literacy** can help an **individual budget** for his or her health care and **identify cost-effective solutions** to health care problems.
- **Negotiation skills** are important for **confidently communicating** one's health goals, one's service or product preferences, and one's health needs. Health literacy and a strong understanding of one's personal health status and needs can be beneficial when practicing negotiation skills in health care.

Criteria for Evaluating and Selecting Health Providers

Criteria for successfully evaluating and selecting health care providers includes staff medical knowledge, insurance coverage, cultural competence, and treatment management recommendations. These criteria can be used to **identify whether the physician is the right fit**; however, one should consider other important attributes prior to visiting. The extent of a **provider's medical knowledge** can be ascertained through a **review of his or her credentials** (e.g., licensing, certifications) and through **reviews by current or former patients**. There are many provider review websites that use overall patient satisfaction to rank or score health care professionals. These websites also often include information on licensing and certification, insurance coverage, and languages spoken. **Insurance coverage** can significantly lower the cost of health services. To determine whether a provider is in-network, one should consult his or her insurer directly. A provider's **cultural competence** can influence the type of care provided and impact the patient's overall experience. A physician who practices culturally competent care treats more than physical health; he or she meets the social, cultural, and linguistic needs of his or her patients.

Interpretation of Signs and Symbols

Sign/Symbol	Interpretation
	Flame: Includes flammable materials and gases and those that are self-heating or self-reactive.
	Corrosion: Includes substances that can cause skin burns, metal corrosion, and eye damage.
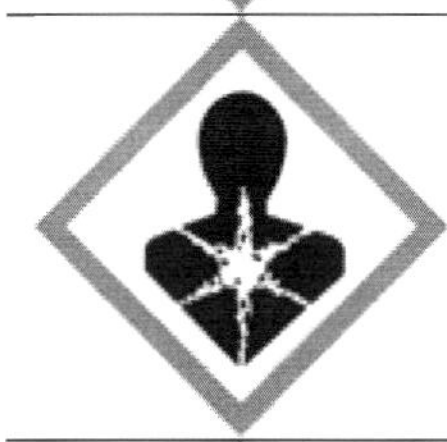	Health hazard: Includes carcinogens, toxic substances, and respiratory irritants.
	Poison: Includes materials, gases, or substances that are extremely toxic and may result in death or severe illness.
	Irritant: Includes material, gases, or substances that are irritants to skin, eyes, and/or respiratory tract, acutely toxic, or have a narcotic effect.
	Biohazard: Includes biological substances, such as body fluids, that pose a threat to humans. Appears on sharps containers that hold contaminated needles.

Consumer Health Protections and Laws

Local Laws, Regulations, and Agencies Related to Consumer Health

Local laws and regulations related to consumer health are often created and enforced by county, tribal, or district-level officials and divisions. Individuals on **local boards of health** are responsible for **establishing and enforcing public health policy** to ensure the protection of human health within their jurisdiction. They may also **make recommendations** for health policy and initiatives to other governing bodies (e.g., the city council). Similarly, local **boards of commissioners** help enforce regulations and ordinances; they are granted the authority by state legislators to impose fines or other penalties for noncompliance. Some counties have a local **office of consumer protection** to protect consumers from scams and deceptive business practices. Each county has a **division of public health** that develops policy and enforces local laws and regulations to protect public safety and wellness. Other local divisions (e.g., water quality division) also provide education, enforce local laws, and monitor the compliance of businesses and consumers. Local policy and agencies related to consumer health can be found on local government websites.

State Laws, Regulations, and Agencies Related to Consumer Health

An **attorney general** is a government official who supervises consumer protection initiatives in the areas he or she represents. His or her **responsibility** is to conduct investigations, manage licensure and certifications of service providers, prosecute those who violate consumer protection laws, and advocate for constituents. Consumers can **file a complaint** against a business if they suspect a health fraud or scam. Most states have a **department of consumer affairs** dedicated to investigating consumer protection violations, educating consumers, licensing professionals, and providing support. The **Deceptive Trade Practices Act** is a law observed by states like Texas, Illinois, Minnesota, and Nebraska that prohibits business fraud and misleading advertising. State and local **departments of justice** and **departments of agriculture and consumer services** are responsible for protecting against fraud and ensuring product safety.

Federal Laws, Regulations, and Agencies Related to Consumer Health

The **Federal Trade Commission (FTC)** is a government agency that is responsible for consumer protection. The FTC's **Bureau of Consumer Protection** is designed to enforce federal consumer protection laws and deliver consumer education. The **Pure Food and Drug Act of 1906** was the first of many consumer protection laws in the United States. Along with creating the FDA, the law banned mislabeled foods, required food and drug labeling (e.g., ingredients on packaging), and established food and drug testing. The **FDA** is a federal agency that oversees the safety of food, pharmaceutical goods, and medical devices. The Consumer Product Safety Act of 1972 established the **Consumer Product Safety Commission (CPSC)**. The CPSC assesses complaints regarding consumer protection, coordinates product recalls, and creates safety standards to minimize consumer harm. However, **other federal agencies** like the US Bureau of Alcohol, Tobacco, Firearms, and Explosives; the US Department of Agriculture; and the US Environmental Protection Agency are responsible for enforcing protective laws, monitoring compliance, and providing education for various health-related products.

How Laws, Regulations, and Agencies Protect Consumers

Health-related consumer protection laws and regulations are often **created in response to violations** against the public's safety and security. They are intended to protect consumers against **predatory business practices, deceptive marketing schemes, and poor production or health practices**. For example, in response to the rampant use of toxic substances in food, the addition of addictive drugs to medical products, and quack medicine during the late 19th century, the United States passed the **Pure Food and Drug Act of 1906**. **Consumer protection agencies** are created to regulate business practices, investigate potential violations of consumer protection laws, award and monitor licensure of health care providers, and educate the public about consumer protection. Many federal agencies that were not exclusively created for consumer protection now contribute to it through monitoring, enforcement, and education and engage in consumer protection advocacy.

Community Health

Common Community Health Problems

The extent of poverty and access to health care services can lead to community health problems like poor nutrition, violence, and unplanned pregnancy. **Community poverty** is associated with distribution of wealth and resources, access to economic opportunity and livable wages, and quality of educational opportunities. Limited financial security can lead to hunger and food insecurity among families, which is associated with **poor nutrition** and **poor health outcomes**. Limited job opportunities and poor academic attainment associated with community poverty can increase the risk of participation in and exposure to **crime and violence** and **unplanned pregnancy**. Limited proximity to health care facilities and providers can influence a community's **access to health care**. Inadequate access to care may result in **poor health education** and promotion, poor health literacy, and insufficient delivery of care. Thus, community members may be **more susceptible to health problems** like poor nutrition and unplanned pregnancy.

Addressing Common Community Health Problems

Upstream solutions (e.g., policy changes, access to affordable housing, and adequate education) that **improve the social determinants of health** are the most effective way to address poor health outcomes; however, they are also often **most expensive and time-consuming strategy**. Community programs like violence prevention awareness campaigns and drug abuse prevention and treatment programs can address community health problems. **Violence prevention awareness campaigns** can provide information to the broader community on the signs and symptoms of violence or abuse and identify resources to escape violence. Similarly, **drug abuse prevention programs** may provide education on the different types of drugs, their effects, and the consequences of drug misuse/abuse. They may also provide helpful information on confronting a friend or family member who is misusing drugs. Both awareness campaigns and prevention programs **empower and motivate individuals** to avoid behaviors that lead to common health problems. Community **drug abuse treatment programs** provide affordable and accessible health care to reduce risk of drug related illness, injury, or death.

Influences on Individual and Community Health

Media Messages

Media messages can **negatively and positively influence** health behaviors and health outcomes. The validity of information delivered through media—television, social media, radio, newspapers, etc.—is not always **verified**. The spread of false or inaccurate information and the messages' deliverer can change or reinforce individuals' health beliefs and practices. For example, false reports and health claims by influential individuals about the origin of the COVID-19 virus, its mode of transmission, and its vaccine efficacy influenced many Americans to discriminate against Asian Americans, renounce masks, and refuse vaccination. As a result, the US experienced a surge in violent crimes against Asian Americans, COVID-19 infections and deaths, and hospitalization rates. However, media messages can also be **powerful tools to improve health outcomes**. Media can be used to **spread valid and verified information quickly and communicate tailored messages effectively to different groups of people**. The anti-smoking truth campaign utilized many different forms of media to elicit a response and shift public opinion of tobacco. It influenced individuals, specifically youth, to reject tobacco and mobilized communities to enact programs and policies aimed at curbing tobacco use.

Technological Advances

Technological advances have significantly **improved health care** precision, delivery, access, and use. Technological advances have improved physicians' ability to accurately diagnose illness or injury (e.g., MRI, genetic testing) and perform minimally invasive and low-risk procedures (e.g., robotic-assisted surgery, endoscopy cameras). **Health care delivery and accessibility** is also improved through technological advances. For example, telehealth and telemedicine provide opportunities for patients to receive care remotely. Various applications and platforms allow patients to **track symptoms or bodily function** (e.g., diabetes testing, symptom tracking) and **order prescription medication** directly to their homes. Technological advances have also improved the ability of epidemiologists to **monitor and track infectious disease**, as well as **measure the occurrence of chronic disease**. As a result, they can mitigate disease transmission and improve short and long-term health outcomes.

Effects of Mandatory Vaccinations

Vaccinations are one of the **most effective** means of preventing disease spread. **Mandatory vaccinations** are not literally compulsory, but are vaccinations that are required as a condition of participating in certain jobs or attending school, with some exceptions. For example, the Polio vaccine and the MMR (Measles, Mumps, and Rubella) vaccine are required for children attending public schools. Those who refuse to comply or present proof of vaccination may be **barred from attendance**. However, **religious and medical exemptions** may preclude certain students from receiving a vaccine. Employer-mandated vaccinations and vaccine mandates for travel are largely dependent on **regional and state policy**. The immunity that one gains from vaccination can **reduce risk of injury or illness** due to infectious diseases and disease-related deaths. **Mandatory vaccinations** increase vaccination rates among individuals, which can **reduce the risk of disease transmission**. Mandatory vaccinations, like the smallpox and polio vaccinations, are attributed with **disease eradication**. The improvements in health outcomes and reductions in disease spread are associated with **lower community mortality rates** and **reduced burden on community health care providers**.

Effects of Workplace Safety Regulations on Community Health

Workplace safety regulations are implemented to protect the health and wellbeing of employees. They are intended to **minimize risk of harm or death** from accidents, work-related injuries, or exposure to hazardous materials. Minimizing injuries reduces individual and employer's expenses related to health care costs and productivity losses. The **Occupational Safety and Health Administration (OSHA)** is a federal agency that regulates safe working conditions through statute and regulation enforcement, inspections, compliance assistance, and training. They **impose workforce safety regulations** that require personal **protective equipment** (PPE) and **hazard prevention** (e.g., exposure limits, infectious disease protections, fall and accident prevention measures). Compliance with OSHA standards can also **protect the general public** from health hazards or accident risks. For example, regulations related to the prevention of infectious diseases (e.g., Hepatitis vaccine), monitoring of accidents (e.g., reporting injuries), and communicating hazards (e.g., using wet floor signs) help minimize exposure to illness or injury in public spaces.

Environmental Health

Impact of Pollution

The health impact of pollution differs by the type of pollution.

- **Air pollution** is a compilation of hazardous gases and particles from sources like wildfires, particulate matter, vehicle emissions, and manufacturing byproducts. They can cause respiratory infections, cardiovascular disease, and cancer. **Smog**—a type of air pollution—can obstruct sunlight and impair visibility.
- **Water pollution** describes chemical or bacterial substances that contaminate water, including wastewater contamination (e.g., sewage, chemical solvents, grease runoff), agricultural fertilizers or pesticides, plastic, and oil. Health impacts include complications from **waterborne diseases** (e.g., diarrhea, vomiting), gastrointestinal diseases, skin irritation, or cancer. Water pollution, specifically **nitrate pollution**, can cause **hypoxic conditions** that create **uninhabitable marine ecosystems**, which can be detrimental to fishing industries and ecosystem health. Oil spills and plastic pollution can also cause harm to marine ecosystems.
- **Noise pollution** refers to disruptive sounds—typically over 85 decibels—that produce harmful effects on human and animal health. Examples include vehicle and air traffic, construction and event sounds, and industrial or manufacturing noises. Noise pollution can cause stress and anxiety, sleep disruption, hearing loss, and memory and attention challenges. In animals, it can impact mating and migratory patterns, predator avoidance, echolocation, and behavior.

Impact of Overcrowding

Overcrowding describes the presence of excessive people in a space that impacts comfortability and health. Overcrowding is associated with **emotional distress, anxiety, and depression**. It can also increase an individual and a community's risk of infectious disease. A higher volume of residents in an area with limited space makes it **easier for diseases to spread** and puts many at **increased risk of disease-related mortality**. Overcrowding can **place stress on existing resources** (e.g., land, water, food) and **infrastructure** (e.g., sanitation and sewage, roads and transportation pathways). This may **increase resource scarcity and risk of accidents or injury**. Overcrowding can place strain on **interpersonal relationships** that may contribute to poor interactions with others. Overcrowded schools can **impact the quality of academic institutions and their capacity to deliver educational services**, which can have lasting impacts on one's academic and professional success. Communities experiencing overcrowding may lack sufficient economic opportunities for all residents and may suffer from an overloaded health care system.

Impact of Hazardous Waste

Improperly managed or stored **hazardous waste** can impact human and environmental health. Hazardous waste may be **toxic** (e.g., carcinogens, mutagenic substances), **reactive** (e.g., corrosive or ignitable waste like batteries), **infectious** (e.g., needles or bandages), or **radioactive** (e.g., nuclear waste). Hazardous waste can cause cancer, organ failure, developmental defects or genetic mutations, and behavioral changes. Hazardous waste can lead to **reproductive complications** in humans and animals and can cause widescale **mortality** in contaminated environments. For example, exposure to toxic waste can cause massive death of marine life and organisms in a lake. Corrosive and ignitable hazardous waste can also lead to **explosions** and **fires** that endanger human and animal life. **Bioaccumulation**—the gradual buildup of chemicals and hazardous waste within a biological organism—can cause serious health complications throughout the food chain. For example, **mercury contamination** from industrial emissions and runoff can accumulate within the tissues of coastal fish. As pregnant mothers consume the mercury-laden tissues, the fetus receives secondhand exposure to mercury, which can lead to possible developmental and infant cognitive impairments. Oftentimes, hazardous waste impacts whole communities or specific demographic groups to produce inequitable health outcomes.

Reducing Environmental Hazards

Water purification describes the process of removing hazardous substances and contaminants from water. Purifying water improves its quality, reduces risk of waterborne disease transmission, and limits exposure to chemical compounds that cause irritation or cancer. **Emissions controls** regulate the acceptable amount and types of pollutants emitted by combustion engines and industrial processes. For example, federal and state automobile emissions regulations may enforce design requirements among vehicle producers, and testing requirements among automobile operators. They are intended to prevent the excessive release of harmful pollutants into the environment and reduce the health impacts of acute or chronic exposure to noxious emissions. Responsible **waste management** can prevent adverse impacts of exposure to toxic substances, medical waste or infectious diseases, and water or air pollution. An example of a waste management practice is recycling or composting to reduce the release of plastic waste and carbon dioxide or methane into the environment. Waste management can also include the responsible disposal of medical waste through sterilization, incineration, and transportation to non-municipal landfills.

Protecting the Environment

Engaging in **policies and practices** that protect the environment can reduce exposure to harm and improve an individual's health outcomes. Healthy ecosystems and physical environments can **ensure access to resources** that fulfill human needs (e.g., clean water, arable farmland, renewable energy, sufficient natural materials for manufacturing). Protecting the environment is also important for **maintaining community health** and **promoting health equity**. Too often, destructive environmental practices take place in under-resourced and marginalized communities. By implementing policies and practices that protect ecosystem health, **governing bodies can ensure equitable access** to environmental goods and services and the health and wellness benefits of living in a healthy environment. Protecting the environment also **safeguards the wellbeing** of plants and animals and preserves the environment for future generations.

Contributing to Improving Community and Environmental Health

Environmental advocacy refers to the practice and promotion of environmentally sustainable practices and environmental stewardship, and the mobilization of people to influence policy and behavior. Examples of environmental advocacy include reducing waste (e.g., recycling, composting, using renewable resources, purchasing used or repurposed items, using biodegradable materials), reducing emissions and industrial pollution (e.g., using alternative modes of transportation like bikes or trains, eating a plant-based diet), and reducing impact (e.g., conserving water and electricity). Advocacy can also include **petitioning** and **protesting** to effect larger systemic change. Altogether, environmental advocacy encourages the use and adoption of sustainable practices to improve the health and wellbeing of all beings within the ecosystem. **Environmental volunteerism** refers to community service that benefits the environment (e.g., community tree plantings, community river cleanups, starting a community gardens). Volunteering improves the natural environment and can improve an individual's sense of place and belonging. It also provides free labor for overburdened community and non-profit organizations which may improve their capacity to further serve their community.

Coordinated School Health Model

A **coordinated school health model** is a systematic approach intended to maximize the health and well-being of the school community through the delivery of health education, programs, and services. All aspects of health (e.g., physical, social, emotional, intellectual) are addressed through coordinated school health programs. Coordinated school health models can **improve academic**

achievement, interpersonal relationships, and student success. A school that utilizes a coordinated school health model simultaneously addresses multiple health areas like a comprehensive health education curriculum, preventative health care, nutrition services, staff health promotion, and psychosocial health opportunities. **Adaptations to the school environment** are also made to optimize physical, social, and emotional health (e.g., installing play areas or green spaces). **Successful coordinated school health programs** include teachers, administration, school counselors and social workers, nutrition staff, community partners, parents and guardians, and students. The inclusion of each stakeholder throughout the planning, implementation, and maintenance of changes is **crucial for buy-in and sustainability**.

Role of the Teacher

All teachers play a role in the planning, implementation, and maintenance of coordinated school health education programs. They are responsible for **creating and delivering lessons** that improve student knowledge and **evaluating content mastery**. Schools that are interested in incorporating health promotion in the traditional classroom setting may benefit from the expertise of health and physical education teachers. Teachers are also important for **assessing students' comprehension of health topics** and **collecting student input**, which can be informative for planning effective schoolwide health interventions. The relationships that teachers form with their students' families and guardians can be useful because those relationships can give teachers **valuable parental insights into a student's health**. Parent-teacher relationships may also be helpful for identifying parents interested in helping plan and support a coordinated school health education program.

Components

The Whole School, Whole Community, Whole Child Model (WSCC) is a popular coordinated school health model that consists of 10 components:

- **Health services** like primary care delivery, referrals, and immunizations are performed at schools to promote student health.
- Through **health education** and **physical education**, students learn how to evaluate and improve their health, prevent illnesses, and set health goals.
- The **physical environment** (e.g., school, land, surrounding community) is safe. For example, hazardous substances are secured, smoke alarms and fire extinguishers are operational, and the campus is visually welcoming.
- The **psychosocial climate** is designed to optimize academic performance and improve social relationships and student engagement. For example, learning and behavior expectations are clear, cultural differences are celebrated, and school activities are inclusive and reflective of the student body.
- **Nutrition services** ensure students receive nutritious foods while at school to maximize student success.
- **Counseling and social services** enhance student psychosocial health, connect students to mental health services, and deliver mental health care.
- **Employee wellness** programs promote healthy practices to improve staff well-being and job satisfaction.
- **Community involvement** and **family engagement** create buy-in, pool community resources, inform needed health programs, and reinforce healthy behaviors beyond the classroom.

Example

CATCH (Coordinated Approach to Child Health) is a widely used coordinated school health program. The program's goal is to **improve the nutrition and exercise habits of students, staff, families, and the community**. This goal is accomplished through **engaging representatives** from all stakeholder groups: health and physical activity educators, health and nutrition services, counseling and social services, staff wellness and healthy school environment initiatives, and families and community members. **Teachers incorporate healthy living** into the lessons that they deliver to students. More **opportunities for moderate to vigorous physical activity** are incorporated into gym classes and traditional classrooms (e.g., games, activity breaks). **Consistent health messaging** is displayed through signage around school campuses, and health campaigns (e.g., "get ur 60" and "get ur H20") encourage the adoption of healthy behavior. Schools host CATCH family events to **engage parents and broaden the reach of health education to families and community members**. Each school implements environmental changes: school gyms are open to students before and after school, and sugar-sweetened beverages are replaced with water.

Relationship Between Health Education and Other Components

A comprehensive health education program can improve the success of other components of a coordinated school health program. Students with strong health literacy and knowledge may be better able to **identify** their personal health problems, **communicate** their health concerns to adults, and **advocate** for necessary school health services. Health education may also make students more **amenable** to participating in school health initiatives or programs. A strong student comprehension of physical, social, and emotional health may **impact health attitudes, beliefs, and knowledge among family members and the broader community**. Students who receive adequate health education are more likely to **select** healthier foods from nutrition services and **engage** in physical activity during their allotted exercise periods. They also may be more likely to practice health behaviors that promote emotional health, which can amplify the benefits of counseling and social services.

Planning and Implementing Coordinated School Health Model

Prior to implementing a school health education program, planners should first **define the population** and **establish health goals**. Next, they must **assess the needs, assets, and capacity** the school has for a health education program. Needs and assets can be identified through a thorough review of school demographics, community and school health data, existing curricula, health knowledge and literacy data, and key informant interviews. Findings should be used to **select health education priorities, create program objectives**, and **determine effective interventions**. Program objectives must be **specific and measurable**. This can be accomplished by clearly stating who is participating in implementation and evaluation and how much or what kind of change is expected. Objectives should also include the **anticipated outputs or outcomes** and how each component of the intervention **contributes to the program's overall goals**. Those planning interventions should consider the school's **capacity for change** (i.e., the number of resources available to implement a program and how realistic the objective is). A school health education program will take time to properly plan, implement, and evaluate. While evaluation findings are not always positive, they create an opportunity to identify barriers to program success and future adaptations to implement.

Important Stakeholders

A **diverse team** that represents all aspects of school health should be included throughout the planning and implementation process of a health education program. A **health assessment** performed prior to the program's implementation can identify key stakeholders. Important actors in a school health education program include faculty, administrators, health care professionals, parents or caregivers, and students.

- **School faculty** provide insight on students' needs and abilities, and they deliver health education to students.
- **School administrators** are important figures in program decision-making and can aid in improving the capacity of a school to effectively implement and sustain a health education program.
- As the recipients of health education programming, **students** can provide valuable information regarding the success of health education initiatives.
- **Parents and caregivers** can provide input about health education programs and help continue education outside of the classroom.
- **Health professionals** may assist in the planning and delivery of health education to ensure that accurate and appropriate material is presented to students.

The inclusion of stakeholders throughout the planning and implementation process can ensure the sustainability of health education programs.

Best Practices for Maintaining a School Health Education Program

A successful school health education program is typically **evidence-based and responsive** to the identified health priorities of the intended population. If program planners **include key stakeholders** (e.g., faculty, administration, caregivers, students, health professionals) throughout the entire process, outcomes are more likely to be attained because a **shared vision** is more likely to be established. Stakeholder inclusion keeps intended recipients of a health education program engaged, accountable, and informed. **Partnerships with local coalitions and community health leaders** can sustain efforts outside of school and secure necessary resources (e.g., funding, space, volunteers) to ensure program success. **Partnerships** can also strengthen the capacity of the school to implement and support the health education program. **Program monitoring and evaluation** help identify problems early, ensure acceptable delivery of the intervention and use of resources, assess program outputs and outcomes, and stay organized.

Considerations for Implementing Health Education Curricula

An **in-depth review of district-level stances on health concepts** (e.g., comprehensive sex education) **and health philosophies** should occur prior to implementation. The use of procedures that are **compatible with school policy** can ensure that the concepts taught and information delivered are permissible. Policy is often implemented to protect students and faculty and to establish acceptable practices for delivering culturally and developmentally appropriate material. Policy can also guarantee that a school's established health priorities are reflected in the curricula. School health policy should be regularly reviewed to ensure that it accomplishes its intended health goals. It is also important to **review state-level education standards related to health**. They can help set clear and measurable learning goals, plan accessible and engaging lessons, measure achievement, and support instruction.

School Health Advisory Councils

School Health Advisory Council (SHAC)

A **school health advisory council (SHAC)** is composed of individuals that advocate for the health and education priorities of a community. The individuals are often **appointed by school district leaders** to advise on school health-related programs and interventions. **Common representatives** may include health and physical health educators, nutrition services staff, social workers, school psychologists or counselors, and administrators. However, an SHAC can include others who are beneficial for understanding and improving student health. The members have a **direct influence** on the health and well-being of students and can **contribute insights** from their daily interactions with students. They can provide an **accurate depiction of student needs** and the resources available within and outside of school to meet health needs. Individuals on SHACs are also important communication links and advocates for the groups that they represent. They can help **solve conflicts** and **clear up misconceptions** that may arise from a newly implemented health initiative.

Mandates Regarding SHACs

Mandates regarding SHACs are often enacted by local or state boards of education. These mandates ensure that **local values and interests are reflected in all health education programs and curricula.** The statutes often mandate that school districts consult the SHAC prior to altering or adopting a new health education curriculum. Every state education code varies, and here are some of the areas that different education statutes might say that SHACs are responsible for providing recommendations on:

- The number of hours of instruction
- Health education graduation requirements
- Appropriate policies, procedures, and initiatives related to preventative health
- Appropriate methods of health instruction related to sexual health, opioid abuse, and violence
- Strategies for integrating school health services, counseling, a safe and healthy school environment, and employee wellness
- Opportunities for collaboration with community organizations and parental engagement and awareness

There are often provisions about **who must be included in an SHAC**. For the most part, SHAC members must represent classroom teachers, school counselors, school administrators, students, health care professionals, the business community, law enforcement, senior citizens, faith-based organizations, nonprofit health organizations, and local domestic violence programs.

Local Health Advisory Councils

A local SHAC's primary role is to **advise the school district on health-related programs and initiatives**. For example, a school district seeking to lower school dropout rates may assemble an SHAC composed of teachers, social workers, academic counselors, administrators, and local education coalitions or organizations to illustrate the problem and offer solutions. SHACs help **collect data on health needs of students and the school community**. Findings from student assessments, informal discussions with students or caregivers, or independent research on student health and development can contribute to a more complete understanding of student health. Individuals on SHACs are often experts in their respective fields, which can add to the group's **comprehension of barriers or motivators** to implementing health education programs (e.g., policy, research, experience). Members of SHACs also have an **in-depth understanding** of the available school or community resources needed or available to address the health problem. Their insight can ensure program fidelity and sustainability.

Strategies for Involving Parents and Guardians

Parent or caregiver involvement when planning and implementing a school health education program can contribute to its success. When **school staff coordinate with parents**, health promotion and messaging can be delivered in a clear and consistent manner outside of school.

Research by the CDC indicates that parents are motivated to engage in their child's education if they believe that their involvement will enhance their child's well-being. Therefore, school health education planners should **clearly state how parents' involvement in health initiatives will benefit student health and education outcomes**. School staff should collaborate with parents to **create a shared school health vision** and **create opportunities for parental feedback** regarding student health (e.g., survey, public forums, interviews). Health education programs and initiatives should incorporate opportunities for parental engagement. For example, parents can provide support through volunteering and leading events or delivering at-home learning. To sustain parental involvement, **a variety of engagement opportunities should be offered to parents** and any **health education events must be hosted at an accessible location and time.**

Strategies for Incorporating Local Culture

The compatibility of a health education program with local culture can determine its success. Local culture refers to a **geographic area or group with a shared identity** (e.g., race, ethnicity, religion). It encompasses **language, beliefs, attitudes, values, customs, and ways of communicating**. Therefore, it is important to **incorporate multiple dimensions of culture** when identifying school health needs and planning interventions. A school health education program that is designed in **coordination with local cultural norms** can improve the community's receptivity and ease regarding the adoption of positive health behaviors. A **situational analysis**—an evaluation of the learner, teacher, school environment, and societal values—can be conducted to understand the local culture regarding health. Findings can **provide context** for local health beliefs and **inform effective strategies** for teaching concepts in a culturally appropriate manner. The inclusion of local community leaders in developing health education programs can illuminate unique health beliefs and strategies for implementation.

Strategies for Addressing Local Needs and Interests

Since SHACs comprise representatives from the school and local community, they can provide useful information about local needs and interests. A **community health needs assessment** provides comprehensive information about a community's health needs, challenges, and health status. **Health needs assessments** utilize quantitative data (e.g., health statistics, demographic data) and qualitative data (e.g., key informant interviews, focus groups, formal surveys, observation) to identify local needs, assets, and interests. Knowledge gained from a health needs assessment can help school health education program planners develop a **community health improvement plan** (CHIP) to create programming that **addresses local needs and interests**. Insights from local health departments can reveal information about the health status of the community, barriers to health care access, and available community resources to address health needs. Health departments' annual community health needs assessments provide a snapshot of community health and what the health department's **key health priorities** should be.

Role of the Health Educator

Communicating the Importance of Health Education

Tailored communication should be used to communicate the importance of health education to students, parents or guardians, and the community. Health education program planners must appeal to each group's drive for involvement, so it is important to **understand each group's motivation for engaging in health education**. For example, a student may be inspired to learn more about how to improve his or her health and prevent the onset of disease. A parent could be motivated to enhance his or her child's learning outcomes and overall well-being. Community members may be interested in improving health outcomes to improve life expectancy, reduce health care expenses, and improve the economic conditions of the community. **Appealing to the local needs and interests** of the school community and broader community can more effectively communicate the importance of health education. **Appropriate delivery of the message** (e.g., messaging medium, communication styles) can help relay the importance of health education. Information should be **presented in a developmentally and culturally appropriate manner** to ensure **maximum comprehension**. Using **multiple communication channels** can ensure a greater number of community members are reached.

Advocating for Health-Related Issues

Health advocates support and promote the health of communities by increasing awareness about **health needs or disparities, helping shape public policy, and creating resources** (e.g., financial, infrastructure, volunteers) to improve access to health care. Individuals involved with SHACs advocate for the health and well-being of the subsections that they represent. There is **no restriction** on who can be a health advocate; any private citizen, public servant, or agency committed to improving the health of the community can advocate for others. Advocates play an important role in expressing the local needs, interests, and health concerns of the community. This can be accomplished through **lobbying for health policy changes, communicating with local legislators or decision-makers** (e.g., school administration, school district staff, state education officials), **launching a health campaign**, or **helping community members overcome barriers to health care**. Advocates may also negotiate with health education organizers to establish programs and curricula that reflect the community's culture, values, and desires.

Role of a Health Education Teacher

Health education teachers are key to **assessing the health needs** of students and staff and **identifying barriers** to health education within and outside of the school. They **help develop curricula and programs** aimed at improving health literacy and health outcomes through education. Health education teachers may also work to **improve the health attitudes, beliefs, and behaviors** of students, staff, parents, and community members. Their roles and responsibilities are accomplished through **collaborating with other stakeholders** to implement health education and healthy living promotion programs and monitor the effectiveness of existing programs. Health education teachers also often coordinate health campaigns to reach and improve the health of their target audience. For instance, a health education teacher may work with health services staff, teachers, and administration to develop a schoolwide physical activity challenge for students and staff. They may **monitor the effectiveness of the program** and **alter components** of it to maximize benefits. Health education teachers deliver health education instruction and communicate health information in an accessible and culturally relevant manner. They are often advocates for health within the school and community.

Review Video: Collaborating with Other Professionals
Visit mometrix.com/academy and enter code: 100351

School Health Education Program

Evaluating a School Health Education Program

Evaluating a school health education program can reveal strengths, weaknesses, threats to program sustainability, and opportunities for growth. A **program evaluation** is a commonly used tool for evaluating a program's impacts, outcomes, fidelity, and value. It is also often used to assess participants' experience, ease of implementation, and impact on health outcomes. Program evaluations **consist of data collection and analysis of program activities and**

recommendations for program improvement. Although the procedures for each program evaluation differ, each typically includes the following steps outlined by the CDC:

1. Engage stakeholders who are invested in the program (e.g., students, staff, parents).
2. Describe the program's purpose, activities, and intended outcomes.
3. Design the evaluation plan (e.g., create an evaluation timeline, finalize the methodology).
4. Gather credible evidence from multiple sources (e.g., pre- and post-program assessments, interviews, literature review).
5. Justify conclusions and generate recommendations.
6. Share findings and lessons learned with stakeholders.

Popular program evaluation tools that can be used to evaluate a school health education program include the **Kirkpatrick model**, the **CIPP evaluation model**, the **SEP model**, **curriculum mapping**, and **needs assessments**.

Data Collection Procedures

When developing data collection procedures to determine health education needs, the health educator must consider the purpose of the data collection, the audience for which the data is intended, the types of questions to be answered, the scope of the research, and the resources available to carry out data collection:

Method	Issues regarding procedures
Direct observation	Observers must be selected and trained as to how to observe and when and how to record observations.
Interviews	Interview questions must be developed and validated and the interviewers given practice time.
Questionnaires	The type of questionnaire, the questions, and the Likert scale must be determined as well as the method of distribution (one-on-one, group, email, Internet).
Record review	A form or checklist should be developed to guide record review and the records selected based on criteria established for the research.
Secondary analysis	The databases to be mined should be selected, and the criteria for the research should be established, including key words, timeframes, and populations.

Modifying a School Health Education Program

Findings from a program evaluation will **reveal strengths and weaknesses** about the school health education program. The findings may also generate information regarding **stakeholders' perspectives on aspects of the program that should be maintained or altered to improve outcomes**. Once a thorough program evaluation is conducted, health education program planners can begin modifications. Although the procedures for modifying a school health education program may vary, the following steps can be used to modify a program:

1. Reengage stakeholders and revisit the purpose.
2. Consider the school and community's capacity for implementation.
3. Implement and monitor modifications.
4. Measure program effectiveness and outcomes.
5. Adapt program to address program weaknesses and threats.

The **inclusion of stakeholders** when designing modifications can improve stakeholders' receptivity of the program and their motivation to be involved. The capacity of the school and stakeholders (e.g., financial resources, staff, time, knowledge) to implement modifications should be considered to maximize impact. **Modifications should be monitored and measured** to ensure fidelity and optimize the program's effectiveness. The modifications should be evaluated to assess whether further adaptations are required.

Health Education Curriculum

Content Areas of Health Instruction

The four major content areas of health instruction are community health, nutrition, mental health, and sex education.

- The purpose of **community health instruction** is to prevent illness and injury through health-management strategies and promote a healthy physical environment to improve well-being. Students learn where to access health-related services and resources, as well as how to advocate for the health and well-being of their community.
- Through **nutrition education**, students learn about maintaining a balanced diet and healthy body weight and how to create and implement health goals.
- Through **mental health education**, students learn about how to identify various mental illnesses and maintain positive relationships and what resources are available for seeking help.
- Students learn about the consequences of engaging in sexual contact and internal and external influences that affect sexual behavior through **sex education**. They may also learn about consent and how to identify and effectively communicate their needs and feelings.

In each major content area, students learn **essential concepts** and **how to analyze influences**, **access valid information**, **communicate effectively**, **make good decisions**, **set goals**, and **practice health-enhancing behaviors**.

Scope Plan for Health Instruction

A **scope plan** is a long-range planning tool that helps an educator identify what a student should know by the end of an academic period. It is often accompanied by a sequence plan. A scope plan includes the **objectives** and **educational milestones** that must be accomplished during the school year for students to demonstrate proficiency in the content covered. A **matrix** is the most used format for scope plans. The purpose of a scope plan is to create a structured and intentional learning experience for students and ensure compliance with content standards. The general components of a scope plan include the **grade group** or level, **education topics** (e.g., community health, nutrition, mental health, sexuality education), **developmentally appropriate skill expectations**, and **performance indicators**. Scope plans should **align with national or state education standards**. They should also **address local health needs or interests** and the developmental status or abilities of the intended audience.

Sequence Plan for Health Instruction

A **sequence plan** is a long-range planning tool that an educator can use to arrange the order of the content that is to be taught. It is useful for **scaffolding learning** and helps educators plan which materials and learning experiences (e.g., activities) are needed to support student learning throughout the unit. Components of a sequence plan include a list of **activities or objectives** to be completed, the **order** they must be completed in, and the **length of time** required to complete each. The order should flow logically, and each objective should be completed in a reasonable amount of time. Sequence plans complement scope plans. When implemented together, scope and sequence plans create a well-planned instructional framework that covers all required standards in a fixed amount of time.

Use of Scope Plan and a Sequence Plan

Together, a health education scope plan and sequence plan **detail the order and rigor of concepts to be taught by the end of each school year**. The knowledge and skills that students acquire become more complex as students progress through subsequent grade levels. Health educators can **use these plans to create lesson units that address multiple health skills** (e.g., decision-making, goal setting) and **reinforce previously acquired health knowledge**. For instance, a scope plan and a sequence plan may place a nutrition unit after units on body systems. Its position will reinforce health concepts from previous lessons and present new information to improve comprehension. A scope plan and a sequence plan can also be helpful for teachers planning across grade groups. A health instructor could use them to **distribute health knowledge and skills at developmentally appropriate age periods**. For example, a health instructor may introduce information about reproductive health and physical changes in adolescence during sixth grade and expound upon those concepts in eighth grade (e.g., discuss STIs in depth) and tenth grade (e.g., discuss forms of contraception). In this scenario, the concepts are reinforced, and more complex information is introduced at developmentally appropriate times.

Integrating the Health Education Curriculum with Other Content Areas

Integrating the school health education curriculum with other content areas like language arts, science, and social studies **promotes cross-curricular learning and produces a more authentic and collaborative educational experience**. To effectively integrate the school health education curriculum, instructors must know the academic standards and instructional strategies for each curricular area. This can reveal any similar methodologies or concepts that could aid in integration. A **concept map** can help teachers chart learning priorities for each curricular area and identify connections between content areas. Teachers can reinforce skills from other content areas, plan thematic units, or engage in project-based learning (PBL). **Thematic units** consist of cross-curricular lessons unified by a theme or topic, and **project-based learning** is an inquiry-based instructional strategy in which students learn through collaborative problem-solving. For example, a health teacher could reinforce narrative writing skills and peer pressure knowledge by asking students to write stories about a time they applied refusal skills. A thematic unit created by social studies and health teachers could explore cultural and geographical nutritional practices and perspectives. Science and health instructors could create a project in which students learn and apply disease knowledge and laboratory skills to test local water sources for *E. coli*.

Planning for Health Instruction

Reflecting the Skills and Abilities of All Students

A **thorough assessment of all students' abilities** at the beginning of the academic period is necessary for planning inclusive health instruction. This includes an evaluation of students' content knowledge and preferred learning styles (e.g., visual, auditory, kinesthetic, reading and writing). By **appealing to students' learning styles** and **implementing a range of instructional modalities**, teachers can create engaging lessons that reflect the skills and abilities of all students. Health teachers can adapt the **delivery of content**, the options for how students **process material** and **demonstrate competency**, and the **learning environment** to teach students with varying abilities. For example, material in a unit on nutrition can be taught using a variety of methods such as realfood.gov's New Pyramid, songs, collage artwork, and cooking demonstrations. **Multiple instructional methods** ensure that the lesson is **accessible to all**. Demonstration of content mastery can also be adapted. For instance, a student tasked with demonstrating mastery of refusal skills could be evaluated through a traditional assessment, a writing assignment, a theatrical skit, or an oral exam. Each option allows students to exhibit comprehension of the material through strengths-based methods.

Visual learners	**Learn best by seeing and reading:** Provide written directions, picture guides, or demonstrate procedures. Use charts and diagrams. Provide photos and videos.
Auditory learners	**Learn best by listening and talking:** Explain procedures while demonstrating, and have the learner repeat. Plan extra time to discuss and answer questions. Provide audiotapes.
Kinesthetic learners	**Learn best by handling, doing, and practicing:** Provide hands-on experience throughout teaching. Encourage the handling of supplies and equipment. Allow the learner to demonstrate. Minimize instructions and allow person to explore equipment and procedures.

Reflecting the Needs and Developmental Levels of All Students

Instructors should **assess content knowledge, educational history, and challenges** when planning health instruction that reflects the needs and developmental levels of all students. These criteria can be evaluated through **beginning of year assessments**, **student surveys**, and **parental input**. Information from evaluations can reveal any knowledge deficits, barriers to learning, and effective strategies utilized by former teachers and/or parents. It can be used to make appropriate instructional or learning environment modifications to meet student needs. Instructors should also **explore health needs and interests** prior to instructional planning. In addition to student and parent surveys, data from the Youth Risk Behavior Surveillance System (YRBSS) and community health data can produce insights on age- and community-specific health needs. **Differentiated instruction** may be used to tailor material to meet the needs and developmental levels of students simultaneously. Regular monitoring of student growth can illuminate deficits in academic progress and opportunities for adaptation. Flexible and responsive shifts in instructional strategies ensure that material is reflective of student needs. A deep understanding of an age group's standard abilities and capacity for learning, as well as the developmental objectives for each age group, is also necessary for responsive instruction.

Review Video: Differentiated Instruction
Visit mometrix.com/academy and enter code: 100342

Reflecting the Interests of All Students

Interest-based strategies for health instruction include encouraging students to identify content and materials related to health topics, allowing students to develop assessment methods, and giving students time to reflect on and practice their strengths. Health instructors could also incorporate strategies or concepts from **other content areas** and present material that **responds to real-world situations**. For instance, a health teacher implementing student-centered design during a unit on risk prevention and management could allow students to collaboratively explore stressors that contribute to conflict and different types of conflict management strategies. Each student can explore the material through a preferred method (e.g., reading a textbook chapter, analyzing data, watching an informational video, or listening to a podcast) and present his or her findings to the class. Students can **demonstrate mastery** of the material **through methods that reflect their academic preferences** (e.g., written report, awareness campaign, play, website) or personal interests. For example, a group of students interested in sports could create a pitch for a basketball intervention program to increase physical activity among their peers. Game-like activities like **choice boards**—a matrix of learning activities that students choose from—and **cubing**—rollable cubes with different activities on each side—**promote choice and honor student interest**.

Reflecting the Cultural Backgrounds of All Students

Materials and visual aids that depict cultural diversity can **promote inclusion** within the classroom. For example, a health instructor can opt for health posters, videos, or other learning materials that include figures of diverse backgrounds, such as people of different ethnicities, races, nationalities, and genders. **Representation** creates a learning environment in which **all students feel welcomed and accepted**. Teachers can also create learning activities that are **culturally relevant** to students. Instructors can include key health practices and cultural perspectives related to health and well-being among different communities to stimulate interest and celebrate cultural differences. Instructors can **incorporate works from notable figures in different cultures** or **use relevant cultural activities to foster interest**. One may consider presenting vocabulary terms in different languages alongside English. Students should be **encouraged to share their cultural perspectives** about health topics to garner understanding among their classmates. However, it is important that instructors **do not mandate or coerce students to contribute**. Teachers should **model respectful speech and tolerance of alternative perspectives**. For example, a health instructor should use a **neutral tone** and **impartial language** when presenting information about sex education. Despite the teacher's opinion, the material should be accurately and respectfully introduced.

Implementing Health Education Curriculum

Implementing and Integrating a School Health Education Curriculum

Learning the **district's academic standards** and **school policy** related to health education is the first step in effectively implementing and integrating a school health education curriculum. A **needs assessment** should be conducted to evaluate learning needs and strengths and any assets for or barriers to learning among students. For example, a needs assessment could identify that a community's robust anti-bullying campaign contributes to student knowledge regarding interpersonal relationships and refusal skills. It could also reveal a lack of student knowledge regarding nutrition and physical health due to staffing issues and poor exercise facilities. Both insights can be helpful for instructors when implementing a health education curriculum. Instructors should also review the effectiveness and adaptability of existing curricula. Next, the curriculum developer(s) must **use findings to establish intended outcomes or objectives**. Information can be organized in a **scope plan** and a **sequence plan**, and planners can begin **developing instructional methods, activities, and assessments**. The curriculum should be **reviewed, tested, and revised** to ensure that it meets the school's and district's requirements and the needs of the students. Evaluation through a combination of formative and summative assessments can determine the impact of the curriculum (e.g., effectiveness, reach, clarity).

Accurate and Age-Appropriate Sources of Information About Health

Students in **different developmental stages** have **different informational needs** related to health topics and need to be able to access accurate and age-appropriate health information. Accompanying textbooks and learning materials provided by the school or school district often serve as appropriate sources of information and are readily available for student use. **School**

health practitioners (e.g., school nurse, school psychologist or social worker, nutritionist) are sources of knowledge related to health and community resources. They can **direct students to age-appropriate and accurate resources** and may have literature (e.g., brochures, one-pagers) that students can use. Physicians may have health-related information for **different age groups**. Physicians are often trained to pare down information to make it more **accessible** and **developmentally appropriate**. **State and federal governmental agencies** (e.g., Centers for Disease Control and Prevention, Food and Drug Administration, local public health offices) distribute reliable, easy-to-read materials that are appropriate for all ages. **Health education teachers** are also reliable sources of accurate and age-appropriate sources of health information. They are often content experts, and instructors can also teach students and families how to recognize accurate sources of health information through media literacy.

Incorporating Accurate and Age-Appropriate Resources and Materials

Textbooks are often purchased to complement each content area's curriculum. Although teachers should use a variety of media in instruction, **textbooks function well to introduce or reinforce health education concepts**. For example, students could use textbooks to learn important vocabulary terms at the beginning of a unit, or they could use them to explore a topic more in-depth during a learning circuit. **School health practitioners**, **physicians**, or **child health advocacy groups** can be invited to speak during class to discuss a topic with students. They can also be a source of knowledge for a student's independent research or provide age-appropriate health materials to integrate into lesson units. Students can use resources from **federal and state governmental agencies** or trustworthy **nonprofit agencies** to process or reinforce information learned in a lesson. Many agencies distribute written materials (e.g., brochures, one-pagers, websites) for children. Some have health-related games, videos, or podcasts to make the learning material more engaging. A health education teacher should incorporate multiple types of resources and materials into health instruction to model responsible information consumption.

Student Health Knowledge and Behaviors

Shaping Students' Patterns of Health Behaviors

A person's knowledge about health-related topics has an **impact on the behaviors that he or she engages in and on his or her motivation to change behaviors**. For instance, a student with **poor nutritional health literacy** may lack knowledge about healthy eating habits or the health effects of a poor diet on physical and emotional health. Without adequate knowledge, the student may **fail to understand the importance** of adopting new health behaviors. Knowledge is acquired through many sources (e.g., education, peer discussions, social media), yet it is important that students receive **adequate experience learning how to assess the validity of health information to ensure the information they receive is accurate**. Health skills are also influential in shaping health behavior, especially one's self-efficacy. **Self-efficacy** refers to a person's belief in his or her ability to adequately enact healthy behaviors. For example, a student with low self-efficacy may believe that they would not be able to refuse alcohol if offered by a peer. If the student received knowledge and opportunities to practice applying refusal skills in a health education course, he or she would be more likely to refuse negative health behaviors if prompted.

How Attitudes Shape Students' Patterns of Health Behaviors

Health attitudes refer to an individual's **favorability of a health behavior** (e.g., smoking, drug use, exercise). They are **influenced by knowledge, experience, observation, and relationships**. For example, a student that has substantial knowledge of the dangers of drug use or has had a negative experience because of drug use may be more likely to have a negative health attitude about drugs. Alternatively, a student whose friends habitually use drugs may have a more positive attitude towards drug use. The **origins of a health attitude** can influence the strength of an attitude and a person's willingness to change his or her health behaviors. For instance, a person who had a traumatic experience at a doctor's office may have a strong aversion to seeking health care. A person whose family or peers believe that health care visits are expensive or inconvenient may also avoid seeking health care. Both may avoid receiving an annual checkup, but the attitude of the individual who experienced a traumatic event is far less likely to change compared to the person whose attitude is shaped by peer influence.

Helping Students Learn and Apply Skills

Students should learn the importance of regularly examining personal health behaviors and influences. **Recurrent reflection** can help students assess their health status and the factors that influence their well-being. This can reveal opportunities for behavior adaptation that are necessary for maintaining good health. **Continuous learning** and strong **health literacy** skills can help students identify accurate and trustworthy sources of health information and build student knowledge about health-related topics. **Robust knowledge about health** (i.e., valid, reliable, and evidence-based health information) is useful for assessing how a behavior contributes to one's overall health and strategies for maintaining good health. Health instructors that teach students **SMART goals** (specific, measurable, achievable, relevant, and time-bound) can help students learn how to maintain health behavior changes. SMART health goals position students for long-term success. They are effective at motivating students to remain focused and improve self-efficacy. Students who learn problem-solving skills and skills for building social support networks can more effectively respond to derailed health behavior goals, temptation, or barriers to success.

Helping Students Locate, Read, Comprehend, and Retain Content

The ability to locate, read, comprehend, retain, and apply content-related information from a range of texts and technologies is referred to as **information literacy**. It can transform a student into a more confident and discerning learner. Instructors should teach students that when locating credible texts and technologies, they should **assess the credibility** of the author or publisher, review the citations used in the resource, identify potential biases, and evaluate when the resource was published. Instructors should teach students **active reading strategies** (e.g., posing pre-reading questions, identifying unfamiliar words, taking notes, creating diagrams, summarizing the main idea of the text). **Active reading strategies** can help students comprehend and retain information regardless of the source. **Reciprocal teaching** is a strategy in which students act as the instructor. This practice can aid in comprehension and retention as students must locate, read, comprehend, and apply content-related information from a resource. Information is then relayed to their peers in an age-appropriate and engaging manner. **Project-based learning** incorporates all skills into a final product. Students must independently locate, explore, retain, and apply information to solve a real-world problem or situation.

Effective Communication in Health Education

Addressing Sensitive or Controversial Health Issues

Sensitive or controversial health subjects include issues related to sex, substance use, abuse, and death. Health instructors who are knowledgeable about school policy and state academic standards can more **effectively address sensitive or controversial health topics**. Sticking to the required health objectives as outlined by state education curricula or policy can prevent noncompliance and act as a well-structured framework to guide teachers through challenging topics. Prior to planning the lesson(s), instructors should consider their own **biases**, **misinformation**, and **questions** about the sensitive topic. This can ensure that teachers adequately plan for student questions and practice presenting information in a nonjudgmental way. Teachers may also **prepare a list of resources** (e.g., age-appropriate materials, list of community health practitioners) that students can access outside of class. **Sensitive subjects should be presented without bias** (e.g., neutral language and tone) and **devoid of the teacher's personal perspective** about the topic. All information shared must be **factual and sourced from credible texts, and all perspectives should be presented.** Students should be given opportunities for reflection to sort through any triggering content, process the material, and express any lingering thoughts and questions.

Importance of Modeling Positive Health Behaviors

Social networks can have a profound impact on health behaviors. The perceptions of those whom one values can influence one's health habits or choices. For example, a child may abstain from underage drinking because his or her parents disapprove of alcohol use. The health attitudes, knowledge, and behavior of individuals within a person's social network can also shape behaviors. A teenager whose peer group lacks knowledge about the dangers of vaping, has a positive attitude toward smoking, and actively participates in vaping may be more likely to adopt the behavior. Peer and parent influences are often the most impactful relationships among youth; however, teachers and other respected adults or role models (e.g., coaches, pastors, tutors) can also influence one's health behaviors. Teachers should routinely model healthy behaviors to increase exposure to healthy habits. For example, a teacher can regularly eat a healthy lunch at school, exercise, or practice healthy communication skills.

Using Communication Skills and Strategies

When teaching health material, teachers can use **precise and accurate health terms to avoid miscommunication**. Clearly and honestly responding to student questions about health topics can **foster effective communication among students**. Teachers can **model positive and effective communication** by building supportive relationships with and among students, motivating students and praising positive behavior, accepting and implementing student feedback, and actively listening to and resolving any problems. An instructor who creates opportunities for **student self-advocacy** can reinforce communication skills. For example, a teacher who encourages students to describe their preferred learning styles, health interests, strengths, and weaknesses provides space for students to actively communicate their needs. Granting students multiple methods for providing feedback or reflecting on content during a unit can encourage them to assert themselves or process thoughts and emotions.

Assessment in Health Education

Identifying Criteria and Methods for Evaluating Student Learning

Teachers can use content criteria and process criteria to evaluate student learning about health. Both types of criteria are effective at evaluating student learning, yet, when applied together, they provide a more holistic assessment. **Content criteria** describes the extent of a student's knowledge about a topic, and **process criteria** assesses how proficient a student is at completing a skill. A health instructor can use **formative** and **summative assessments** to evaluate student knowledge of a health topic before, during, and after a lesson unit. **Content criteria** can be generated directly from academic standards or learning objectives outlined through scope and sequence plans. These assessments are used to **measure student knowledge and growth**. **Skill proficiency** is a type of content criteria, but is usually assessed through **performance-based assessments** (e.g., application of refusal skills, creating a health goal). Process criteria can be assessed through student **self-assessment**. For example, a student can evaluate his or her own performance on a project.

Self-assessments allow students to reflect on their strengths, weaknesses, and abilities. Information can be used to evaluate lapses in health knowledge and guide future instructional strategies. Regardless of the assessment, students should receive a grading rubric and understand the purpose of the evaluation.

APPLYING STUDENT ASSESSMENT RESULTS

Results from student assessments can be used to adjust teaching strategies, identify or adapt instructional tools, differentiate instruction, and tailor lessons to meet the needs of all students. For example, a **summative assessment**, which is an assessment that takes place at the end of a unit, may reveal that most students performed poorly on the topic of communicable and noncommunicable diseases overall. If the assessment was **standards-based**, an instructor can determine which learning objective(s) students did not master. He or she should reflect on the methods used to teach the learning objectives that students mastered or did not master and any accompanying materials or instructional tools (e.g., diagrams, games, written text). The instructor can use these findings to research alternative instructional methods to implement in subsequent lessons. **Results** from assessments can also be used to **tailor instruction** for individual students or subsets of students that perform poorly. When used in conjunction with information on student demographics, health needs, community culture, and learning styles, this information can help an instructor create **differentiated learning opportunities** that are relevant, engaging, and accessible to all students.

> **Review Video: Formative and Summative Assessments**
> Visit mometrix.com/academy and enter code: 804991

Professional Foundations of Health Education

CONTINUING EDUCATION

NCHEC

One resource for continuing education knowledge and credits is the **National Commission for Health Education Credentialing (NCHEC), Inc.**, accredited by the National Commission for Certifying Agencies (NCCA). NCHEC offers workshops, seminars, and conferences in various health education topics. These include:

- Lung summits sponsored by the American Lung Association
- Conferences on annual public health, annual mental health and aging, and breastfeeding
- Seminars and workshops on teen contraceptive counseling approaches, age-related dementia, creating aging-friendly communities, trauma, and addiction
- Nutritional training
- Medical school tobacco treatment specialist trainings
- Wellness and health coaching workshops and certification courses
- Family planning health worker courses
- Asthma educator certification courses
- Programs on Medicare, diabetes, women's gender-specific treatment, technology use integrating sexual and reproductive health with primary care, behavioral healthcare in the criminal justice system, worksite wellness certification and health promotion, nonprofit finance, project management, etc.

Health educators can also take self-study courses for wellness coaching certification training and information about physical activity, nutrition, weight control, injury prevention, skin assessment, wound care, suicide prevention, grief, mental health, PTSD, substance abuse, addiction recovery, peer education, teen health risk behaviors, weight control, trauma, prevention, health equity, program evaluation, qualitative research, social media, and more from diverse sponsors, for certification, knowledge, and credits.

SOPHE

The **Society for Public Health Education** (SOPHE) is a national nonprofit organization dedicated to providing **continuing education** for health and education professionals. It includes an affiliate membership program with local chapters. SOPHE is designated by the National Commission for Health Education Credentialing (NCHEC) as a multiple event provider of Continuing Education Contact Hours (CECH). SOPHE is approved by the National Board of Public Health Examiners as a provider of renewal credits for the Certificate in Public Health. SOPHE is one of the largest continuing education providers for Certified Health Education Specialists (CHES). Health educators can take advantage of continuing education opportunities SOPHE offers, including attending local chapter events; attending the SOPHE Annual Meeting; pursuing eLearning including taking online courses, Journal Self-Study Tests, playing back meeting webcasts, marketing and promotion videos, archived webinars, and streaming live webinars; publishing and/or reviewing manuscripts in SOPHE Journals; and participating in Journal and Meeting Calls for research. Health educators can create accounts and profiles at SOPHE's updated Center for Online Resources and Education (CORE), log in, and earn CE credits via courses and other activities.

Professional Development Opportunities for Health Educators

Resources offering health educators **PD opportunities** include National Education Association's (NEA) Educational Support Professionals (ESP) PD; US Centers for Disease Control and Prevention's (CDC) Division of Scientific Education and Professional Development (DSEPD); ShapeAmerica.org, aka American Association for Health, Physical Education, Recreation, and Dance (AAHPERD); American Public Health Association (APHA)'s Center for PD, Public Health Systems and Partnerships; and health and education departments of many state and private universities and colleges. Shape America offers a webinar series covering topics including Adapted Physical Education (APE); APE for autism; sport coaching; Common Core State Standards (CCSS); Early Childhood Education (ECE); PE e-learning, etc.; a Researcher's Toolkit; a Distinguished Lecture Series; and workshops on fitness, PE, and the Presidential Youth Fitness Program (PYFP).

The CDC Learning Connection includes thousands of public health learning products and continuing education (CE) courses, many free, through CDC TRAIN, online educational resources, Quick-Learn Lessons for mobile devices, and links to Facebook and Twitter posts on public health topics. NEA offers its ESP National PD Conference; Leaders for Tomorrow program; and trainings in results-oriented job descriptions, crisis action plans, leadership, air quality action plans, collective action, mentoring, and school community team-building.

OHDSI

The **Observational Health Data Sciences and Informatics Program (OHDSI)** is an interdisciplinary collaborative initiative among disciplines including biomedical sciences, physics, informatics, epidemiology, computer science, and statistics. This initiative has multiple stakeholders, including healthcare providers, academics, medical product manufacturers, payers, and government agencies. Its purpose is to use large-scale analytics to demonstrate the value of **observational health data**. With its coordinating center headquartered at Columbia University, OHDSI has developed an international network of observational health databases and researchers. In 2014, at the EDM (Electronic Data Methods) Forum in San Francisco, OHDSI released Achilles, its first open-source software application. OHDSI has produced a two-minute YouTube video to welcome new participants, and has published a paper in the Drug Safety periodical. Those who can benefit from participating in the OHDSI community include scientists exploring large-scale data methodologies, clinical researchers using OHDSI's network for answering clinical questions, members of organizations that have healthcare data (for more effectively using their data), members of healthcare systems (for improving the efficiency and quality of healthcare using OHDSI's tools), and software designers and developers (for contributing to projects to enhance patient health).

Participants in the Observational Health Data Sciences and Informatics Program (OHDSI) are developing **open-source software tools** to analyze, characterize, and evaluate health data, medical product safety, healthcare quality, and comparative effectiveness, and to build predictive patient-level modeling. They are also developing an **international data network** to use large-scale analytical methods for extracting evidence from observational health data. OHDSI's Columbia University center will house open-source summary statistics to share throughout the network, enabling all stakeholders to learn from real-world evidence. OHDSI aims to evaluate the reliability of the evidence it produces by systematically assessing observational analysis methods performance. This collaboration holds weekly webinar teleconferences where members present current research including proposals, works in progress, and final products for collaboration, feedback, and review. At these meetings they also review funding and publication opportunities and topics of shared interest. OHDSI has formed specific workgroups for design and implementation of the Observational Medical Outcomes Partnership Common Data Model, version 5 (OMOP CDMv5) specifications and vocabulary standard, data characterization, patient-level prediction, population-level estimation, the knowledge base, a phenotype library, and visualization/communications.

Valid, Reliable Online Databases

The US Department of Health and Human Services (HHS) includes the National Institutes of Health (NIH). The NIH offers a number of **public databases** that users can search for valid, reliable **health-related data**. These databases include:

- NIH RePORTER, the database of RePORT (Research Portfolio Online Reporting Tools)
- NIDB (NeuroInformatics DataBase) Resources
- NCBI (National Center for Biotechnology Information) Literature Databases
- PubMed Central
- PubMed Medline
- Research.gov
- Community of Science (COS)
- Science.gov
- World Wide Science
- ClinicalTrials.gov

The Centers for Disease Control and Prevention (CDC) have interactive database systems on their website for these topics: birth defects and developmental disabilities; child and adolescent health; chronic disease; crosscutting; diabetes; disabilities; environmental health; global health; health risk behavior; HIV, STIs, and viral hepatitis; infectious disease; influenza; injury; maternal and child health; occupational safety and health; oral health; and population.

The World Health Organization (WHO) has an online database of survey information from health and human rights organizations, established through collaboration with the Harvard School of Public Health's Program for International Health and Human Rights. WHO also offers an online library catalogue, WHOLIS, for searching WHO's printed publications collection from 1948 to the present, historical medicine and public health monographs, and international health literature.

YRBSS Database

The YRBSS is the (National) **Youth Risk Behavior Surveillance System** used in the National Youth Risk Behavior Survey conducted by the Centers for Disease Control and Prevention (CDC). Data from this survey are available online in ASCII and Access® file formats for download and use. The YRBSS website also offers SPSS® and SAS® programs for converting ASCII data into datasets compatible with SPSS® and SAS® use. Users can access YRBS national high school data files from as far back as 1991 online, including user's manuals for each year. Every year of data has its own format library. The website includes instructions for using the data files in the different formats, plus methodology of the YRBSS, a review of analysis software, best practices and guidance for combining YRBS data from multiple years (for conducting trend analyses of the data) and interpreting the trend data, information for how groups can conduct their own YRBS surveys, and frequently asked questions (FAQs).

ShapeAmerica Resources and AMA Database Licensing

The **American Alliance for Health, Physical Education, Recreation, and Dance** (AAHPERD.org), aka **ShapeAmerica**, offers databases and other resources, including: a database with regularly updated information about available research and program grants from the NASPE (National Association for Sport and Physical Education); a database where research fellows can enter and update their information; a database of grassroots contacts, through its Legislative Action Center Tutorial PDF; and its Library/Shared Files Exchange for lesson plans, assessment tools, etc. from which educators can access, contribute, and share. The **AMA** has offered healthcare community access to its Physician Masterfile for over 60 years to benefit the medical industry and public good. Today, **Database Licensees** contract with the AMA to arrange access to a variety of databases containing health-related research activities and marketing services. Medical schools, hospitals, pharmaceutical manufacturers, medical supply and equipment companies, consultants, insurance companies, market research firms, and commercial organizations all use the AMA Masterfile. The AMA reviews data requests from Database Licensees daily to monitor licensing agreement compliance. Physicians can restrict their prescription information from pharmaceutical sales representatives, and request no contact and no release restrictions to their AMA Physician Masterfile records.

CSHP

A **coordinated school health program** (CSHP) should include comprehensive health education (K–12), health services, psychological and socials services, safety initiatives/safe environment, physical education, nutritional services, and beneficial partnerships (e.g., with local public health staff, parents, state and community agencies and organizations). The purpose of the CSHP is to recognize that **academic success** and **physical and emotional health** are linked and that all components must be integrated and work together for the benefit of the students' health and well-being as well as health promotion for the staff. The CSHP helps to focus attention on behaviors that have a negative impact on students' health and achievement, such as risk-taking behaviors. Some of the goals of this program include better attendance, improved academic outcomes, fewer dropouts, fewer behavior problems (including bullying/violence), better nutrition, increased physical activity, and increased participation by family, educational staff, and other members of the community.

Healthy People 2030

Healthy People 2030, enacted in 2020 and released by the US Department of Health & Human Services, is a 10-year guide to national public health practice and objectives. *Healthy People 2030* is based on previous initiatives, including *Healthy People 1990, 2000, 2010,* and *2020. Healthy People 2030* is particularly relevant to the health educator because many funding sources are tied to these objectives and educational materials are developed in support of them. Additionally, one section addresses **adolescent health** with the goal of promoting "healthy development, healthy behaviors and well-being across all life stages." This section addresses public health and social problems (such as unintended pregnancies), environmental influences on behavior and outcomes, and emerging issues. *Healthy People 2030* can be used to guide the focus of instruction because it includes a framework for health promotion and disease prevention and measurable objectives, such as increasing the proportion of students who graduate with a regular diploma after four years of high school.

HEALTH SCIENCE RELATED TO ADOLESCENT HEALTH RESOURCES

Resources for keeping informed about current knowledge in health science include the following:

- **Internet**: The government has many websites devoted to current knowledge, such as CDC.gov. A valuable online resource is the E-Updates and News in Adolescent Health provided by *the Office of Adolescent Health* (HHS). Major news sites, such as CNN.com, have daily health news. *Medical News Today* provides links to medical news articles.
- **Professional journals**: Journals such as the *Journal of School Health* and the *American Journal of Health Education* provide health information of particular interest to health educators.
- **Public health/Local health agencies**: These agencies provide updates to the community about issues of current concern, such as outbreaks or emerging infections.
- **Professional organizations**: Organizations such as the American School Health Association (ASHA) and the American Association for Health Education (AAHE) carry out research and provide information and support to members as well as sponsoring state and national conferences, various workshops, and informative websites.

ROLE OF HEALTH EDUCATORS IN ADVOCATING FOR HEALTHY SCHOOL ENVIRONMENT

The health educator has the primary role of communicating, promoting, and **advocating** for a healthy school environment and should take every opportunity to do so, beginning with **increasing awareness** within the classroom through a variety of means: panel discussions, guest speakers, demonstrations, project-based learning, debates, experiments, and role playing. The health educator should carry out an **assessment** and report to the school board about the school's environment, highlighting areas in which the school is performing well as well as those that need improvement. The health educator must also establish close working relationships with **administrators**, whose support is critical, and with teachers and other staff members, stressing how their roles are made easier in a healthy school environment and ways in which they can support taking steps to improve the situation at the school. The health educator should monitor and report progress.

Chapter Quiz

Ready to see how well you retained what you just read? Scan the QR code to go directly to the chapter quiz interface for this study guide. If you're using a computer, simply visit the online resources page at **mometrix.com/resources719/oaehealth** and click the Chapter Quizzes link.

OAE Practice Test

Want to take this practice test in an online interactive format?
Check out the online resources page, which includes interactive practice questions and much more: **mometrix.com/resources719/oaehealth**

1. The CDC suggests six strategies to prevent adverse childhood experiences (ACEs). Implementing family-friendly work policies is an example of which strategy?

a. Ensuring a strong start for children
b. Connecting youth to caring adults and activities
c. Strengthening economic supports to families
d. Intervening to lessen immediate and long-term harm

2. Which of the following practices is NOT an example of a population-level intervention to prevent chronic diseases?

a. A local public health department launches a healthy eating campaign.
b. A tobacco company prints warning labels on its products.
c. A city votes to implement a soda tax.
d. A group of coworkers form a running group that meets up twice a week to exercise.

3. School-based health clinics provide each of the following health services EXCEPT:

a. WIC enrollment
b. Behavioral health care referrals
c. Vaccinations
d. Sexual health education

4. Which of the six essential nutrients helps repair and build tissue?

a. Carbohydrates
b. Fats
c. Protein
d. Minerals

5. Which of the following is NOT a professional, legal, or ethical practice regarding sensitive issues?

a. Distributing parent permission forms before a sexual health education unit
b. Sharing information with a caregiver about a student's question related to contraception
c. Reporting sexual abuse
d. Offering professional development training about child protection issues

6. Frank's housemate has neglected to complete his share of the household chores for the past few weeks. Frank confronts him by saying, "I feel frustrated that I have been doing the majority of the work around the household the last few weeks because I have been very busy at work. I would like our household workload to be equal. Is there anything that has prevented you from completing your share of the work?" What communication style is Frank practicing?

a. Assertive
b. Passive
c. Aggressive
d. Avoidant

7. Which health career should be considered by a person who is interested in identifying disease risk, conducting disease surveillance, and facilitating disease transmission prevention efforts?

a. Public health nurse
b. Biostatistician
c. Epidemiologist
d. Community health worker

8. Suzanne is exploring contraception options. She is sexually active with her long-term partner but does not plan on having children for the foreseeable future, so she would prefer a long-lasting and low-maintenance method. She also would rather use a nonhormonal contraceptive. Which type of contraception is the most appropriate for her preferences?

a. Female condom
b. Depo-Provera shot
c. Progestin implant
d. Copper intrauterine device (IUD)

9. Reciprocal determinism is one of the constructs in which behavioral change theory?

a. Theory of Planned Behavior
b. Health Belief Model
c. Social Cognitive Theory
d. Transtheoretical Model

10. Mrs. Abdallah is planning a lesson on the five food groups (fruits, vegetables, grains, protein foods, and dairy). Students are divided into five groups and tasked with working together to research their assigned food group. The students are reorganized into different groups to report their findings to the other "nonexperts." Which instructional strategy is Mrs. Abdallah implementing?

a. Cooperative learning
b. Direct instruction
c. Guided discovery
d. Brainstorming

11. A man with a history of bipolar I disorder and opiate abuse reports suicidal thoughts with a plan to his therapist. He was recently in a car accident and broke his leg. The patient says that he had one suicide attempt by overdose five years ago. He is actively using intravenous drugs and has a history of sexual trauma during childhood. Which factor listed is NOT a risk factor of suicide?

a. History of childhood sexual abuse
b. Active substance abuse
c. Past suicide attempt
d. His recent car accident

12. Janice is assigned to write a paper for her health class about heart disease. Which of the following is NOT an example of a valid source of health information?

a. An American Heart Association article about Heart-Check certification
b. A well-known health enthusiast's post summarizing the CDC's recommendations on heart-healthy exercises
c. A peer-reviewed journal article about the relationship between diabetes and heart disease
d. A fact sheet on frequently asked questions about heart disease from the Office on Women's Health at the Department of Health and Human Services

13. What does body composition refer to?

a. The measure of a person's body fat based on the ratio of height to weight
b. The ratio of a person's waist circumference to weight
c. The percentage of adipose tissue in a person's body
d. The percentage of bone, water, muscle, and fat in a person's body

14. During one phase of the menstrual cycle, the corpus luteum raises levels of progesterone that thicken the uterine lining to promote implantation. What is the phase that precedes this?

a. Menstrual
b. Luteal
c. Ovulation
d. Follicular

15. Fresh water is a finite resource, yet reserves are being depleted far faster than they can be naturally replenished. Which of the following water conservation methods has the potential to preserve the greatest volume of water?

a. The US government provides a federal subsidy to support the installation of drip irrigation and subsurface irrigation systems on US farms.
b. A country enforces lawn watering restrictions for all water sources.
c. A federal mandate requires leak detection systems in all newly constructed homes.
d. Native corn crop varieties are introduced to reduce the need for artificial watering.

16. A teenager who is creating her first social media profile may jeopardize her health or safety through which action?

a. Personalizing the default privacy settings
b. Accepting friend requests from individuals she has met in-person
c. Enabling location services on her photos
d. Using a password management service to create a password

17. Which conflict resolution strategy involves an unbiased third-party facilitator who guides both parties toward a mutually beneficial resolution?

a. Mediation
b. Negotiation
c. Litigation
d. Reconciliation

18. According to attachment theory, a person whose parents rejected his or her social-emotional needs during childhood is most likely to develop which of the following attachment styles that is characterized by independence, intolerance of close relationships, and evasion of emotional situations?

a. Secure attachment
b. Anxious attachment
c. Disorganized attachment
d. Avoidant attachment

19. Mrs. McMullen wants to assess how effective her instruction was during the first academic quarter. Specifically, she wants to learn how to enhance student engagement, strengthen teacher-student relationships within her classroom, and improve her classroom climate. Which of the following reflective processes of teaching is LEAST likely to produce the findings she seeks?

a. Journaling
b. Parent interviews
c. Observing other teachers
d. Student surveys

20. Each of the following behaviors is associated with reducing the risk of chronic disease EXCEPT:

a. Eating a diet high in unsaturated fats
b. Exercising at least 150 minutes per week
c. Consuming no more than one to two glasses of alcohol per day
d. Sleeping at least seven hours per night

21. A young woman is drinking for the first time and consumes five alcoholic drinks within a one-hour period. Which consequence is LEAST likely to result from her risky behavior?

a. Extreme dehydration
b. Alcohol addiction
c. Self-harm
d. Unintentional injuries

22. Which of the following behaviors is an example of an adaptive coping skill?

a. A person experiencing stress related to eating and weight gain restricts his or her food intake.
b. A person experiencing performance anxiety practices breathing techniques before a test.
c. A person who becomes easily nervous making new friends avoids social gatherings.
d. A person who experiences stress about a new health issue avoids going to the doctor.

23. A student who is practicing a new skill that is outside of her comfort zone but is excited about the prospect of accomplishing this feat may be experiencing which type of stress?

a. Eustress
b. Acute stress
c. Distress
d. Academic stress

24. A community health educator wants to implement a health promotion campaign to reduce rates of vaping among older female adolescents (ages 15 to 19) in the local school district. Which health promotion method is most appropriate for this scenario?

a. A TikTok video campaign led by social media influencers that warns viewers about the dangers of vaping
b. A one-page graphic about the long-term physical effects of vaping posted on the school district's Facebook page
c. A pamphlet in the school counselor's office about how to apply refusal skills when pressured to vape
d. A guest lecture about vaping by the community health educator at the local high school

25. A person weighs the pros and cons of changing his or her eating habits to lose weight. Which stage of change is depicted by this scenario?

a. Action
b. Contemplation
c. Preparation
d. Precontemplation

26. Use the DECIDE model to respond to the following question: Yeslia is the supervisor of four staff members. She notices that one of her employees has been less productive the past few weeks. The employee's performance has begun affecting the other employees she manages. What is the most appropriate first step?

a. Meet with the employee to brainstorm strategies for improving his or her productivity.
b. Establish the criteria that Yeslia will use to assess her employee's productivity.
c. Define any challenges or stressors that impact the employee's productivity.
d. Implement biweekly check-ins to ensure that the employee stays on track.

27. Human papillomavirus (HPV) causes nearly 90 percent of all cases of cervical cancer, yet it can be avoided through which preventative practice?

a. Antiprotozoal drugs
b. Antibiotics
c. Vaccination
d. Antiviral drugs

28. Tom is driving Louisa home after their first date. As they approach Louisa's house, Tom begins to make unwanted sexual advances toward Louisa. Which of the following is the LEAST effective strategy for refusing sexual advances?

a. Louisa remains quiet and hopes that Tom will pick up that she is uncomfortable.
b. Louisa tells Tom that she is not interested.
c. Louisa makes a joke to defuse the tension.
d. Louisa exits the car and heads to a neighbor's house until Tom leaves.

29. Waste is removed throughout the body by each of the following body systems EXCEPT:

a. Excretory system
b. Respiratory system
c. Endocrine system
d. Integumentary system

30. Which of the following data sources and databases monitors youth health risk behaviors that contribute to mortality and disability?

a. Youth Risk Behavior Surveillance System (YRBSS)
b. Society of Health and Physical Educators (SHAPE America)
c. KIDS COUNT
d. National Survey of Children's Health (NSCH)

31. Delirium tremens (DTs) is a potentially fatal form of alcohol withdrawal that causes tremors, confusion, hallucinations, and high blood pressure. What type of drug is a person who is experiencing DTs withdrawing from?

a. Stimulants
b. Hallucinogens
c. Depressants
d. Opioids

32. Jessica goes to the gym locker room after completing her workout and finds a woman lying on the ground. After she checks the scene for safety, she checks for responsiveness, breathing, and bleeding. The woman does not appear to be conscious or breathing, and Jessica cannot feel her pulse. Jessica calls 911 and places the woman on her back. Jessica is not CPR-certified. What is the next step the 911 operator should direct Jessica to take?

a. Immediately initiate chest compressions while calling for help.
b. Conduct a blind swipe of the mouth to remove any possible foreign objects.
c. Deliver a cycle of 100 chest compressions before checking for signs of life.
d. Find and attach an automated external defibrillator (AED).

33. What is the first step in beginning a needs assessment?

a. Establish the roles and responsibilities of the research team.
b. Design the data collection methodology.
c. Identify and engage stakeholders.
d. Determine the purpose of the needs assessment.

34. According to Jean Piaget's theory of cognitive development, at which stage does a person achieve the ability to perform abstract reasoning (e.g., respond to hypothetical situations, perform deductive reasoning)?

a. Sensorimotor stage
b. Preoperational stage
c. Concrete operational stage
d. Formal operational stage

35. A man arrived at a hospital experiencing chest and arm pain. Upon examination, his doctors determined that atheromatous plaque accumulated along his heart's blood vessels causing narrowed arteries that partially restricted blood flow to his heart. Aside from diagnosing him with angina, what else would his doctors diagnose him with?

a. Pulmonary embolism
b. Coronary artery disease
c. Cardiac arrhythmia
d. Cardiac arrest

36. Each of the following statements regarding sexual abuse is true EXCEPT:

a. Communities that have strict gender roles have higher rates of sexual violence.
b. Children with developmental disabilities are at a greater risk of sexual violence.
c. Former victims of sexual abuse are less likely to become perpetrators of sexual violence.
d. Academic achievement is a protective factor for sexual violence perpetration.

37. Mr. Sulliman is planning a lesson unit on the 10 major body systems and introduces the essential question, "How do the body systems interact to fulfill a person's needs?" He then separates students into groups and gives each group an array of manipulatives and instructional resources to collaboratively explore the essential question. Students are given a list of questions to spark conversation about the material and invited to share their insights. Which instructional strategy is Mr. Sulliman implementing?

a. Guided discovery
b. Role playing
c. Brainstorming
d. Direct instruction

38. An assertive person is LEAST likely to do which of the following?

a. Use "I" statements to express his or her feelings
b. Seek to understand a speaker's point of view
c. Withhold his or her opinions or feelings from others
d. Set boundaries with others

39. Martha wants to reduce her carbon footprint. Which of the following strategies will likely produce the greatest carbon reductions?

a. Martha adjusts her thermostat to be five degrees cooler in the winter.
b. Martha opts to drive eight hours for the holidays rather than take a flight.
c. Martha chooses to purchase her clothes from a thrift shop and upcycles outdated clothing items.
d. Martha purchases a tumbling composter to reduce the volume of food waste.

40. Leopold has noticed a scaly, circular rash that itches forming on his upper thigh. Which personal hygiene practice could have prevented the condition?

a. Rinsing his skin daily with a nonabrasive cleanser to eliminate comedonal acne
b. Washing his bedsheets weekly to kill scabies mites
c. Being aware of and avoiding possible areas with poison ivy
d. Washing his exercise clothes after each use to prevent tinea

41. According to Raymond Cattell's theory of intelligence, fluid intelligence refers to problem-solving, abstract thought, and the ability to learn new things. At which life stage does fluid intelligence peak?

a. Adolescence
b. Early adulthood
c. Middle childhood
d. Late adulthood

42. Which of the following is NOT an example of a societal consequence of opioid abuse?

a. Perceived social isolation
b. Higher incarceration rates
c. Reduction in labor force participation
d. Increased rates of hepatitis C transmission

43. Bernice works in a rural county health department. After conversations with community members, she learns that many residents are unaware of health-related resources in the area. Residents also note that inadequate public transportation and limited hours at the local health clinic prevent many from accessing primary health care (e.g., wellness screenings). Which of the following opportunities for health education advocacy could Bernice use to respond to community feedback?

a. A health professional conference
b. A community resource guide
c. A school assembly
d. A health fair

44. Which of the following risk factors does NOT contribute to noncommunicable diseases?

a. Gender
b. Unhealthy diet
c. International travel
d. Tobacco use

45. Use the DECIDE model to respond to the following question: Jonathon has noticed that he and his partner, Charles, have been fighting regularly lately. Jonathon shares his observation with Charles, who tells Jonathon that he feels like Jonathon prioritizes work over their relationship. After talking more, they decide that they would like to increase the amount of time they spend together each week to ensure that both parties' needs are met. They would also like to avoid future related conflicts. After they discuss their needs, what is the most appropriate next step?

a. Consider the amount of time each will dedicate and the types of activities they can do together
b. Identify the best solution that meets both of their needs
c. Determine the root cause that is contributing to their conflict
d. Develop a schedule and implement a plan to spend more time together

46. Research suggests that a person who wants to prevent a communicable disease should do which of the following?

a. Avoid unprotected sex
b. Avoid tobacco use
c. Rinse his or her hands with water for 10 seconds after using the restroom
d. Consume fewer processed foods

47. Each of the following is an example of an effective way to assess learning needs EXCEPT:

a. A teacher conducts in-depth interviews with parents to determine students' cognitive abilities and preferred instruction strategies.
b. A teacher administers a post-assignment survey to identify students' experiences learning and applying the content.
c. A teacher uses prior knowledge gleaned from previous interactions with individuals of a cultural group to assess learning needs.
d. A teacher conducts a learning needs assessment for each student to evaluate content knowledge and preferred learning styles at the beginning of the year.

48. What is a confounding variable in research?

a. A characteristic that cannot be quantified
b. A factor that distorts the relationships between the causes and effects of phenomena
c. The condition that a researcher manipulates to produce a result
d. The outcome of an experiment

49. __________ is a complication that occurs during the second trimester in which a mother develops high blood pressure.

a. Breech birth
b. Preeclampsia
c. Gestational diabetes
d. Rh incompatibility

50. Unhealthy family dynamics are associated with poor attachment, poor communication, and emotional dysregulation. Which of the following risk factors related to family dynamics is LEAST likely to contribute to unhealthy relationships?

a. Rigid expectations of children
b. Intrusive parents
c. Preferential treatment among children
d. Diverse family structures

51. The first stage of Erik Erikson's psychosocial development theory occurs from birth to 18 months. During this stage, a person experiences his or her first conflict: trust vs. mistrust. Infants whose caregivers behave in ways that promote or reinforce mistrust are more likely to experience each of the following EXCEPT:

a. Difficulty regulating emotions
b. Poor decision-making
c. Memory problems
d. Formation of attachment bonds with untrustworthy people

52. A health teacher is planning a curriculum for her elementary school health course. She presents content that supports students across different age groups and developmental abilities. The content increases in complexity as students progress in the class and through grade levels. She also complements lessons with developmentally appropriate materials and age-appropriate activities. This refers to the ______ of the curriculum.

a. Sequence
b. Differentiation
c. Scope
d. Continuity

53. A new teacher is planning health lessons for the school year. What is the recommended first step to ensure that his curriculum aligns with the school's academic expectations?

a. Consult the Common Core standards for healthful living.
b. Refer to the Society of Health and Physical Educators (SHAPE America) national standards and grade level outcomes.
c. Review the National Commission for Health Education Credentialing (NCHEC) competencies.
d. Familiarize himself with district standards.

54. Each of the following is an example of self-analysis in the reflective pedagogical approach EXCEPT:

a. Keeping a journal
b. Reflection-in-practice
c. Teacher observations
d. Recording a class session to watch back

55. Individuals with low health literacy are often less likely to comply with a physician's medical directions, which could result in adverse health outcomes. Which strategy should a physician use to confirm a patient's comprehension?

a. The physician should summarize critical information at the end of the appointment.
b. The physician should use diagrams or draw pictures to explain complex medical concepts.
c. The physician should offer the patient multiple types of educational materials (e.g., pamphlet, visual diagram, video).
d. The physician should ask the patient to teach-back the health instructions.

56. A teacher wants to incorporate a kinesthetic activity into her lesson on the circulatory system. Which of the following activities best achieves her goals?

a. A student uses colored pencils to trace the circulation of blood through the body.
b. A student learns how to perform a blood pressure test to assess heart health and explain results to a patient.
c. A student listens to a song that describes the circulatory system (e.g., associated organs, characteristics, purpose).
d. A student writes a summary of the textbook chapter on the cardiovascular system.

57. Which of the following is an example of a responsible decision-making model?

a. Objectives and Key Results model
b. SODAS and ICED models
c. Decision tree
d. SMART framework

58. Which of the following is NOT an example of a curricular or extracurricular program that addresses student health needs?

a. Team sports
b. School health policy
c. Student health council
d. Cross-curricular health project

59. Dwayne is enjoying a meal with his family at a restaurant. His eight-month-old daughter begins coughing weakly, emitting soft and high-pitched sounds when she tries to inhale, and turning blue. What is the first step Dwayne should take?

a. Sweep the infant's mouth with a finger
b. Lay the infant face down along his forearm and strike with the palm of the hand
c. Use one hand to perform the traditional Heimlich maneuver on the infant's stomach
d. Deliver chest compressions along the infant's sternum with two or three fingers

60. "Sliding vs. deciding" is a concept used to describe the practice or absence of intentional decision-making in relationships, usually with specific regard to romantic relationships. A sliding decision may be the result of impulsivity, internal and/or external pressure to comply (e.g., personal or cultural values, peer pressure), poor communication, or convenience. Each of the following is a strategy to prevent sliding in a romantic relationship EXCEPT:

a. Discussing personal values and relationship goals early in the relationship
b. Exploring the advantages and disadvantages of a mutual decision before it is made
c. Dividing decision-making responsibilities equitably between partners
d. Establishing clear and healthy relationship boundaries with your romantic partner

61. Malaria is an infectious disease that is primarily spread from person-to-person when female mosquitoes infected by Plasmodium parasites bite humans. Which of the following is NOT used to prevent the spread of malaria?

a. Antimalarial drugs
b. The use of large water drums to trap mosquitoes
c. The use of protective clothing and bed netting
d. The use of insecticides

62. Which of the following healthy lifestyle goals adheres to the SMART goal model?

a. By the end of next month, I will lose 10 pounds by skipping breakfast three times per week.
b. Sometime in the next week, I will eat three servings of fruits and vegetables per day.
c. By the end of next month, I will work with a personal trainer to lose 30 pounds by exercising two hours per day.
d. By the end of three months from today, I will quit smoking cigarettes by using nicotine replacement therapy and creating a stress management plan.

63. Which of the following is NOT appropriate educational material from a professional organization, agency, or association that meets the needs of diverse audiences?

a. A scholarly article from the Journal of the American Medical Association
b. A closed-caption video on how to perform CPR from the American Heart Association
c. An interactive map that provides state-level data about health behaviors from the CDC
d. An infographic about positive nutrition habits from the US Department of Agriculture

64. A student is experiencing stress related to an upcoming exam. Which of the following is a poor coping strategy to alleviate stress?

a. Relaxing test performance expectations
b. Practicing meditation and breathing techniques
c. Reaching out to the teacher before the exam for extra help
d. Eliminating study breaks until the student gets all of his or her study guide questions correct

65. The sixth stage of Erik Erikson's psychosocial development theory occurs during young adulthood (i.e., between ages 18 and 40). Which of the following represents the developmental task a person experiences during this life stage?

a. A person develops intimate relationships outside of the family.
b. A person creates or nurtures things that will outlast himself or herself.
c. A person grows more confident performing work independently.
d. A person establishes an identity separate from their relatives.

66. Mr. Lewis is told that his lesson plan does not contain SMART objectives:

> Students will be able to identify the purpose and parts of the reproductive system by correctly labeling a graphic organizer containing male and female reproductive organs.

Which of the following components of a SMART objective is lacking from the original learning objective?

a. The objective is not time-bound.
b. The objective does not contain a way to measure student knowledge.
c. The objective is not achievable.
d. The activity is not relevant to the lesson.

67. Which of the following is NOT a modifiable health risk that can lead to obesity?

a. Polycystic ovary syndrome (PCOS)
b. Excessive consumption of processed foods
c. Too little sleep
d. A sedentary lifestyle

68. What is the first step in the DECIDE model?

a. Define the criteria
b. Decide to act
c. Develop a plan of action
d. Define the problem

69. Many drugs, such as nicotine, are addictive. Which neurotransmitter do these drugs cause the brain to release?

a. Endorphins
b. Dopamine
c. Adrenaline
d. Serotonin

70. What type of communication might a person use to reinforce messages and information conveyed in his or her casual speech?

a. Verbal communication
b. Written communication
c. Visual communication
d. Nonverbal communication

71. Which of the following organs is NOT involved in the release of hormones that initiate the development of secondary female sexual characteristics?

a. Pituitary gland
b. Hypothalamus
c. Gonads
d. Thyroid

72. Which of the following interventions is best suited for reducing the harmful long-term effects of exposure to adverse childhood experiences (ACEs)?

a. Increased access to affordable, high-quality childcare
b. Parenting skills classes that promote positive approaches to child discipline
c. Trauma-focused cognitive behavioral therapy
d. Legislation aimed at reducing corporal punishment

73. A teacher wants to establish behavioral expectations at the beginning of the school year. She values student input and wants to make sure that her classroom rules reflect student needs and expectations while also promoting student accountability. Which of the following classroom management strategies most aligns with her vision?

a. Collaborative classroom agreement
b. Positive behavioral interventions and supports
c. Classroom economy system
d. Individual behavior plan

74. The prefrontal cortex undergoes significant maturation during which developmental stage?

a. Early childhood
b. Middle childhood
c. Late childhood
d. Adolescence

75. A __________ assessment is a formal evaluation that is administered to students at the end of a lesson unit to assess student learning. Student performance is usually measured by an academic standard or benchmark.

a. Formative
b. Norm-referenced
c. Performance
d. Summative

76. A teacher confronts a student who is misbehaving during class. When confronted, the student explains that there is no point completing his assignment since he has yet to get the correct answer. Which of the following character education virtues should the teacher focus on to help the student?

a. Intellectual
b. Civic
c. Moral
d. Performance

77. After expressing her dissatisfaction with the unfair distribution of household chores to her parents, a young woman is told that children should be "seen and not heard." This expectation affects how comfortable she feels speaking up about injustices that she faces. Which type of factor best describes this influence?

a. Genetic
b. Cultural
c. Environmental
d. Intrinsic

78. Which part of the peripheral nervous system is responsible for directly controlling voluntary muscle movement and processing sensory information?

a. Somatic nervous system
b. Autonomic nervous system
c. Central nervous system
d. Sympathetic nervous system

79. During his second year of college, Omarion begins experiencing a growing and overwhelming feeling of hopelessness and notices drastic changes to his sleep patterns. Although he previously had high grades and participated in intramural soccer, he has suddenly lost all interest in going to class or exercising. He lacks motivation to get out of bed and has lost pleasure in most things he used to enjoy doing. After Omarion is evaluated, his doctor diagnoses him with major depressive disorder. Each of the following is a well-documented risk factor for major depressive disorder EXCEPT:

a. History of trauma and/or abuse
b. Perceived social isolation
c. Second-degree relative with a mood disorder
d. Traumatic brain injury

80. Which of the following is NOT true about the factors that influence diet?

a. Women require greater amounts of calcium and iron than men.
b. Older adults need fewer calories and more nutrients as they age.
c. Athletes should consume more calories and nutrients than nonathletes.
d. Pregnant women require the same number of calories as before pregnancy.

81. During the 12-month wellness check for Maria's infant, the doctor asks Maria about the infant's dental hygiene routine. The infant has two teeth that have erupted through the gums. Maria cleans her infant's gums and teeth after every feeding with water and a soft washcloth. She does not give her infant any beverages other than water and formula. The infant regularly eats solid foods with the family. Maria always tests the temperature of the bottle before giving it to her infant to make sure that the infant does not burn her gums. Which of the following habits should Maria alter to promote good oral health?

a. Maria should use a toothbrush on the infant's teeth instead of a washcloth.
b. The infant should not eat solid food.
c. Maria should give her infant orange juice fortified with vitamin D to promote teeth growth.
d. Maria should first take a small sip through the bottle when feeding the child to check its temperature.

82. Which of the following is NOT an effective strategy to demonstrate active listening skills while communicating with school staff, students, parents, or the community?

a. Repeating or summarizing the speaker's statements
b. Refraining from interrupting
c. Asking questions to clarify
d. Refraining from using facial expressions

83. Tuberculosis is an example of an illness caused by which living single-celled disease-causing agent that reproduces through binary fission?

a. Bacteria
b. Parasitic worms
c. Virus
d. Fungi

84. Identify the communication strategy used in the following scenario: a teacher helps two students identify the root of their dispute and guides them as they set boundaries that satisfy the needs and wants of both students.

a. Mediation
b. Negotiation
c. Active listening
d. Arbitration

85. How do state and district standards differ from national standards?

a. National standards are often more rigorous than state and district standards.
b. State and district standards may be more relevant to local norms.
c. National standards are based on findings from educational research, whereas school district standards are not.
d. State and school district standards are easier to align with course curriculum.

86. Individual responsibility to the environment refers to the actionable steps that a person takes to minimize his or her impact on the environment. Which behavior or strategy has the greatest potential to improve environmental health?

a. Recycling plastic waste
b. Supporting environmental networks and organizations
c. Retrofitting one's home with renewable energy sources
d. Consuming fewer animal-based foods

87. Which of the following is the strongest predictor of childhood obesity?

a. Sedentary lifestyle
b. Excessive calorie intake
c. Parental obesity
d. Irregular sleep patterns

88. After graduating from high school, Omar decides to pursue a degree in music theory. His parents share that they are disappointed with his career choice and attempt to persuade him to change his mind; however, they eventually tell Omar that they can "live with it." All three acknowledge their differences in opinion and do not discuss his decision further. This scenario is an example of which characteristic of healthy relationships?

a. Acceptance
b. Understanding
c. Tolerance
d. Empathy

89. Which of the following would NOT be a violation of the Family Educational Rights and Privacy Act (FERPA)?

a. A teacher accidentally discloses a student's grade to another student
b. A teacher discusses a middle schooler's grade with the student's parent
c. A teacher shares with another student that a student is absent from class because they have been suspended
d. A coach tells the rest of the team that the team captain will not be playing in the next game because they are failing too many classes

90. The FITT principles can be used to improve a person's workout plan. The difficulty of a person's workout refers to which element?

a. Frequency
b. Intensity
c. Time
d. Type of exercise

91. Dr. Fleishman is conducting a nine-month wellness check when she notices that despite normal past wellness checks, the lethargic infant avoids eye contact and does not smile or make any vocal sounds. Since the last wellness check, the infant's weight has drastically declined. After running a few tests, Dr. Fleishman diagnoses the infant with non-organic failure to thrive. Which of the following interventions would be most effective at preventing exacerbation of the child's condition?

a. An anomaly scan to screen for genetic disorders
b. Breastfeeding classes
c. Consult with a social worker to ensure that the infant's family has enough food to eat
d. A barium swallow to test for gastrointestinal abnormalities

92. Spina bifida is a neural tube defect that is clinically evident from birth and occurs when a fetus's spinal cord does not develop properly in utero. What type of disease is spina bifida?

a. Infectious
b. Congenital
c. Hereditary
d. Lifestyle

93. Yoga best exemplifies which of the four types of exercise?

a. Flexibility
b. Balance
c. Endurance
d. Strength

94. Markel is a school health educator who is interested in improving parent involvement in student health education. Prior to implementing an intervention, Markel should take which of these actions?

a. Administer a community health assessment to evaluate parental health status.
b. Conduct a teacher focus group to collect information about teachers' perspectives of parental interest.
c. Invite parents to facilitate after-school health education programs.
d. Host a listening session to gather opinions from parents about health-related curricula and out-of-school activities.

95. A community health assessment (CHA) contains information about a community's health status, needs, assets, and barriers to well-being that is collected by state, local, and tribal health entities. CHAs are often used to influence local and state health policy. Each of the following factors that impact health policy is assessed in a CHA EXCEPT:

a. Demographics (e.g., age, race, gender)
b. Socioeconomic status (e.g., poverty rate, academic achievement)
c. Total community health-related expenditure
d. Available community resources

96. A middle school has recently seen a major uptick in the frequency of fights between students throughout the past month. Which of the following is the best policy response to implement in this situation to prevent further violent incidents?

a. Increasing the security presence on campus
b. Implementing a zero-tolerance policy that assigns suspensions to anyone involved in fights
c. Implementing a universal school-based prevention program for violent or aggressive behavior
d. Performing regular behavioral risk assessments to identify and discipline students at risk for violence

97. An eighth-grade health education teacher is planning a new unit on sexual health to incorporate into her classroom curriculum. She should pay attention to each of the following factors to ensure the lessons are compliant with academic regulations and ethical considerations EXCEPT:

a. Developmental and emotional maturity of students
b. Content standards
c. Student interest
d. Parental approval

98. In conjunction with individual therapy and medication, which of the following strategies is most effective at reducing hospital readmission and relapses in symptoms and improving overall social functioning in individuals with schizophrenia?

a. Electroconvulsive therapy
b. Supported employment
c. Supportive family therapy
d. Group psychotherapy

99. Harry and Matt are working together on an upcoming school project. Harry wants to make sure that their work is equitably distributed and completed before the due date, so he decides to delegate tasks and assign project milestones. As the project due date inches closer, Harry notices that Matt has not completed any of his work. Harry has had a hard time reasoning with Matt before, so he decides to work alone to avoid a dispute. Which type of decision-making does Harry use to resolve the conflict?

a. Unilateral decision-making
b. Collaborative decision-making
c. Third-party intervention
d. Joint decision-making

100. A/an __________ teaching style creates a classroom in which students are highly involved and engaged, yet the teacher has very little control over his or her students.

a. authoritarian
b. uninvolved
c. authoritative
d. indulgent

101. Which of the following is NOT one of the CDC's eight components of coordinated school health?

a. Health education
b. Nutrition services
c. Healthy and safe school environment
d. Health insurance

102. "Love bombing" is a manipulative tactic used by a person to force dependence on and gain control over another person. Each of the following is an example of an unhealthy relationship trait associated with love bombing EXCEPT:

a. Excessive affection
b. Constant communication
c. Withholding romantic feelings
d. Possessiveness

103. A woman with a family history of breast cancer who wants to lower her risk of cancer should do all the following EXCEPT:

a. Get genetic testing to see if she has a BRCA mutation
b. Regular breast cancer screenings
c. Limit alcohol consumption
d. Refrain from breastfeeding her infant

104. Which of the following represents a primary preventative strategy for mental illness?

a. A safety plan for a person experiencing suicidal thoughts
b. A mental illness awareness campaign
c. A depression screening for a person with a history of self-harm
d. A school suicide hotline for students after the death of a peer

105. Which of the following strategies does NOT appeal to the needs of diverse audiences?

a. The inclusion of complementary photographs, simple illustrations, or other visual media
b. The use of technical language
c. The use of bulleted text to break up long paragraphs
d. The use of targeted messages that address the cultural needs of the intended audience

106. Which of the following is NOT one of the 10 components of the Whole School, Whole Community, Whole Child (WSCC) model?

a. Employee wellness
b. Community health policy
c. Family engagement
d. Physical environment

107. Using the DECIDE decision-making model, identify the next step a student should take in the following scenario.

A 17-year-old student goes over to a close friend's home for a sleepover. After talking for a while, the friend excuses herself and returns with two beers. The student hesitates when the friend offers her a beer. The friend explains that her parents let her drink whenever she wants and pressures the student to drink with her. After defining the problem (underage drinking) and establishing the criteria (avoid harm or injury, maintain relationship with friend), what should the student do?

a. Develop a plan of action.
b. Identify the best solution
c. Consider the possible choices
d. Evaluate the results

108. A 33-year-old man has recently been diagnosed with prediabetes. He smokes two cigarettes per day and eats a sandwich, chips, and a cookie for lunch most days. He plays soccer for two and a half hours after work once per week. Which modifiable behavior can he adopt to most significantly reduce his risk of developing type 2 diabetes?

a. Replace processed meats with lean beef cuts
b. Quit smoking
c. Exercise more
d. Replace refined sugars with 100% fruit juice

109. Tyler and Jose have recently moved in together. Conflict arises between the two when they discuss splitting the cost of their living expenses. Jose makes a significantly higher salary than Tyler yet thinks that they should split their bills evenly. Although Tyler does not believe that it is fair, he forgoes any dispute and obliges Jose to resolve the conflict as soon as possible. What style of conflict management is Tyler using?

a. Avoidance
b. Compromise
c. Collaboration
d. Accommodation

110. Intimate partner violence (IPV) refers to abuse that occurs within an intimate or romantic relationship (e.g., physical violence, sexual violence, stalking, aggression). Which of the following is NOT generally considered a risk factor for IPV?

a. Witnessing IPV between parents during childhood
b. Living in impoverished communities
c. High self-esteem
d. Prior history of victimization

111. A person with a/an ____________ communication style effectively and respectfully expresses his or her wants, needs, and emotions and considers the needs of others.

a. assertive
b. aggressive
c. passive
d. passive-aggressive

112. Which of the following research methods can be easily administered to a large sample group to collect health data yet may be subject to sampling or nonresponse bias?

a. Case studies
b. In-depth interviews
c. Observations
d. Surveys

113. You are attending a conference on a complex topic and are engaged in a conversation with one of the presenters during a break. How can you show that you are actively listening to the presenter's ideas and facilitate further conversation?

a. Provide direct solutions to the speaker's problem.
b. Ask open-ended questions to clarify what the speaker means.
c. Agree with everything the speaker says to show support.
d. Share personal anecdotes that relate to the topic at hand.

114. A middle-aged man wants to reduce his risk of heart disease. Which preventative strategies should he consider using to reduce or prevent the onset of heart disease?

a. Aim to eat 3.5 oz (about 99.22 g) of red meat per day.
b. Maintain a more sedentary lifestyle to avoid stressing his heart.
c. Eat foods that lower his LDL cholesterol levels.
d. Aim to lose 30 lb in one month.

115. A teacher seeking to evaluate his or her advanced knowledge of health education should pursue which of the following continuing education and professional development strategies?

a. Participate in the Physical Activity Leader (PAL) Learning System training from the Society of Health and Physical Educators (SHAPE America)
b. Pursue a Certified Health Education Specialist (CHES) certification from the National Commission for Health Education Credentialing (NCHEC)
c. Attend a Center for Online Resources and Education (CORE) conference from the Society for Public Health Education (SOPHE)
d. Participate in self-studies with the American School Health Association's (ASHA) Journal of School Health (JOSH)

116. A teacher is creating a grading rubric for an upcoming project on disease types and prevention. He will be grading students on several project components (e.g., content knowledge, presentation skills, teamwork). The teacher wants the rubric to clearly and adequately define the expectations and provide grading flexibility. Which of the following rubrics aligns best with his vision?

a. Holistic
b. Checklist-form
c. Analytic
d. Developmental

117. What type of disease is described in the following example: a person contracts norovirus after having direct contact with an ill person experiencing similar symptoms (e.g., stomach pain, vomiting, and diarrhea)?

a. Chronic
b. Infectious
c. Secondary
d. Congenital

118. Which of the following is LEAST likely to reduce the risk of sexually transmitted diseases?

a. Intrauterine device
b. Female condoms
c. HPV vaccine
d. Abstinence

119. According to group dynamics theory, ________ groups are formed voluntarily among individuals with similar interests and shared goals.

a. friendship
b. interest
c. task
d. functional

120. Social responsibility and ethics theory suggests that a person has a duty to act in a way that benefits and protects the best interests of the local community. Which of the following examples best represents directly fulfilling this civic responsibility to one's community?

a. A person receives the flu vaccine to reduce rates of transmission in his family.
b. A member of a local congregation tithes 10 percent of her income to support her church program.
c. A regional grocer donates a portion of the business's earnings to a local food bank to increase food access to low-income populations.
d. A person reduces the number of products he or she purchases that contain single-use plastics to reduce plastic pollution.

Answer Key and Explanations

1. C: Implementing family-friendly work policies (e.g., remote work, paid childcare, flexible work schedule) is an example of strengthening economic supports to families because these policies allow parents to fulfill their duties as an employee and caregiver more effectively. Higher minimum wages are also an example of strengthening economic supports.

2. D: Population-level health interventions are strategies that are delivered to a large group of individuals aimed at preventing or addressing known causes of disease. While physical activity is known to reduce the risk of many chronic diseases, the preventative or curative effects are limited to the participating members of the running club. Health promotion, health education, and policy are examples of population-level interventions that can prevent chronic diseases within a population.

3. A: WIC programs are government nutritional subsidies for women, infants, and children. WIC enrollment is typically performed at local health agencies (e.g., WIC office, local health department, social service agencies). A school health clinic practitioner may refer a parent to a WIC enrollment location. School-based health clinics provide a range of health services (e.g., mental health, eye and dental care, sick visits, sports physicals, and health education). However, they should not be used as a replacement for primary care.

4. C: Protein is needed to build and repair cells and body tissue. Carbohydrates are the main energy source. Fats also provide energy for the body but also protect organs, support cell function, and absorb nutrients. Minerals and vitamins support growth and development and help body systems function. Water helps regulate temperature, carries nutrients and oxygen, and protects organs like the brain.

5. B: A teacher has no professional, legal, or ethical responsibility to share student questions about contraception with a parent or caregiver. Permission slips offer parents the opportunity to opt out of school-led sensitive education topics. Teachers are mandatory reporters, which means that they are required to report any form of abuse.

6. A: Frank is practicing assertiveness. He uses "I" statements to express his frustration and shares why he feels that way. He clearly expresses his needs, and he also seeks to understand what is preventing his housemate from doing his fair share of the household chores. By seeking to understand, he is demonstrating his respect for his housemate's feelings and needs while establishing an opportunity to collaboratively solve the problem.

7. C: An epidemiologist is responsible for disease surveillance and disease risk assessment. A person interested in health education and health advocacy should consider a career as a community health worker. Public health nurses and other medical practitioners are responsible for illness and injury prevention, health promotion, and health education. Biostatisticians use statistics to conduct public health research (e.g., develop public health research methodologies, collect and analyze data, and communicate results to influence programs and policy).

8. D: A copper IUD is a 99 percent effective nonhormonal contraception that lasts up to 12 years. It is the most appropriate option since Suzanne would like a long-term solution that requires little maintenance. While progestin implants are equally effective and last up to five years, implants release the hormone progestin to prevent ovulation and obstruct sperm by thickening cervical mucus. Depo-Provera shots—also called Depo shots or birth control shots—are also 99 percent effective. However, birth control shots must be administered every three months. Female or internal condoms are less than 80 percent effective and must be used every time that a couple has sexual intercourse. Similarly, male condoms must be used every time but are slightly more effective (approximately 87 percent effective). Condoms are the only contraceptive option of those listed that also prevent STD transmission.

9. C: Reciprocal determinism is one of the key constructs in Social Cognitive Theory (SCT). According to reciprocal determinism, a person's actions influence and are influenced by individual factors (e.g., beliefs, attitudes, cognition, skills), behavioral factors, and environmental factors. For example, a student who dislikes reading because he does not perform at grade level (individual factor) and his teacher is rude to him (environmental factor) refuses to participate in class (behavioral factor).

10. A: The instructional strategy described in the scenario—a jigsaw activity—is an example of cooperative learning. Students collaborate to become "experts" in the subject area content and then are reorganized into new groups. They present their research to the members of their new group. Students must employ listening skills, problem-solving skills, effective communication, and accountability.

11. D: Although being in a car accident can certainly cause stress, it is not a risk factor of suicide. Risk factors include previous suicide attempts, history of mental illness, serious or chronic illness, criminal or legal problems, financial problems, substance use, and history of abuse in childhood. Although the car accident could contribute to a risk factor of suicide (e.g., causing financial problems), it is not a risk factor itself.

12. B: Although the health enthusiast has a keen interest in heart health, he or she is not a credible source of information since the health enthusiast holds no formal certification. Since the information is presented through a personal blog post, the information may be misrepresented, inaccurate, or biased. Valid sources of health information can be found through government websites and materials. Nonprofits and medical or health-related associations are also valid sources of health information.

13. D: Body composition refers to the percentage of muscle, fat, water, and bone in a person's body. It is often separated into lean mass (i.e., all nonfat components like muscle, bone, and water) and fat. Body composition is a helpful tool to assess health since excess fat can contribute to and exacerbate symptoms of chronic diseases. Body mass index (BMI) is the measure of a person's body fat based on the ratio of height to weight. While BMI is a tool frequently used to evaluate healthy weight status, it does not always accurately depict body composition. Muscle is much denser than fat, so a person with a high percentage of lean muscle may be inaccurately classified within the overweight or obese BMI categories.

14. C: During the luteal phase, the corpus luteum—a cell mass that produces progesterone—thickens the lining of the uterus to encourage a fertilized egg to implant. If no implantation occurs, the body transitions into the menstrual phase. During this stage, progesterone and estrogen levels decline and the uterine lining sheds. The follicular phase begins when the hypothalamus cues the release of follicle-stimulating hormone (FSH) from the pituitary gland. In response to FSH, follicles containing immature eggs are created in the ovaries and one egg begins to mature. Estrogen hormone levels rise to accommodate the egg, which signals the release of luteinizing hormone (LH) from the pituitary gland. The presence of LH prompts the beginning of the next phase: ovulation. During this phase, the mature egg travels toward the uterus via the fallopian tube for fertilization and the body transitions back into the luteal phase.

15. A: Agriculture consumes the largest amount of water in the US. Therefore, a water conservation intervention that incentivizes the installation of highly efficient watering systems has the potential for greater impact than the other strategies.

16. C: Photos with attached metadata (e.g., location, date, and time the image was shot) may contain personal information. Social media posts with a tagged location can also provide a person's exact location. By disabling location services, unwanted contact can be avoided.

17. A: Mediation is a conflict resolution strategy in which a third-party facilitator assists with reconciliation. Negotiation is conflict resolution that takes place between two parties. Litigation is a type of conflict resolution that takes place in court.

18. D: Avoidant attachment style typically occurs when a child experiences distant or unavailable caregivers. His or her strong sense of independence and self-sufficiency emerges as he or she learns to self-soothe, yet he or she is often unable to form deep relationships with others when he or she is older. Anxious attachment occurs when caregivers are inconsistent, which causes the child to develop confusion and anxiety. Those with anxious attachment are overly attentive to their partners and constantly seek their approval. Disorganized attachment develops when a child experiences trauma or abuse. Individuals with disorganized attachment long for closeness and intimacy, yet they often push others away. Those with secure attachment experience appropriate care and support and will usually cultivate healthy relationships.

19. B: Although parent interviews may elicit insightful information about her instructional practices, it is the least effective reflective process of teaching compared to the other answer choices. Journaling allows Mrs. McMullen to assess what parts of her lesson went well and did not go well. Peer observations can provide examples of effective instructional strategies and classroom engagement ideas, and student surveys generate feedback from those who are most directly impacted by her teaching.

20. C: Recent reports from organizations like the World Health Organization and the World Heart Federation state that any consumption of alcohol can increase the risk of chronic disease (e.g., heart disease, cancer) and injury. For those who partake, health practitioners recommend one to two drinks at most on days when alcohol is consumed. Behaviors that reduce the risk of chronic disease include regular exercise; abstaining from tobacco use; regularly consuming unsaturated fats, whole grains, and fruits and vegetables; regular health screenings; practicing good oral hygiene; sufficient sleep; knowing one's family health history; and limiting stress.

21. B: The woman described in the scenario is binge drinking, which is associated with dehydration, alcohol poisoning, unintentional injury, and risk-taking behaviors. Alcohol is also a mood-altering drug and can lead to intentional self-harm if the person is in poor mental health. Although repeated binge drinking can lead to alcohol addiction, it is unlikely she would develop an alcohol addiction after one instance of binge drinking.

22. B: Adaptive coping skills are behaviors that help a person manage or relieve stress in a healthy way (e.g., meditation, mindfulness, breathing, exercise, problem-solving). Maladaptive coping strategies are negative behaviors that relieve immediate stress but worsen stress overall. Examples include avoidance or procrastination, substance use, and self-harm.

23. A: Eustress is positive or good stress. It is often short-term and motivates or energizes a person to change (e.g., learn a new skill, start a new job, move to a new place). Distress is negative stress that causes anxiety and hinders performance (e.g., interpersonal conflict, unemployment, divorce). Acute stress is short-term and generally caused by a situational stressor. Academic stress refers to distress experienced by students related to school-related internal stressors (e.g., poor study habits and time management, academic achievement expectations) and external stressors (e.g., difficult assignments or high workload, poor teaching performance by educators). Like other forms of negative stress, academic stress can result in poor motivation, academic performance, and sleep hygiene along with an increased risk of depression and anxiety.

24. D: The target group—older female adolescents in a specific school district—is far more likely to receive the health message in a classroom setting by a health professional. The lecture may contain a combination of multiple methods (e.g., visuals, videos, written texts, games or interactive activities) that engage the target audience. Although many individuals within the target group are likely TikTok users, the app's content is curated to reflect viewers' interests. The videos are also less likely to be contained to the target group (i.e., adolescents attending school in a specific district). One-page graphics are an effective medium to share inclusive educational material since they contain images, diagrams, and short or bulleted text, among other features. However, the students may not use Facebook or follow the school district's Facebook page. A pamphlet is another useful method for delivering health messages; however, the pamphlet is not readily available to all individuals in the target group.

25. B: Contemplation follows precontemplation—the stage in which a person does not recognize or is uninterested in modifying his or her behavior—and precedes preparation—the stage in which a person commits to changing his or her behavior. Contemplation is the correct answer because the person has already acknowledged that his or her weight is unmanaged yet has not committed to actively losing it. In this stage, the person reviews the negative aspects of a health behavior and considers the benefits of behavior change.

26. C: According to the DECIDE model, the most appropriate first step is to define the problem. Yeslia should consult with the employee to define the challenges that he or she faces and any stressors causing his or her loss of productivity.

27. C: A vaccine contains an inactive virus that imitates infection and triggers an immune response. Vaccines help the immune system identify and mount an immune response when the virus is encountered in the future. Antibiotics are used to treat illnesses caused by bacteria. Antivirals can be used to lower viral transmission from an infected person to a noninfected person (e.g., HIV antivirals) and help the immune system fight off a virus once it has infected the host. However, antiviral treatments for HPV are not currently available. Antiprotozoal drugs are used to treat infections caused by protozoa.

28. A: Assuming that Tom will stop any unwanted sexual advances based on Louisa's nonverbal cues is the least effective strategy. Effective refusal skills include making excuses, making a joke, saying "no," redirecting the conversation, proposing alternative activities, and physically leaving the situation.

29. C: The endocrine system is responsible for making, releasing, and regulating hormones that affect mood and development. The respiratory system removes gases like carbon dioxide through gas exchange, the integumentary system removes waste through sweat glands in the skin, and the excretory system removes nitrogen-based wastes like urea through the kidneys and bladder.

30. A: The YRBSS is generated from the results of a survey administered to students in ninth to 12th grade every two years. Data related to violence, sexual behavior, alcohol and drug use, diet, and exercise are collected. The survey is conducted by the CDC and various state, local, tribal, and territorial governments. Since the survey is administered by government agencies, it is considered a valid and reliable data source.

31. C: Alcohol is a type of central nervous system depressant, and DTs is a severe form of alcohol withdrawal. It occurs most often among individuals who abruptly halt alcohol use after consuming excessive alcohol daily for more than one month, and it typically begins two to three days after the onset of withdrawal. Death can occur from high body temperatures and seizures.

32. D: The first step a person should take when encountering a scenario like this is to call 911 and follow the dispatcher's instructions. Usually, the second step is to find an AED as it can help to guide a trained or untrained person through CPR, monitor vital signs, and administer shocks if necessary. In this situation, After checking for responsiveness, breathing, and pulse and calling 911, Jessica would most likely be guided by the operator through the use of an AED. AEDs are intended to be usable by anyone, even if the individual is not CPR-certified. The American Heart Association recommends that an untrained person administer hands-only CPR. Hands-only CPR consists of chest compressions delivered at a rate of 100 beats per minute and a depth of two inches. Blind swipes of the mouth to remove foreign objects are no longer encouraged due to risks for further lodging the object into the airway. Conventional CPR consists of giving two breaths after every 30 compressions.

33. D: School health needs assessments collect data (e.g., achievement data, health status, health attitudes and behaviors of school stakeholders, community input) to determine the perceived or actual health needs and establish strategies for addressing those needs. Results may be used to establish school health goals, determine priorities for school health programs, and assess school health needs. Defining the purpose of the needs assessment (e.g., how it will be used, who will participate, defining the target population) is the first step in conducting a needs assessment.

34. D: During the formal operational stage, an individual achieves abstract thought. This stage typically begins around age 11 and continues through adolescence and adulthood. Sensorimotor stage occurs from birth to two years old. Infants learn about their environment through their senses, engage in basic problem-solving, and begin communicating. During the preoperational stage (ages two to seven), children begin to understand identity and cause-and-effect relationships. The third stage—concrete operational stage—occurs from ages seven to 11. During this stage, children master concrete thinking and improve their classification skills and spatial understanding.

35. B: Coronary artery disease develops when plaque accumulates within a person's coronary arteries and causes restricted blood flow to the heart. Coronary artery disease can lead to angina—pain due to restricted blood supply to the heart—and a heart attack (also called a myocardial infarction)—a complete blockage of blood to the heart that causes damage to the heart muscle. Cardiac arrest occurs when an electrical issue causes the heart to stop beating (e.g., ventricular fibrillation). Cardiac arrhythmia is an atypical heartbeat that happens when the heart beats irregularly (e.g., tachycardia, bradycardia). A blockage that develops in an artery in a person's lung is called a pulmonary embolism. It can inhibit blood flow to the lungs, causing lung damage, decreased blood flow to the heart, increased blood pressure, and death if left untreated.

36. C: There is insufficient data about whether or not victims of sexual abuse go on to become perpetrators of sexual violence. Risk factors for being a victim of sexual abuse include low self-esteem, loneliness, poor refusal skills, unmonitored computer and social media use, having a disability, identifying as LGBTQ+, experiencing prior domestic abuse, and substance use and/or abuse. Sexual abuse is more frequent in cultures and societies that hold discriminatory gender stereotypes, strict gender roles, and/or have poor institutional support or lack anti-sexual violence legislation.

37. A: This activity is an example of guided discovery. Guided discovery is a student-centered, inquiry-based instructional strategy that encourages students to explore the material independently or collaboratively.

38. C: A person who avoids sharing his or her opinions or feelings is exhibiting passive communication. Using "I" statements and seeking to understand the speaker's point of view can promote understanding and compassion within both parties. Setting boundaries can establish acceptable behavior and encourage accountability.

39. B: According to the EPA, a single round-trip flight across the country equates to nearly 20 percent of the greenhouse gases that a person's car generates in a year, making choice B the most effective. Adjustments to a person's thermostat produce the greatest energy savings in the home since HVAC appliances account for nearly 40 to 50 percent of one's electricity use. Avoiding fast fashion by purchasing used or vintage clothes and composting food waste are also effective strategies for reducing one's carbon footprint. However, they are not as effective as replacing flying with driving.

40. D: Leopold most likely has tinea (also known as ringworm) since the rash is itchy, scaly, and circular in shape. Tinea often develops from skin-to-skin contact or indirect contact (e.g., touching a contaminated surface) and thrives in hot and moist conditions. Regular bathing, handwashing, and washing clothes can prevent the spread of the fungal infection. Since tinea fungi thrive in moist and hot environments, keeping the skin clean and dry is an effective preventative method. Those who engage in heavy exercise or are prone to excessive sweating should wash their clothes regularly to avoid infection. Animals are frequent carriers of tinea, so regularly checking animals' skin for signs of infection and handwashing before and after touching animals can prevent tinea.

41. B: Fluid intelligence peaks in early adulthood (approximately ages 20 to 30) before declining slowly; however, different components of fluid intelligence peak at different ages. For example, information processing typically peaks around ages 18 to 20, and short-term memory plateaus around age 25 before declining around age 30. Crystallized intelligence—the other type of intelligence in Cattell's theory of intelligence—refers to knowledge and facts acquired throughout a person's life.

42. A: Perceived social isolation is an example of an intrapersonal or individual-level consequence of opioid abuse. As with other forms of substance abuse, individuals with opioid addictions experience stronger feelings of loneliness. Higher rates of drug-related incarceration, reduced labor and economic participation, and increased rates of drug-related disease transmission are examples of consequences that impact the broader community. Physiological consequences differ based on the substance ingested but can include weakened immunity, poor memory and decision-making, brain damage, liver damage, and heart conditions. Psychological impacts of substance abuse are paranoia, aggression, impulsiveness, and poor self-control and judgement. Substance abuse can lead to arrests and fines, which can impact a person's ability to secure employment and maintain healthy relationships.

43. D: The purpose of a health fair is to provide information about health, share local resources, and offer basic preventative medical screenings for participants. Although the community resource guide is a useful tool for those seeking services, the community expressed a need for medical screenings and basic preventative care. Health professional conferences and school assemblies may be used to deliver health education, but the target population is limited to health practitioners and the school community, respectively. A health fair could be held at more convenient times and locations to better accommodate the community.

44. C: International travel can be a risk factor for communicable (infectious) diseases. There are three broad risk categories for noncommunicable (chronic) diseases: nonmodifiable factors (e.g., gender, race, age, genetics), modifiable factors (e.g., diet, exercise, stress, sleep patterns), and metabolic risk factors (e.g., obesity, high blood pressure).

45. A: Jonathon and Charles have defined the problem (Charles feels Jonathon is more focused on work than their relationship) and established the criteria (Jonathon and Charles will increase the amount of time they spend together each week to ensure both of their needs are met). The next step in the DECIDE model is to consider the possible choices; therefore, the next best step is to consider the amount of time they will dedicate each week and the types of activities they can do together.

46. A: Safe sex (e.g., wearing a condom, seeking regular STI tests) can prevent communicable diseases transmitted through sexual activity. Consuming fewer processed foods and avoiding tobacco use are effective practices for preventing chronic diseases. Regular handwashing is crucial for staving off communicable diseases. However, in order to prevent communicable diseases, one should lather for at least 20 seconds with soap and water instead of only rinsing. Other behaviors to prevent infectious diseases include immunization, isolating when sick, quarantining when exposed to an infected person, cleaning surfaces often, and preparing food safely.

47. C: While interactions with individuals of a different cultural group can unearth new perspectives, a teacher should discuss cultural norms and beliefs with current students to assess learning needs. In-depth interviews with parents, pretests and learning needs assessments, and posttests are effective strategies for assessing learning needs. Teachers may also consult previous teachers and content standards to determine a student's actual and anticipated developmental progress and cognitive abilities.

48. B: Confounding variables are factors that distort the relationship between the independent variable (the cause) and the dependent variable (the effect). For example, confounding variables like metabolic rate, gender, or calorie intake could skew the results of research on the relationship between exercise and weight loss. If confounding variables are not considered, they may lead to inaccurate interpretations of data.

49. B: Preeclampsia is a pregnancy complication that typically occurs after 20 weeks of pregnancy. Mothers with preeclampsia develop hypertension that persists throughout the remainder of their pregnancy and occasionally after the birth. Mothers with gestational diabetes develop high blood sugar levels that typically cease after birth, but it can increase the mother's and child's likelihood of developing type 2 diabetes later in life. The Rhesus (Rh) factor refers to the negative or positive designation after a person's blood type (e.g., O positive, AB negative). Rh is a protein on the surface of a person's red blood cells. Rh incompatibility is a pregnancy complication that occurs when an Rh-negative mother carries an Rh-positive fetus. The mother's immune system may misidentify the Rh-positive red blood cells as foreign material and produce antibodies that attack the fetal red blood cells. The mother does not experience any complications, but the fetus can develop hemolytic anemia. A breech birth refers to the position of the infant during delivery (e.g., infant is delivered feetfirst or buttocks-first).

50. D: Diverse family structures refer to different formations of family beyond the conventional nuclear family. Examples include single-parent, foster-parent, or adoptive parent families; blended families (e.g., half siblings, relatives by marriage); non-parent relatives or intergenerational households; or LGBT parents. Although some family structures may increase stress (e.g., single-parent households) due to the loss of a caregiver or financial security, diverse family structures are not associated with producing unhealthy relationships.

51. C: Infants whose caregivers violate their trust (e.g., fail to meet physical or emotional needs, expose the infant to unsafe environment) often fail to develop appropriate or trusting relationships with others. They are more likely to be mistrustful of others or form relationships with untrustworthy individuals since their caregivers failed to model trust to them as infants. They are also more likely to have poor emotional regulation and decision-making and experience depression or anxiety. Although memory problems can be often associated with conditions like depression and anxiety, memory is not typically impacted by unresolved trust vs. mistrust conflicts.

52. A: Sequence refers to the order that skills are taught, whereas scope refers to the topics and amount of content. Since the teacher is creating a curriculum that is ordered by developmental abilities and content knowledge, this refers to the curriculum sequence.

53. D: Each district may have its own set of academic standards that educators are expected to follow. The local district must also satisfy state and national standards, so the local standards are the strictest level of standardization and the most helpful for a teacher to be familiar with to ensure he or she is meeting the school expectations. District standards may be based on SHAPE America's standards. Common Core does not have health-related standards, and the NCHEC competencies refer to the roles and responsibilities of Certified Health Education Specialists (CHES).

54. C: Teacher observations are a common reflective teaching strategy that consist of another educator or administrator observing a teacher's class. They typically evaluate the success of a teacher's instructional strategies, the clarity of his or her lesson delivery, student participation, and classroom management. The observer debriefs with the teacher afterward. Each of the other strategies constitute self-analysis.

55. D: The teach-back method is an effective strategy to gauge patient understanding. It can be helpful for embedding important instructions and correcting any inaccurate information. Summarizing critical information, using visual aids, and offering multiple complementary educational materials are helpful strategies for reinforcing health education, but not necessarily for confirming comprehension.

56. B: Kinesthetic activities are those that require students to physically manipulate or touch something or move their own bodies. Writing and drawing, though they require students to use pencils or pens, are not usually considered kinesthetic activities. Listening is not a kinesthetic activity.

While learning styles do vary some from person to person, all people do need learn from visual information, auditory information, and by hands-on learning. Different materials lend themselves to a different format, but where possible, the best practice when presenting information to others is to use a mixture of formats, including hands-on materials, visual, and auditory information to keep the materials engaging to all learners.

57. B: SODAS (situation, options, disadvantages, advantages, and solution) and ICED (identify the problem, create alternatives, evaluate the alternatives, and decide on the best solution) are decision-making frameworks that guide students through responsible decision-making. Decision trees and other flowcharts can help students visually organize components of a decision-making model; however, they are not frameworks. The Objectives and Key Results model and the SMART framework are used for setting goals.

58. B: Although school health policy is an effective means of addressing student health, it is not a curricular or extracurricular program. Curricular and extracurricular activities like health and physical education, social-emotional learning, after-school programs, team sports, and community service programs can improve health knowledge, build self-efficacy, and promote positive health habits.

59. B: If an infant shows signs of severe choking, such as struggling to breathe, weak or ineffective coughing, high-pitched or no sounds when trying to breathe, and turning blue, you should use a sequence of back blows and chest thrusts. Do not perform abdominal (Heimlich) thrusts on infants. The infant should be laid face down on the rescuer's forearm, supported on the thigh, with the head lower than the body, and receive five firm back blows with the heel of the hand between the shoulder blades. If the object does not dislodge, turn the infant face up and give five chest thrusts with two fingers on the sternum; alternate back blows and chest thrusts until the object is expelled or the infant becomes unresponsive.

60. C: Sliding can be avoided by discussing personal values and visions or goals for the relationship, exploring the pros and cons, logistics, and possible outcomes of a potential decision, and establishing healthy boundaries and conflict resolution strategies. Although decision-making should be shared, both parties should be active and present for each decision. This can prevent miscommunication of wants, needs, and values as well as potential conflict.

61. B: Standing water is the ideal breeding location for mosquitos—large water drums full of stagnant water may attract mosquitoes and encourage reproduction. Antimalarial drugs are commonly used to prevent malaria and alleviate symptoms experienced by an infected person, and protective clothing and bed netting prevent mosquito bites.

62. D: SMART is an acronym for specific, measurable, achievable, relevant, and time-bound. Answer D is the correct answer because the person identifies a specific goal to stop smoking cigarettes. The goal is also measurable since progress can be assessed by counting how many cigarettes have been smoked. The goal is achievable because three months is a reasonable amount of time to quit smoking cigarettes. Nicotine replacement therapy and stress management plans are relevant strategies for achieving the goal. The goal is time-bound because the individual has three months to complete the goal. Although answer C contains many of the elements of the SMART model, exercising two times a day and losing 30 pounds in one month is not an achievable goal for most. Answer A is not correct because skipping breakfast three times per week is not relevant or achievable.

63. A: Although a scholarly article from the Journal of the American Medical Association often contains in-depth research about a health topic, it is not accessible to diverse audiences. The article is likely to include scientific jargon, long block text, and few graphics. Materials and practices that are generally supportive of diverse audiences include those that use closed-captions or transcripts of videos and audio-based materials, use 12-point or larger font, chunk content or use bullet points, omit technical jargon, and use a colorblind-friendly palette. A teacher can make educational material more inclusive by omitting any culturally specific references to idioms and incorporating a range of diverse identities and experiences.

64. D: Answers A, B, and C are all positive coping skills that can ease the stress related to the student's test. Putting limits on activities and refraining from well-needed breaks can add to the stress the student is already experiencing.

65. A: Young adults experience a conflict between intimacy and isolation in Erikson's sixth stage. During this stage, young adults begin to develop extrafamilial bonds. Success depends on a strong formation of identity that occurs in stage five. Failure to form relationships with others leads to isolation and loneliness, which can affect later stages: generativity vs. stagnation in stage seven and integrity vs. despair in stage eight.

66. A: SMART goals are used in a variety of industries to ensure that goals are well designed. SMART refers to specific, measurable, achievable, relevant, and time-bound. Mr. Lewis' original learning objective is not time-bound. To fix this, he should include a target date or period of time that students will be able to achieve the learning objective. For example, he could include, "by the end of the lesson" or "by the end of the lesson unit."

67. A: PCOS is not a modifiable health risk. Although the exact cause is unknown, the condition is likely connected to abnormal hormone levels and heredity. PCOS can cause some weight gain, but since the condition is not curable, it is not a modifiable behavior. Modifiable behaviors for obesity include diet, physical activity, sleep, and stress.

68. D: The DECIDE model can be used to guide users through responsible decision-making. DECIDE is an acronym for define the problem (D), establish the criteria (E), consider the possible choices (C), identify the best solution (I), develop and implement the solution (D), and evaluate the solution (E).

69. B: Dopamine is the neurotransmitter responsible for pleasure and reward. The brain releases dopamine naturally when an individual does something pleasurable or satisfying, and it is intended to reinforce life-sustaining behaviors (e.g., eating). Some mood-altering drugs cause an immediate surge of dopamine in the body that produces intense feelings of pleasure. Although drugs like MDMA cause the brain to release large quantities of serotonin, this is not associated with addiction.

70. D: Verbal communication is the primary means of communication, whereas nonverbal communication is frequently used to reinforce messages or convey unspoken information (e.g., raising eyebrows to show surprise, maintaining eye contact to show active listening). Nonverbal communication consists of body language and facial expressions, and it can be intentional or unintentional.

71. D: Secondary sex characteristics (e.g., breast development, pubic and underarm hair growth, widening hips) develop during puberty due to the presence of female sex hormones such as estrogen and progesterone. These hormones are released by the gonads (ovaries). The ovaries release these hormones when the pituitary gland releases luteinizing hormone (LH) and follicle-stimulating hormone (FSH). The pituitary gland releases LH and FSH when exposed to gonadotropin-releasing hormone (GnRH), which is released by the hypothalamus. Although the thyroid is an endocrine organ, its hormones do not affect the development of secondary sex characteristics. Instead, thyroid hormones primarily regulate metabolism.

72. C: Trauma-focused cognitive behavioral therapy (TF-CBT) is an evidence-based treatment associated with reductions in depression, post-traumatic stress disorder, anxiety, and behavioral challenges in children. Participants in TF-CBT learn to challenge unhealthy and distorted thought patterns. Legislation aimed at reducing corporal punishment can change social norms and criminalize harsh punishment of children, yet it does not reduce consequences among children already exposed to ACEs. Similarly, parenting skills classes and increased access to affordable, high-quality childcare are preventative approaches.

73. A: Creating a collaborative classroom agreement is an effective classroom management strategy that incorporates student input and promotes a culture of peer accountability. Students collaboratively create behavioral expectations, establish positive reinforcements for those who follow rules and disciplinary actions, and generate a shared understanding of the purpose of each rule.

74. D: Adolescence takes place between ages 13 and 18. During this stage, teenagers undergo significant physical changes and hormonal development. Their prefrontal cortexes—the part of the brain responsible for decision-making and judgement—undergo significant maturation. The prefrontal cortex is one of the last regions of the brain to mature and typically finishes around age 25.

75. D: Summative assessments evaluate student comprehension and learning progress at the end of a lesson unit, academic quarter, or grade level. They are considered formal and high stakes. Formative assessments are usually informal continuous assessments of student comprehension. They are considered low stakes and consist of activities like entrance and exit tickets, sticky note self-assessments, thumbs-up responses, or anonymous polls. Performance assessments measure learning through application of content or tasks. They may be formal or informal. Norm-referenced assessments measure student knowledge compared to the "norm" (e.g., students of a similar age or developmental level).

76. D: Character education consists of intellectual (e.g., curiosity, autonomy), civic (e.g., engagement, consideration), moral (e.g., honesty, compassion), and performance (e.g., motivation, perseverance) virtues. The teacher should focus on performance virtues since the student's misbehavior is a result of lack of motivation due to low confidence.

77. B: This scenario is an example of how culture influences family dynamics. These dynamics vary widely within societies and often have generational effects. This type of response may condition the children in this family to be more submissive to adults and other authorities in general. The type of response that individuals have to their family dynamics can vary widely, as individuals may either retain their family views or develop contrary beliefs that they bring into their own relationships and new family units later in life. Genetic factors are not conditioned by behavior but are biological and inherited. Environmental factors are a broader category that refer to external influences, including culture, but also include the physical environment and access to resources in society. Finally, intrinsic factors are personal motivations that are not influenced by external situations.

78. A: The nervous system consists of the peripheral and central nervous systems. The peripheral nervous system is made of nerves and contains the somatic and autonomic nervous systems. The somatic nervous system controls voluntary movement (e.g., walking, talking) and transmits sensory information to the brain. The autonomic nervous system controls involuntary processes (e.g., breathing, digestion). The autonomic system is further divided into the sympathetic and parasympathetic system. The sympathetic nervous system adjusts body processes to respond to stress or danger (e.g., fight or flight), while the parasympathetic nervous system slows down body processes (e.g., rest and digest). The brain and spinal cord make up the central nervous system, which is responsible for decision-making and information processing.

79. C: Risk factors for major depressive disorder include adverse childhood experiences (e.g., death of a loved one, abuse, trauma), low social support, and traumatic brain injuries. A person with a first-degree relative (e.g., parent, sibling) has a two to three times greater risk of developing major depressive disorder. There is little evidence demonstrating an association between second-degree relatives (e.g., aunt, uncle, grandparents) and an increased risk of developing a mood disorder like major depressive disorder.

80. D: Women require a greater number of calories and nutrients when they are pregnant to ensure optimal fetal development. Older adults need fewer calories, but they need more nutrients since nutrient absorption slows with age. Athletes need more energy and nutrients to replenish burned calories and maximize recovery. Women require more calcium because they are more prone to bone deterioration. They are also at a greater risk of anemia due to blood loss during menstruation.

81. A: It is generally recommended to begin using a toothbrush as soon as the first tooth erupts. A moistened washcloth is recommended for infants before they develop their first tooth. Infants can eat solid food usually after around 6 months. Juice and milk are acceptable but should be given in moderation. Unlimited access to juice and milk, especially unsupervised in a crib, increases the risk of dental caries. Bacteria that causes dental decay is transmissible from an adult to an infant; therefore, it is recommended that Maria avoid putting her mouth on the bottle.

82. D: Using facial expressions can demonstrate that the listener is engaged and actively listening. It is one way in which a person can use body language to show that he or she is interested in the conversation.

83. A: Bacteria are unicellular, prokaryotic microorganisms that exist nearly everywhere. Some are pathogenic (like the bacteria that causes tuberculosis), yet most are helpful (e.g., aid in digestion, nitrogen fixation). Viruses are nonliving agents that infect host cells and reproduce as the host cell replicates. Fungi are multicellular eukaryotic organisms that rely on spores to reproduce. Parasitic worms are multicellular organisms that drain nutrients from their host.

84. A: The teacher is acting as a mediator in the scenario. Although mediation and negotiation are both used to resolve disputes between two parties, mediation requires the use of a third party to facilitate resolution whereas negotiation is only between the two disputing parties. Active listening is a tool that one can use when mediating or negotiating since it helps build trust and understanding between parties.

85. B: State and district standards are often more relevant to local norms, and they may be more reflective of local interests. Neither state, district, nor national standards are necessarily more rigorous, easier to implement, or less based on research than the others.

86. B: Individual actions on climate change are less effective than the implementation of larger-scale programs, governmental regulations (e.g., placing a cap on carbon emissions), and corporate responsibility legislation (e.g., restrictions related to environmental health for companies). By supporting environmental networks and organizations, one can be a part of these large-scale solutions. Although each of the other behaviors listed are helpful to the environment, they are not as effective as organized or systemic movements.

87. C: All of the answers are predictors of childhood obesity, but parental obesity is one of the strongest predictors. Parental obesity encompasses genetic, environmental, and family factors that contribute to childhood obesity. For example, obesity can alter the biochemical and hormonal environment in an expecting mother, which can impact fetal growth and development. Parents control what a child consumes and model eating patterns. Their health attitudes and health knowledge regarding nutrition and infant development can impact their child's dietary behaviors.

88. C: This scenario is an example of tolerance. Omar's parents tolerate his decision even though it is different than what they want. Omar's parents would have demonstrated acceptance if they affirmed his decision without trying to dissuade him. Neither Omar nor his parents attempted to understand each other's perspectives or empathize.

89. B: Discussion of a student's grades with their parent or guardian is allowed under FERPA as long as the student is under the age of 18 and is not attending a post-secondary educational institution. Each of the other answer choices are FERPA violations. Even if the violation is accidental, the teacher or staff member can still be held liable for violating FERPA.

90. B: Intensity refers to how difficult one's workout is. Frequency is how often a person works out, time is how long a person's exercise session is, and type refers to the type of exercise (e.g., cardio, strength training).

91. C: Both organic and non-organic failure to thrive (FTT) lead to stunted physical and mental development (e.g., being underweight, fatigue, delayed motor skills). Unlike organic FTT, which is caused by an underlying physical condition, non-organic FTT is commonly caused by neglect. Infants who develop non-organic FTT often have mothers suffering from depression, excessive stress, and/or substance abuse that inhibits their ability to properly care for their infant. Prenatal classes about infant feeding skills or needs (e.g., how to breastfeed, infant nutritional needs) can prevent non-organic FTT. Since the infant has likely transitioned to eating solid foods, breastfeeding classes would do little to treat non-organic FTT in this situation. Consulting with a social worker can help identify any social or economic barriers to infant feeding and connect the infant's family to community resources to improve the infant's condition.

92. B: Congenital disorders are caused by inherited or environmental factors in utero and are present from birth. Since spina bifida is a malformation syndrome that is apparent from birth and can be caused by genetic, environmental, or nutritional factors, it is considered a congenital disorder. Hereditary diseases can only be caused by genetic mutations.

93. A: A well-rounded exercise program consists of flexibility (i.e., range of motion), balance (i.e., body coordination and stabilization), endurance (i.e., cardiorespiratory function), and strength (i.e., muscle mass and bone health). Although yoga can build strength and balance, it is most associated with flexibility.

94. D: Prior to implementing an intervention, Markel should collect data from the target population (e.g., host a listening session for parents to share their opinions about health education). A community health assessment is useful for understanding health status, needs, and barriers within a school; however, it is unlikely to illuminate parental perspectives about improving engagement in health education. Information about parental interest collected from a teacher focus group may be biased and inaccurate. Inviting parents to facilitate after-school programming is an example of an intervention. Without proper research on the feasibility of an intervention, the program may lack community interest and be ineffective.

95. C: Total community health-related spending is not typically included as a core component of CHAs. Available community resources, existing health programs and interventions, and other community assets are typically listed in the CHA to display how health issues are addressed. Demographics, socioeconomic statuses, and health data are collected to show a health snapshot of the community. Oftentimes, the data collected is used to demonstrate the need for policy change and how funds should be allocated to improve health outcomes.

96. C: A universal school-based violence prevention program delivers lessons and activities aimed at reducing violence and classroom disruption among students (e.g., social and anger management skills, problem-solving and conflict resolution, counseling). Programs are implemented schoolwide rather than on an individual level for identified students. Additional components like collaborative classroom activities, parental and community involvement, and school environment modifications can generate a stronger impact. There is little to no evidence that increasing the security presence or implementing punitive policies and approaches (e.g., zero-tolerance, suspension, expulsion, loss of privileges) reduce violent incidents in schools. In fact, these approaches can lead to poor academic performance and engagement, along with an increased risk of legal consequences or exposure to violence. Students that are not white, able-bodied, heterosexual, cisgender, or whose first language is not English are also disproportionately impacted by punitive policies. Behavioral risk assessments are used to prevent school violence by evaluating the severity and seriousness of a student's threat of violence. Behavioral risk assessments can be an effective preventative intervention if identified students are given mental health, safety planning, and conflict resolution services. Disciplinary action should be limited when implementing behavioral risk assessments as it may incite violence or aggression.

97. C: Although student interest is an important factor when creating relevant content for school health education, it is not considered an academic or ethical consideration. Required content standards are set by school districts, are used to guide instructors, and are academically and developmentally appropriate. Parental approval is a crucial ethical consideration since parents often have the authority to excuse their child from comprehensive sexual health education.

98. C: Aside from medication compliance and individual therapy, the most effective treatment strategy is supportive family therapy. Supportive family therapy instructs families on how to best support their loved one with schizophrenia, identify signs and symptoms that indicate an impending relapse, educate family members on medication and treatment, and provide emotional support to family members. It promotes empathy and strong social ties within the family unit, which will help reduce hospital readmission and symptom relapse and improve the overall social-emotional functioning of the patient.

99. A: Since Harry makes the decision to work alone without consulting Matt, this is an example of unilateral decision-making, which refers to a decision made by one party. Harry's decision to avoid dispute by working alone could cause further conflict between the two. Harry should have collaboratively assigned roles and created the plan for completing the project. Matt's input on the project from the onset may have increased his participation.

100. D: There are four categories of classroom management styles: authoritarian, authoritative, uninvolved, and indulgent. Each differs based on the level of student engagement and control over the classroom. Teachers with an authoritarian teaching style have high control and low student engagement, which means that the classroom environment is highly structured with few disruptions, yet the teachers make little effort to form bonds with the students. Authoritative teachers have a high level of control over the classroom and are highly invested in each student's success. They set and reinforce behavioral expectations and forms strong connections with the students. Uninvolved teachers have low control over the classroom and low involvement with students. They often fail to set or maintain classroom rules or punish poor behavior. They are also often ill-prepared for teaching and fail to meet student needs. Teachers with an indulgent teaching style demonstrate a genuine interest and care for their students. Students trust and feel connected to their teacher, which often enhances student engagement. However, teachers with an indulgent teaching style lack the assertiveness and discipline necessary to control their classrooms.

101. D: According to the CDC, a coordinated approach to school health contains eight components: health education, physical education, nutrition services, healthy and safe school environment, health promotion for staff, family and community involvement, health services, and psychosocial services. Health insurance is not one of the eight components.

102. C: A person who is love bombing displays excessive affection and attention toward his or her partner, constantly communicates, expresses deep romantic feelings, and exhibits possessive behavior. He or she may also use guilt and isolation to control his or her partner.

103. D: Genetic testing, regular cancer screenings, regular physical activity, and maintaining a healthy weight can reduce the risk of or prevent breast cancer. A nutritious and well-balanced diet that consists of little to no alcohol consumption is also associated with breast cancer prevention. Breastfeeding has been associated with a lower risk of breast cancer and ovarian cancer. Exclusive breastfeeding is also associated with a lower risk of childhood cancer, asthma, obesity, type 1 diabetes, and sudden infant death syndrome (SIDS).

104. B: Primary prevention strategies address mental health challenges—typically at the community level—before they occur (e.g., awareness campaign, parenting skills classes, mental health education, legislation). Early detection and early intervention are key aspects of secondary prevention (e.g., depression screenings, suicide hotlines, crisis management interventions, safety plans). Tertiary prevention refers to treatment that occurs after a mental health episode aimed at preventing further damage (e.g., medication, therapy, peer support groups).

105. B: Technical language or jargon can be difficult for audience members to understand. Teachers should use words or concepts that are age and developmentally appropriate to maximize comprehension.

106. B: The WSCC model is a multidimensional coordinated school health model that addresses all aspects of student health. Stakeholders from the school and community collaborate to direct resources and create programming that improves the health and well-being of the whole child. The 10 components of the WSCC model are physical education and physical activity, nutrition services, health education, social and emotional climate, physical environment, health services, counseling and psychological services, employee wellness, community involvement, and family engagement.

107. C: The next step once the student has defined the problem and established the criteria is to consider the possible choices (e.g., t*aking the drink, rejecting the offer, telling her parents, or leaving the situation). While considering the possible choices, she should evaluate the potential consequences of her decision* (e.g., getting in trouble, getting sick from the alcohol, losing a friend). The next steps would be to identify the best solution, develop and implement the solution, and evaluate the results.

108. B: Individuals who smoke cigarettes are 30 to 40 percent more likely to develop diabetes than nonsmokers. Quitting smoking is a modifiable behavior that can reduce the risk of developing type 2 diabetes. Consuming refined carbohydrates and sweetened beverages, including beverages with natural sugars like fruit juice, can increase the risk of type 2 diabetes. Eating processed meats and red meats is associated with a higher risk of prediabetes. Although exercise is a protective behavior against type 2 diabetes, the man's exercise habits already meet recommendations. In general, individuals should aim to exercise 150 minutes (about two and a half hours) per week.

109. D: Tyler is using accommodation to manage conflict. Although he disagrees, Tyler bends to the will of Jose to prevent further conflict and maintain favor with him. Those who practice avoidance ignore the conflict altogether. Two parties using compromise will attempt to end their conflict by meeting in the middle. This style can be a quick way to resolve conflict, yet both parties must sacrifice their needs, wants, etc., to appease the other. Collaboration strives to create a win-win situation. Those using this style collaborate to meet a resolution that satisfies all their needs; however, it can be a time-consuming process.

110. C: Individual risk factors for IPV include low education, low socioeconomic status, drug use, impulsivity, poor behavior management skills, history of experiencing abuse, hostility toward the opposite gender, stress, and social isolation. Relationship risk factors include witnessing abuse between parents, disrupted family dynamics (e.g., divorce, separation), and friendships with aggressive or violent peers. Community risk factors include high poverty rates, limited economic opportunities, high unemployment, high crime rates, and high rates of drug use. High self-esteem is generally a protective factor.

111. A: Assertive communication is the most effective communication style. Those who practice assertive communication can communicate their needs and feelings in a considerate manner while also respecting the needs of others. Aggressive communicators are often loud and demanding. They may use intimidation tactics to attain control over others. Passive communicators suppress their feelings and needs to avoid confrontation. Passive-aggressive communicators may outwardly display passive nonverbal or verbal communication techniques yet indirectly express negative or aggressive feelings.

112. D: Surveys are an effective research method when exploring phenomena from a large, predetermined population. They allow researchers to collect a broad range of data (e.g., demographics, health attitudes, behaviors, opinions) in a relatively short period of time. Surveys can be administered online, over the phone, or in-person, yet they must be standardized to ensure reliability.

113. B: Active listening involves verbal and nonverbal cues. In a conversation about a complex topic, a listener can demonstrate active listening by asking open-ended questions that help clarify and explore the speaker's ideas. This shows that the listener is engaged and interested in understanding the speaker's perspective. Providing direct solutions or agreeing with everything the speaker says can actually hinder the conversation by shutting down further exploration and critical thinking. Sharing personal anecdotes may be appropriate in certain situations, but it is not necessarily an indicator of active listening. Overall, asking open-ended questions is a powerful technique for demonstrating active listening in complex conversations.

114. C: High levels of LDL cholesterol can lead to atherosclerosis, or the buildup of plaque, in a person's arteries. If untreated, atherosclerosis can lead to heart disease, heart attack, or stroke. Consumption of red or processed meats, fried foods, and full-fat dairy products can contribute to high levels of LDL cholesterol in the body. It is recommended that those who eat red meat limit their consumption to less than 3 oz one to two times per week. A sedentary lifestyle increases the likelihood of developing heart disease. Although excessive body fat can increase the risk of heart disease, a person should always consult a doctor to discuss what his or her ideal weight should be to prevent heart disease. Losing 30 pounds in one month is likely too extreme to be done safely.

115. B: A CHES certification is attained through passing a competency-based examination. It indicates that the recipient has completed coursework specific to and is an expert in all eight areas of responsibility for health education specialists. SHAPE America's PAL Learning System is a workshop that instructs attendees on how to ensure students meet the recommended 60 minutes of physical activity per day. SOPHE's CORE contains many professional development and virtual learning activities (e.g., webinars, courses, journal self-studies, conferences). ASHA also provides many professional development options.

116. C: An analytic rubric provides detailed descriptions of each criterion and its corresponding grade. It is usually presented in matrix form with the components listed on one axis (e.g., content knowledge, presentation skills, teamwork) and the different levels of achievement on the other (e.g., beginning, developing, accomplished, exemplary). The boxes in the center detail justification for the scale and category. For example, the description of "accomplished" in the teamwork category might contain the following description: "student engages in conversation with peers, regularly participates in group discussion, and contributes equal effort in project duties." Analytic rubrics promote clear expectations, accountability, and flexibility.

117. B: An infectious disease is transmitted from an infected person to a noninfected person. Common modes of transmission include animal vectors, contaminated surfaces, skin-to-skin contact with an infected person, droplets or airborne pathogens, and fecal-oral transmission. Chronic diseases are long-lasting conditions. In public health, the term often refers to long-term noncommunicable illnesses (e.g., diabetes, heart disease) that are not typically spread from person to person. Secondary diseases refer to illnesses that result from another disease (e.g., developing pneumonia after an upper respiratory infection). Congenital disorders develop in utero and result from genetic or environmental factors.

118. A: An intrauterine device prevents unwanted pregnancy but does not protect against STDs. Abstinence is the most effective method for avoiding unwanted pregnancy and STDs. Male and female condoms prevent most STDs, yet a person can still contract infections like herpes or HPV from skin-to-skin contact during sex. The HPV vaccine protects against HPV strains most likely to cause cervical cancer.

119. B: An interest group is comprised of individuals with similar goals who are participating voluntarily. Typically, they share a common mission and actively work toward increasing awareness and acceptance of their interest among others. Friendship groups are comprised of individuals who are bonded by a shared experience. Task and functional groups include individuals who work together to achieve a common task or goal.

120. C: Each of the answer choices is an example of a type of social responsibility in which an individual takes responsibility to serve other people. However, only choice C represents an action taken to serve the local community. The person receiving the flu vaccine is doing so for his family, not for his community. Tithing may benefit the larger community if funds are used for community service, but donations to the church vary from church to church and do not directly relate to the community at large. Tithing is also fully elective and related to religious motivations; therefore, it is not typically considered a civic responsibility for civilians. A person altering his or her buying habits to reduce the amount of carbon he or she consumes and the amount of plastic released in the environment is an example of individual environmental social responsibility but would not count as civic duty, as it does not directly relate to serving the community at hand.

Online Resources

Due to our efforts to try to keep this book to a manageable length, we've created a link that will give you access to all of your online resources:

mometrix.com/resources719/oaehealth

It's Your Moment, Let's Celebrate It!

Share your story @mometrixtestpreparation